Alias Bill Arp

Alias Bill Arp

Charles Henry Smith and the South's "Goodly Heritage"

David B. Parker

The University of Georgia Press

Athens and London

© 1991 by the University of Georgia Press
Athens, Georgia 30602
All rights reserved

Designed by Kathi L. Dailey
Set in Ehrhardt by Tseng Information Systems
Printed and bound by Thomson-Shore

The paper in this book meets the guidelines for
permanence and durability of the Committee on
Production Guidelines for Book Longevity of the Council
on Library Resources.

Printed in the United States of America

95 94 93 92 91 C 5 4 3 2 1

Library of Congress Cataloging in Publication Data

Parker, David B.
    Alias Bill Arp: Charles Henry Smith and the South's
"Goodly heritage" / David B. Parker.
        p. cm.
    Includes bibliographical references and index.
    ISBN 0-8203-1310-6 (alk. paper)
    1. Arp, Bill, 1826–1903. 2. Dialect literature, American—
Southern States—History and criticism. 3. Southern States—
Popular culture—History—19th century. 4. Humorists,
American—19th century—Biography. 5. Journalists—
United States—Biography. 6. Southern States in literature.
7. Georgia in literature. 8. Georgia—Biography. I. Title.
PS2859.S5Z84   1991
814'.4—dc20   90-45162
                                                        CIP

British Library Cataloging in Publication Data available

Title page illustration: Charles Henry Smith, c. 1890;
photograph in *Bill Arp: From the Uncivil War to Date,
1861–1903*, Memorial edition (Atlanta, 1903).

Contents

Preface

When I began my first graduate research seminar some years back, I decided that my project for the semester should be a historical study of southern humor, including an analysis of the characteristics that distinguish that genre. Professor George B. Tindall gently suggested that this might be too large a topic for a thirty-page seminar paper and that perhaps I should limit myself to a study of one southern humorist. I took his advice and chose Charles Henry Smith, a Georgia essayist and humorist who wrote under the pseudonym of Bill Arp. The seminar paper grew into a master's thesis, a doctoral dissertation, and finally this book. I am still in Professor Tindall's debt for that push in the right direction.

My first desperate idea for a topic, the study of southern humor that Professor Tindall advised me to put on the back burner for a while, remains on the back burner, and I plan to keep it there for a long time. I believe it was E. B. White who once compared the analysis of humor to the dissection of a frog: you can do it, he said, but you tend to kill the frog in the process. I have no desire to kill southern humor. As it turns out, I never dealt with Arp's humor as such. I looked instead at the topics he discussed—his family and farm, the Georgia folk, his boyhood, industrialization, race relations, sectional reconciliation, and so forth—and tried to figure out how all these things fit together, both for Arp himself and for his readers.

In presenting my interpretation of Bill Arp in this book, I quote extensively from his writings. Typesetting in the late nineteenth century was a tedious process, and typographical errors crept into many of Arp's newspaper pieces. I have silently corrected obvious errors of this nature when quoting Arp, but I have left intact his intentional misspellings and the various mistakes I assumed to be his, not the printer's.

Stylistic concerns prohibit me from beginning every sentence with the phrase "According to Bill Arp." I hope readers will understand that many of the views expressed in the second part of this study are Arp's, not mine.

Many kind people in Georgia went to great lengths to make a research trip there in the spring of 1986 both enjoyable and productive. My wife and I especially enjoyed the time we spent with Marilu Munford of Cartersville, Charles Henry Smith's granddaughter and the epitome of southern hospitality and graciousness. "Miss Marilu," as she insisted we call her, died a couple of years ago, and I am glad we had the chance to meet her. I also want to thank William Brown and Celestine Sibley of Atlanta, the Gwinnett County Historical Society, the Atlanta Historical Society, and the staffs of the libraries of Agnes Scott College and Emory University. Several people allowed me to see and use items in their possession. Among them are Liz McCole of Duluth, Georgia; W. T. Maddox of Rome, Georgia; and Marian Granger Stout of Nova Scotia. I read most of Arp's *Atlanta Constitution* columns on microfilm supplied by Perkins Library at Duke University through the University of North Carolina at Chapel Hill's courteous and efficient interlibrary loan service.

Two chapters of this study were first published, in revised form, in *Southern Studies* and the *Georgia Historical Quarterly*. I first offered my interpretation of Arp's *Atlanta Constitution* columns in a paper read at the Citadel Conference on the South in 1985 and later published in *Southern Historian*. I am grateful to the editors of these publications for permission to reprint some of the materials here. The Department of History and the Graduate School of the University of North Carolina at Chapel Hill financed part of my research, and a six-month fellowship from the Graduate School gave me enough free time to finish writing. The good people at the

University of Georgia Press—Malcolm L. Call, Madelaine Cooke, Nancy G. Holmes, and the rest—performed the miracle of turning the resulting manuscript into this book.

George B. Tindall has been a valuable advisor for this study from the beginning. Peter Walker, Peter Coclanis, Joel Williamson, Louis D. Rubin, Jr., and Kimball King offered useful advice as members of my graduate committees. Gary R. Freeze, now at Erskine College, Wayne Mixon of Mercer University, and William Garrett Piston, a colleague at Southwest Missouri State University, gave the manuscript the most thorough readings that it is ever likely to receive. The book is better for the assistance of these scholars.

Despite all the help I received from these fine people, it was only when Chantal, my wife, read the first part of the manuscript and said she liked it that I knew everything would be all right. I sometimes suspect that she grew tired of hearing about Bill Arp long ago, but she always pretended to be interested, and I thank her for that. Her encouragement over the years has meant more than I can say in a few lines, and this book is for her. It is also for Bryce and Elizabeth Parker and for Gentry and Kathleen Wright, our parents, who have been supportive in many ways. Finally, it is for Katie Mae and Gentry, our children, for occasionally going to bed at a decent hour and letting me finish this. Thanks, everybody.

Introduction

On June 3, 1969, Celestine Sibley, a columnist for the *Atlanta Constitution*, told her readers that a student had written to her for information on Bill Arp. Sibley admitted that she knew very little about her predecessor of the previous century and had not read his works, but after checking into the matter she could confirm that many years ago the *Constitution* had indeed printed a weekly letter from a man who wrote as "Bill Arp." "Fashions in humor have changed," she told the student, "and the things that made Georgians wait by their mailbox for their morning Bill Arp 75 years ago might not be funny anymore." [1]

The response to this column was immediate and almost overwhelming, Sibley later said. A few days after it appeared, she wrote a column titled "Everybody Knows Bill Arp" in which she reprinted comments from some of the many people who had gotten in touch with her. "Not know Bill Arp! Shame on you!" wrote a man from South Carolina. "He was one of the greatest names in Southern newspapers—and the reason my family subscribed to the . . . Constitution." An eighty-year-old Georgia woman said that "*everybody* who professes to be literate should know his name if not his works." [2] Sibley took the admonitions to heart. She learned more about Arp, acquired one of his books, and developed a taste for his writings. Every year or two after that, she mentioned Arp in one of her columns; and when she compiled *Day by Day with Celestine Sibley* in 1975, a book of quotations (with her comments) for each day of the year, she included, along with passages from Benjamin Franklin,

Mark Twain, Ralph Waldo Emerson, George Bernard Shaw, and others, nine excerpts from the works of Bill Arp.

Despite his prominence in Sibley's book, Charles Henry Smith, the essayist and humorist who wrote as Bill Arp, was a minor southern writer, and this book is not an attempt to raise his status to that of Mark Twain or Edgar Allan Poe. Such an attempt would be foolish. Nevertheless, a study of Smith and his writings is worthwhile for at least two reasons. First, Smith was prolific. He took his pen name at the opening of the Civil War, and for the next dozen years or so wrote about a hundred pieces that addressed issues of the war and Reconstruction, often in a humorous way. From 1878 to 1903, Smith contributed a weekly letter to the *Atlanta Constitution* in which he discussed whatever was on his mind—politics, farm life, the race problem, industrialization, his family, and a multitude of other topics. The result is a fairly detailed record of the views and opinions of one southerner through four decades of his region's history. Second, Smith's Bill Arp was extremely popular, especially in the South. A large part of this study will therefore look at Bill Arp's writings with an eye toward exploring the reasons for that popularity.

The three chapters that make up part 1 of this book are biographical. When Annie May Christie set out in the 1940s to write a dissertation on Smith, she found few good biographical sources for her research. Most of Smith's private papers had gone up in smoke when a grandchild's house burned a few years before.[3] Christie managed to find a few letters and other papers scattered among Smith's descendants. She collected these and later donated them to Agnes Scott College, where she taught for many years. The Agnes Scott collection of Smith's papers, numbering some forty items, is therefore the largest such collection in existence.

Christie found other sources for her life of Smith—the memoirs of two daughters and those of friends, for example, and the autobiographical writings of Smith himself—and from these constructed what was until now the only full-length study of Smith. When James C. Austin wrote *Bill Arp*, a thin volume in the Twayne

Introduction

United States Authors Series, he noted that Christie had been his "most important source of information" and that almost all of his biographical information on Smith came from Christie's study.[4]

This book focuses more on the writings of Bill Arp than on the life of Charles Henry Smith. Still, given the general paucity of published information on Smith, a biographical sketch seems to be in order. Christie's pioneering efforts provided a good foundation for this study, but I have tried to go beyond her work at a few points in her telling of Smith's life (and later at many points in her interpretation of his writings). The reader is forewarned that this biographical sketch does not raise a great number of issues that will be crucial in the later discussion of Smith's writings; rather, it simply presents a short description of the life of Charles Henry Smith, the man who created Bill Arp.

Part 2 shifts the focus from Charles Henry Smith to Bill Arp. Chapter 4 describes Arp's Civil War and Reconstruction writings. Smith first used his pen name in April 1861 when President Abraham Lincoln issued a proclamation calling out the militias of the loyal states and ordering the rebels in the South "to disperse and retire" immediately. Smith's satiric response to the proclamation was written in the language (supposedly) of a Georgia cracker: "Mr. Linkhorn—Sur: These are to inform you that we are all well, and hope these lines may find you in *statue ko*. We received your proklamation, and as you have put us on very short notis, a few of us boys have konkluded to write you, and ax for a little more time. The fact is, we are most obleeged to have a few more days, for the way things are happening, it is utterly onpossible for us to disperse in twenty days." Smith continued in this vein for several paragraphs, and then signed the letter "Bill Arp."[5]

Other Bill Arp letters appeared in the newspapers during the war, ridiculing Lincoln and the Union army, censuring those people whose actions hurt the Confederate war effort, describing Smith's experiences as a refugee during Sherman's march to the sea, and cheering the South on, even in the bleak last days of the war. Arp continued to speak for large numbers of southerners after the war as he criticized northern attempts to reshape southern society and demanded that southern bravery and honor be acknowledged.

Almost all of Arp's war and Reconstruction letters were written in the dialect that was so fashionable among mid-nineteenth-century American humorists. Dialect writing, which had been fairly common since about 1830, reached its peak of popularity about the time of the Civil War with the "Phunny Phellows," a group that tended "to macerate grammar; to mix metaphors; to commit malapropisms, spoonerisms, and 'unintentional' puns; and to use eccentric sentences, which readers found funny." Three of the best of these Phunny Phellows who joined in what Walter Blair has termed "the misspelling bee" were David Ross Locke, Henry Wheeler Shaw, and Charles Farrar Browne.[6]

Locke, a journalist associated with the *Toledo Blade* for many years, wrote his first "Petroleum V. Nasby" letter in April 1862. Locke often used the device of misspelling as a way to attack the evils he saw in society, among them slavery, intemperance, political corruption, and the lack of women's rights. John M. Harrison has contended that Locke was more of a satirist than a humorist.[7] This is a useful distinction, for Locke always wrote with a mission; his primary goal was reform, not laughter, and some of his pieces were hostile enough in their satire to lose most of their humor.

One of Nasby's funnier sketches was one in which Locke ridiculed the Democratic party. "I wuz born a Whig," he wrote, but later in life became a Democrat. He described the conversion:

Liftin my hands 2 heven, I vowed 3 vows, to-wit:

1. That I wood devote my life to the work uv redoosin the Afrikin 2 his normal speer.

2. That I wood adopt a perfeshn in2 wich I cood steel without bein hauled up fer it.

3. That the water I hed consoomed while in doorance vile, wuz the last that wood ever find its way, undilootid, in2 my stumick.

Hentz, I jined the Dimocrisy, and whoever eggsamines my record, will find that I hev kep my oaths![8]

Charles Henry Smith, who as a southerner and a Democrat stood for many of the things Locke despised, did not think highly of the northern Republican humorist. "I dont know Nasby. I dont know whether he is a knave or a fool, and I dont care," he wrote in 1884 in response to a Petroleum V. Nasby essay attacking southern race relations. "Nasby's disease has become chronic and he cant be cured. . . . He was born hatin us I reckon and cant help it."[9]

If Locke used misspelling as a vehicle for political thought, Henry Wheeler Shaw's use of the same device had just the opposite effect. Shaw, a Massachusetts native who finally settled in New York, was a man of many trades. He began writing humorous pieces for publication about 1858 and took his pen name, "Josh Billings," a few years later. Shaw realized he was on the right track as a dialect writer when his humorous sketch "Essay on the Mule," which had raised little interest at first, became a hit when revised as "Essa on the Muel, bi Josh Billings." (The essay began, "The mule is haf hoss, and haf Jackass, and then kums tu a full stop, natur diskovering her mistake.")[10]

Josh Billings was the master of the amusing aphorism, such as, "Musick hath charms tu soothe a savage; this may be so, but i wud rather tri a revolver on him fust," and "When a feller gits a goin down hil, it dus seem as tho evry thing had bin greased for the okashun."[11] Aphorisms such as these were largely responsible for the success of *Josh Billings' Farmer's Allminax*, his most popular work, published annually from 1869 until 1879. Billings rarely wrote on political matters.

Smith liked Josh Billings. "He did much good, for he gave a passing pleasure and gave it frequently, and left the odor of good precepts that lingered with us," Smith wrote in a tribute following Shaw's death in 1885. "He was Aesop and Ben Franklin, condensed and abridged. . . . It is curious how we are attracted by the wise, pithy sayings of an unlettered man."[12]

"Artemus Ward" was the pen name of Charles Farrar Browne. "I hav no politics," he wrote. "Nary a one. I'm not in the bisiness."[13]

Browne did occasionally write on political topics, but those writings were softened by a moderation Locke could never achieve. Browne, a reporter and editor for the Cleveland *Plain Dealer* (and later an editor at *Vanity Fair*), took the name of Artemus Ward in an 1858 letter to the Cleveland paper. Browne's character was a traveling showman who asked the *Plain Dealer* for assistance in advertising his show: "i hav a show consisting in part of a Calforny Bare two snakes tame foxies &c also wax works my wax works is hard to beat." [14] The letter was so popular that he wrote more to the newspaper, detailing his experiences with his show in New York, Chicago, Utica, and other places around the country.

The reception of the showman letters and Artemus Ward's other humorous pieces was such that he (like Josh Billings and Bill Arp) took to the lecture platform. His most famous lecture, "Artemus Ward Among the Mormons," kept him on the road for over two years. When he gave the lecture in Macon, Georgia, in 1866, he sent Smith a complimentary ticket and an invitation to meet him there. (Tickets for the Mormon tour said, "Admit Bearer and One Wife.") It is not known whether Smith went to Macon, but in any case he admired Ward, calling him a "man of infinite jest." [15]

The Phunny Phellows were, in Brom Weber's words, "uniquely individual writers," but they shared certain characteristics. They were, as David B. Kesterson has reminded us, "*Literary* Comedians," generally well-educated and well-read in the classics. They also shared, of course, the ability to make people laugh. Abraham Lincoln, himself no mean joke-teller, enjoyed the Phunny Phellows. When he met with his cabinet in 1862 to discuss his Emancipation Proclamation, Lincoln read aloud one of Artemus Ward's showman letters and said, "Gentlemen, . . . with the fearful strain that is upon me night and day, if I did not laugh I should die, and you need this medicine as much as I do." Lincoln once declared that he would trade the presidency for Nasby's comic genius. Lincoln's opinion of the third member of the trio was similarly high: "Next to William Shakespeare, Josh Billings is the greatest judge of human nature the world has ever seen." And it is said that Lincoln laughed upon reading Bill Arp's first open letter to him.[16]

Attempts to trace literary influences can be confusing and inconclusive, "like chasing will-o'-the-wisps in cypress swamps," wrote Alan Gribben, a Mark Twain scholar. Twain is a good example of this difficulty. Scholars have debated for years over the major influence in his writings: whether it was the southwestern humorists (writers such as Augustus Baldwin Longstreet, Johnson J. Hooper, George W. Harris, and Joseph G. Baldwin) or the Phunny Phellows.[17] A similar debate, admittedly of lesser magnitude, has gone on concerning the early writings of Bill Arp. One scholar said that Arp "began his career in the footsteps of the Old Southwestern humorists," while another asserted that "the most immediate influence on the Bill Arp letters" was Phunny Phellow Artemus Ward.[18] The latter view probably hits closer to the mark. It is true that Charles Henry Smith's Bill Arp, "the apotheosis of the cracker," would have made a wonderful character for a southwestern humorist. It is also true that Smith belonged (geographically, at least) to what Louis D. Rubin, Jr., has called "one of the most long-lasting and powerful literary genres in southern literature: Middle Georgia humor," a "genre" that included a number of southwestern humorists. Still, Smith's early writings (1861–1872) fit firmly into the Phunny Phellow tradition.[19]

A year or two after the war, Mark Twain told a newspaper reporter that Bill Arp was "one of the few real American humorists," and Twain apparently kept his high opinion of Arp. In 1880, a publisher approached Twain with the idea that he compile an anthology of humor to be sold by subscription; Bill Arp's name was first on Twain's list of possible humorists to be included.[20]

As popular as Arp's early dialect humor had been, Smith abandoned that mode of writing when he began his weekly column in the *Atlanta Constitution* in May 1878. Compared with his earlier pieces, Arp's letters to the *Constitution* must have seemed tame. Many were what scholars have come to call "homely philosophy," delightful sketches of his farm and family, the common folk of Georgia, and the past. Smith also wrote on subjects that were not homely philosophy—race relations, sectional reconciliation, and industrialization, for example. Smith collected a number of his homely philosophy pieces in three books, but few of his columns on other subjects were reprinted. This has led recent scholars to misread his later writings. These scholars have mistakenly seen in Arp's homely philosophy the expressions of a contented man looking optimistically to the future rather than mournfully to the past.

The remainder of this study offers a new interpretation of Bill Arp's *Constitution* columns. Chapter 5 describes Arp's writings on the themes of industrialization and diversified, scientific agriculture. Arp promoted the New South program of Henry W. Grady and others throughout his quarter-century at the *Constitution*. These columns seem to support the generally held view of his post-1878 writings: that the once bitter and frustrated humorist had resigned himself to the Confederacy's defeat and was prepared to accept, even to welcome, the coming of a new age in the South. This is at best half true, however, because while Arp certainly supported Grady's New South, he often felt ill at ease in the new age. The next chapter therefore looks at the other side of Bill Arp—a side scholars have ignored. Using primarily the columns in the *Constitution* that were not reprinted in book form, chapter 6 shows a Bill Arp who was very dissatisfied with the society of the New South, which he said lacked the virtues of the Old South and the traditional values of hard work, morality, and self-reliance. At times, in fact, Arp's columns were sharply critical of the new age. If we see Arp as having apparently contradictory views of the New South— supporting a program of modernization through industrialization and improved agricultural practices on the one hand, criticizing the society brought about by modernization on the other—then his homely philosophy letters cannot be the writings of the contented man scholars have seen. Instead, Arp's writings on his family and farm, the Georgia folk, and the past were an implicit criticism of the new order, because in them he emphasized the values and virtues he saw missing in the New South.

The virtuous Old South that Bill Arp described was not necessarily the Old South of W. J. Cash, William R. Taylor, Bertram Wyatt-Brown, Frank L. Owsley, or any of the other capable historians who have examined antebellum southern culture.[21] I make no attempt to evaluate the validity of Bill Arp's Old South, or to fit it into other historiographical models. For the purposes of this study, what the Old South really was is much less important than what Bill Arp said it was.

Two topics of special concern to Bill Arp were race relations and sectional reconciliation, and chapters 7 and 8 review his writings on these subjects. Although his views were no doubt shaped by various and complicated forces, it is interesting that he often expressed them in terms of Old South virtues. This is strong evidence reinforcing the interpretation of Arp expressed in chapter 6.

Finally, the last chapter looks at "The Meaning of Bill Arp." Much recent scholarship has addressed the question of change or continuity in southern history, and historians on both sides of the debate have gathered impressive amounts of evidence to support their interpretations. Regardless of the outcome of this controversy, Arp and presumably many other southerners *perceived* great changes in southern society. These perceptions created anxieties that some people relieved by turning in one way or another to the past. This is what Smith did in his Bill Arp letters, and the popularity of those letters suggests that his readers used his writings to relieve their own anxieties.

Charles Henry Smith's Bill Arp was popular from the day of his birth in April 1861 through the days of Reconstruction partly because his letters were funny, but even more because he spoke for a large number of southerners. Arp continued in this role during his years with the *Constitution*, addressing the frustrations and anxieties of his fellow southerners as they all faced the changes of the New South.

Part One

Charles Henry Smith

One

Lawrenceville: 1826–1851

Charles Henry Smith was born in Lawrenceville, Georgia, on June 15, 1826. His father was Asahel Reed Smith, a Vermont native who had taught at a small school in Leicester, Massachusetts, until about 1818. That year, the elder Smith and a friend decided to seek their fortunes by chartering a ship and carrying a load of brick from Newburyport to Savannah, where they knew it would fetch a premium price. The young men were in sight of the Savannah harbor when a terrible storm blew up. Fearful for their lives, they threw most of the bricks—and all of their profits—into the water. His companion returned North, but Smith stayed. He worked first as a clerk in a Savannah grocer's store, then as a teacher in a nearby academy.[1]

In 1822 Asahel Smith decided to try his hand as a merchant in Lawrenceville, Georgia. Lawrenceville, some thirty miles northeast of what would later become Atlanta, was a small town, having been incorporated only in December 1821, but it was growing rapidly; by the end of the decade it would have forty houses, ten stores, ten machine shops, three law offices, three doctors, three churches, and a school. Smith's store, a log building on the northwest corner of the town square, almost failed at first. Smith had little business experience, and he quickly lost all his capital and was forced to bor-

3

row a thousand dollars. His creditors were lenient, however, and helped him get back on his feet. The store began to prosper, and in 1823 he married Caroline Ann Maguire, one of his former academy students. Their first house was fairly humble—one large room, a smaller one to the side, and two attached shed rooms without ceilings. A year or so after their marriage, the first of their ten children was born.[2]

As Smith's family expanded, so did his standing in the community. In December 1822 he became the town's postmaster, a position he held until 1840 and then again from 1846 to 1849. (Smith was a Democrat, and Whigs controlled the patronage in the early 1840s.) The position paid about $200 a year, and it made Smith's store more of a public place and thus gave him an edge over his competitors. Within a few years he was able to move his growing family to a larger house just outside of town. Smith was elected a justice of Gwinnett County's Inferior Court, serving from 1826 to 1833 and from 1837 to 1841. (The five justices of the Inferior Court were usually farmers, merchants, or physicians rather than lawyers.) In 1824 he was named to a commission to raise money for the Gwinnett County Academy. He was one of the largest original stockholders in the Lawrenceville Female Seminary, established in 1837. In 1835 he helped found the Gwinnett Manual Labor Institute, a school based on the idea that students should exercise their bodies as well as their minds, and which therefore allowed them to pay for their board by working on the school farm. When the Institute folded a few years later, Smith lost everything he had invested in it, a considerable sum of money.[3]

In Georgia, the New England native overcame an early aversion to southern slavery. He gradually acquired a few slaves himself, listing one in the censuses of 1830 and 1840 and five in 1860. The early records of the Inferior Court describe an interesting decision in the July 1830 attachment case of *Asahel R. Smith v. John Mosley:* "On motion showing that said attachment has been levied on an old negro woman slave by the name of Phillis, and that the property is of a perishable nature, it is ordered that the sheriff do proceed to sell the said negro woman as perishable property." Within a few years Smith convinced five of his seven brothers and sisters to join him, and paid the way south for several of them.[4]

Caroline Ann Maguire, the young woman Smith married in 1823, was the daughter of James Maguire, a coconspirator in Robert Emmett's failed rebellion in 1803 for Irish independence, and Emily Barrett, a Charleston, South Carolina, woman Maguire had met when he fled to this country. In 1813, Maguire and his wife died in a yellow fever epidemic, orphaning Caroline, then seven, and her nine-year-old brother James. In the panic of the epidemic, well-meaning adults accidentally separated the children. James ended up at an orphanage in Boston, where a year later a wealthy shoe manufacturer adopted him. Caroline was carried to Savannah; eventually the grandmother of Frank Goulding, author of *The Young Marooners*, took her into her home. Unaware of James's fate, Caroline grew up, married her former teacher, moved to Lawrenceville, and began a new family.

Caroline's efforts to find her lost brother were, for many years, unsuccessful. She and Asahel placed advertisements in newspapers in the South and in New York and Philadelphia, but James, who had made several trips to Charleston looking for his sister, did not see them. In 1833 the Smiths tried once more, sending the advertisement to Boston, St. Louis, and New Orleans. This time the advertisement worked, and after two decades of separation, brother and sister were reunited. Charles Henry Smith, who was seven years old at the time, wrote of the reunion seventy years later in a sketch entitled "A Pretty Story."[5]

Little record remains of Charles Henry Smith's early days. Later, however, he would often write in his weekly *Atlanta Constitution* column of the days of his youth, and from these columns we can presume that his childhood was a happy one. As a boy, Smith attended the Lawrenceville Academy and the Gwinnett Manual Labor Institute. At the latter school he worked three hours a day on the school farm to pay for his board. When Smith was eighteen, his father gave him an interest in the store. A year later, Smith entered

Franklin College (the University of Georgia) in Athens. There he
became active in Phi Kappa, a literary and debating society, and
was Junior Orator in 1847. He also organized and edited a college
newspaper that "kept the boys in a ferment of fun and expectation."
But Smith's college days ended, just months short of graduation,
when his father became ill and he had to leave school to take care of
the store. During this illness, and perhaps because of it, Asahel had
financial difficulties. His health and his finances both recovered,
however, and he lived until 1875.[6]

While selling goods back at Lawrenceville, Smith noticed a girl
he had known as a child, "a pretty, hazel-eyed lassie" who "had
grown out of her pantalets and into long dresses, and was cast-
ing sly glances at the boys about town." She was Mary Octavia
Hutchins, eldest daughter of Nathan Louis Hutchins, a wealthy
planter and lawyer who served five terms as state senator and for
eleven years (1857–1868) was a distinguished justice of Georgia's
Western Circuit. Octavia's father, a man of humble origins, had
moved to Gwinnett County in 1822 or 1823, about the same time as
Asahel Smith. By 1860 he owned a plantation of almost 2,300 acres
and forty-nine slaves, down from sixty-five (the most in the county)
ten years before. In addition to the plantation, he owned a home,
Mitford Cottage, on the outskirts of Lawrenceville. Hutchins had
acquired part of his wealth through marrying into the well-to-do
Holt family. Smith's children, while doing research on their family
tree in 1893, discovered that Octavia was related on her mother's
side to William H. Seward, Lincoln's secretary of state, a fact that
surprised the family. Smith kidded Octavia about this, but, as he
pointed out, he could not push the joke too far, because of his own
ancestry: "We are about even now . . . half yankees all around."[7]

Smith knew that Octavia liked him because she visited his store
often, trading not only for the Hutchins family, which included
eleven children, but for some of the neighbors as well. He almost
got rich off of her before they were married, he said. A page that has
survived from Smith's account book lends credence to the story; it
shows that many of the Hutchins transactions at the store from May

to November 1848, including the purchase of "Ladies shoes," lace, thread, ribbon, and "1 pr super kid gloves," involved Octavia. She soon caught Smith's eye, and, as he later recalled events, "it didn't take me long to fall desperately in love, nor did it take a long siege for me to take that fort, for I was a right handsome youth myself, and was smart and doing well."[8]

Few would deny that Smith was "a right handsome youth." Average in height and build, with black hair (already thinning at the top), a neatly trimmed beard, dark eyes, and what a journalist would later call "rather a grave expression of countenance," Smith was a good-looking young man who appeared older than his years.[9] He bought a toupee to cover his balding pate sometime during the 1850s, but the experiment proved a failure. One of the first times he wore it, he was acting as a pallbearer at a funeral. He passed under some trees at the cemetery, he later recalled, "and one of them took off my hat and my scratch with it, and my bald spot showed no hair apparent to the crown, and excited too much levity for the solemn occasion." According to his daughter, Smith "never tried a toupee again but went balder as time wore his hair off." As Smith's bald spot grew, his remaining hair gradually turned gray. In 1891 an editor of the *Atlanta Constitution* joked that Smith "so closely resembles President [Benjamin] Harrison that when the latter stopped [in Cartersville] it was hard to tell them apart."[10]

Charles and Octavia were married at Mitford Cottage on March 7, 1849, when she was sixteen, he twenty-two. It was a small wedding, with no diamond ring, fancy trousseau, or long lines of attendants. "My wife cost me $25, that's all," he wrote in 1892. "Ten dollars for a ring and $10 for the preacher and the rest for a fancy marriage certificate." As a wedding present, Hutchins gave them several of his slaves. The couple went to Gainesville, Georgia, for their honeymoon. When they returned, young Charles and Octavia lived first with one set of parents, then with the other, until he built a two-room house for them.[11]

Smith impressed his father-in-law with his business sense and his quick wit, and Hutchins convinced him to study law and join his law firm. "So I placed my mercantile interests in other hands," Smith later explained, "and began to peruse Blackstone. In two or three months I was admitted to the bar on the promise of continuing my studies, which promise I kept, and in due time began to ride the circuit at the tail of the procession." [12]

Meanwhile, town officials in Lawrenceville were having trouble with the courthouse square; the fence surrounding the square was in a continuous state of disrepair and, in the absence of a stock law, cattle, goats, and hogs were frequent unwelcome guests at the courthouse. The justices of the court decided to give the corner lots of the square to four of Lawrenceville's "smart lawyers" with the understanding that the attorneys would keep the fence in good shape. As an added inducement, the justices permitted the lawyers to build brick office buildings on those lots. Smith received the deed to the southeast lot on November 28, 1849, and, in the course of eighteen months, erected an office building on the site. Hutchins, Smith's father-in-law, got the southwest corner.[13]

On January 16, 1850, Charles Henry Smith and his father-in-law formed a partnership to combine their practices in Lawrenceville. Hutchins agreed to furnish the office and pay two-thirds of the operating expenses in return for two-thirds of the profits. Presumably Smith's one-third share in the firm would have been lucrative, but in 1851 he "took the Western fever" and moved his family (which now numbered four, since two children had been born in Lawrenceville) some seventy miles west to Rome, a rapidly growing industrial and commercial center and the seat of Georgia's Floyd County.[14]

Two

Rome:
1851–1877

When the Smiths moved to Floyd County in 1851, they lived at first in a house about two miles outside of Rome near the present location of Berry College. Within a few years, however, Smith's business in town had grown so much that he had to move closer to his office. Their new home on Fourth Avenue extended the length of the block, from East Third to East Fourth streets, and stretched back to the campus of Shorter College. It was called Rose Hill for the many beautiful flowers that surrounded it. "The land and improvements are valuable," Smith wrote his brother-in-law in 1856, "and I can sell the same for $12,000 to Col. Cothran but design to remain there for life. I have spent a good deal of money in improving it for that purpose, and wish to secure Octavia & the children a home beyond contingencies." [1]

In 1852 or 1853, Asahel and Caroline Smith moved to Rome. They lived in a house one block behind the home of their son and his family. Although it is not exactly clear why the parents followed the son to Rome, Smith later wrote that it was only after his father had left Gwinnett County that he recovered from the "great infirmity" that had afflicted him for several years. Asahel apparently had some type of store in Rome before the Civil War, and he was appointed postmaster in 1866 and 1867. [2]

Once in Rome, the Smiths added eleven children to their family, making a total of thirteen, ten of whom survived infancy. According to a family story, the Smiths had run out of names by the time the last child came along, and they decided to have a "naming party" to take care of the problem. Guests put their choices in a hat, and the first two drawn became the baby's name. The first piece of paper pulled from the hat said "Jessie," which had been Charles's choice. The second, contributed by Martha Grady (Henry W. Grady's sister), said "Winfred." So the Smiths' youngest daughter was named Jessie Winfred.[3]

In addition to their own large family, the Smiths took care of four children of close relatives, and two of these should be counted as full-fledged family members. Harriet Hutchins Iverson (Mrs. Smith's sister and the wife of Confederate general Alfred Iverson) died in 1861, leaving two daughters, Minnie Caroline (then two) and Julia Octavia (then four), in the care of their aunt. The Smiths raised them after that. When one of the girls got married, Smith said: "She was not our child, but was almost, for Mrs. Arp [his wife] was the only mother she ever knew, and we loved her."[4]

At the birth of each of the older children, Hutchins would send over one or two more slaves as a present. "It used to make Charlie so mad," Smith's wife remembered. "He didn't want the care of them. Just like so many children to watch and feed and clothe." Few of Smith's antebellum comments on slavery have survived, but he addressed the subject several times in later years. "I never could make the account balance until the war was over," he wrote in 1891, although elsewhere he admitted that he somehow "managed to support 'em until Abe Lincoln come along and kindly relieved me from the burden. Blessings on old Abe. He dident know what he was doing, but he lifted a load off of me sure, for the darned niggers wasent worth a darned cent to me."[5]

Whether or not the ownership of slaves was financially worthwhile, Smith kept them, ending up with about nine at the time of the Civil War. Smith had sold several in 1856, but in 1863—in the middle of the Civil War—he bought one. Anderson, a neighbor's slave, was married to Mary, who belonged to Smith. Anderson was unhappy being apart from Mary and ran away from his owner. Smith bought Anderson while he was still a runaway, thinking that he might come in from the woods if he knew he could be with his wife. The trick worked; shortly after Smith told Mary that she and her husband could now be together, Anderson returned.[6]

Despite his occasional troubles with the South's peculiar institution, Smith later wrote that he appreciated slavery in general and several of his own slaves in particular. "I've seen the day, oh, blessed day, when I strutted around my darkies like a patriarch," he once said. "I felt like I was running an unlimited monarchy on a limited scale." He noted elsewhere that "there was something about that good old patriarchal institution, when properly conducted, that was mighty pleasant." Smith wrote kindly of several of his slaves, such as Frances and Mary: "The children loved their black mammy better than they did their mother. Many a time have I seen mother try to coax her child to come to her from the nurses' arms." His favorite, however, was clearly Tip (short for Tippecanoe). "Tip was never our slave but was our friend," he wrote in 1891. "Tip grew up with the children and was one of them. Tip was my trusted confidential servant." "There are thousands of white men whose chances for heaven are not so good as Tip's," he wrote elsewhere. Although Smith "had to whip some of the other servants occasionally," he "never whipped Tip."[7]

Smith was known in Rome for his sense of humor. Sometimes he wrote humorous letters for his friends over the name of Sam McCrackin, a wise but witty old Irish well digger.[8] At other times he used his own name. In January 1860, agents for the Delaware State Lottery sent Smith an offer to try his chances at a special reduced price. Smith had that letter, along with his response (his first known published satire), printed in one of the Rome newspapers. First, the lottery company's letter to Smith:

> Dear Sir: We take the liberty to enclose you a scheme of the Delaware State Lottery, for which we are general agents, our object being

to try and sell you a prize so as to create an excitement in your locality that will tend to increase our business. With this end in view, we offer you the preference to purchase a very finely arranged package of 25 tickets. . . . This package gives you the advantage of $31.25 worth of tickets for the cost of only $20; and to convince you of our confidence in its success, we will guarantee you another package of our extra lotteries free of charge if the above fails to draw a prize, the lowest being $200. . . . We make this offer in good faith, with a desire to sell you the Capital, $37,000. Should you think favorably of it, enclose us $20, and the package will be sent by return mail, the results of which we confidently think will be satisfactory to you.

And Smith's response:

I send you my note for $20, instead of the cash, as it will save exchange, and there is really no necessity of sending money to Baltimore and having it sent back again in a few days. This arrangement, I confidently think, will be satisfactory to you, for it is done in good faith.

I really feel under many obligations that you have chosen me as the object of your liberality and do assure you that when that $37,000 prize comes to hand, the excitement which it will raise in this community will swallow up and extinguish the John Brown raid, and you will sell more tickets here than traveling circuses and monkey shows take off in 20 years. This is a good locality for such an experiment, for there is a vast number of clever people who are in the habit of racking their brains to devise some way to get money without working for it, and I know very well that when they are satisfied they can do so through your company, they will cheerfully give you that preference which you have shown to me. . . .

You are hereby authorized to deduct $20 and send the remainder to me by Adams & Company's Express.

Attached was Smith's note: "On demand I promise to pay Gilbert & Co. twenty dollars, provided the finely-arranged package of tickets which they have selected for me draws a prize of not less than $200."[9]

Smith joined John Underwood's law practice shortly after moving to Rome. Theirs was a happy association that lasted for thirteen years, until Underwood was elevated to the bench. Business was good for Underwood and Smith but, Smith wrote to his brother-in-law, another lawyer, "We have a large amount due us for fees but collections in litigated cases are very slow as you well know. It takes all the proceeds of plain collections to support our families and if I had not [made] considerable money in outside transactions I could not have got along." These outside transactions were probably primarily in real estate; he mentioned in this letter that he had been unable to sell his "town property." He told Hutchins that unless he could sell the property quickly, he would have to ask him for a loan of about $2,000. "My assets are abundant and increase continually," Smith wrote, "but still I am embarrassed." [10]

Smith also became involved in civic affairs and, more briefly, politics. He helped found the city's board of education and waterworks system and was a member of the chamber of commerce. He was an elder in the Rome Presbyterian Church and occasionally represented that congregation at various conferences. Citizens of Rome elected Smith city council clerk in 1852 and city alderman six times between 1860 and 1873. Smith was a leading figure in the local chapter of the International Order of Good Templars and was president of the Rome Sons of Temperance. Following the Civil War, he served one term as state senator (1865–66) and one term as Rome's mayor (1867–68). [11]

Despite his father's northern background, Smith's sympathies were clearly with the South as sectional tensions increased in the years just prior to the Civil War. In February 1860 Smith served on a committee of Rome's citizens that passed a resolution of nonintercourse with the North, this being, according to Smith and others, "the surest plan to bring the Northern fanatics to their senses." The committee resolved "that the merchants and mechanics of this city and county be requested to patronize Southern manufacturers, Southern markets and direct importations to Southern ports, to the exclusion of all others." "I hollered and shouted with the boys for secession," Smith bragged later, but his role in secession beyond the nonintercourse resolution is not known. [12]

When war broke out in the spring of 1861, Smith was a member of the Rome Light Guards, a local militia formed in 1858. The Confederate government accepted the Rome Light Guards for service and sent them to the Virginia front in May 1861, but Smith did not go with them. The first week in July he went to Virginia with Reuben S. Norton, a kinsman, to visit the Light Guards, then part of the Eighth Georgia Regiment. After spending a few days with their friends, Norton and Smith prepared to return to Georgia. Just before they left, however, a member of Gen. Francis Bartow's staff told Smith that he had been appointed to Bartow's brigade commissary. Smith immediately tried to get a leave of absence so he could return home, but this was refused. Norton went home alone, and Smith found himself in the army.[13]

When Bartow was killed in action at Manassas, Smith was transferred to Gen. George Thomas "Tige" Anderson's brigade. During the peninsular campaign of 1862, Smith "saw more of the horrors of war than ever before or after." He later recorded some of his memories:

> I recall a soldier who sat upon the ground with his back erect against a tree, his rifle grasped with rigid hands and the muzzle resting on the ground. He was sitting just where he fell, but his head was gone, entirely gone, and the blood still oozing from his neck. I have seen the army wagons crossing the shallow trenches where the dead of the battle of Seven Pines had been buried a few days before, and as the wheels crashed down into the soft wet clay, an arm or a leg would be forced up and fall again, and sometimes a ghastly, swollen face would show itself as the heavy wheels passed upon the shallow covered breast.[14]

During one of these battles, Anderson sent Smith to Gen. Robert E. Lee's headquarters for instructions about troop movements. As he entered Lee's tent, Smith saw a man under the tables, asleep in the straw. It was Gen. Thomas "Stonewall" Jackson, an officer explained, who had gone without sleep for forty-eight hours. When he fell exhausted by the table, Lee would not have his rest disturbed. "Reverently I gazed upon him for a minute, for I felt almost like I was in the presence of some divinity," Smith wrote. "What a scene for a painter was that—the two greatest generals of the army, yes, of the age, together; one asleep on the straw, worn out with fatigue and excitement, the camp tables set above him; while the other, with his staff, dined in silence over him and watched his needed rest." [15]

Fever sent Smith to a Virginia hospital for a short while. Tip, his favorite slave, was there to help nurse him back to health. Hines, Smith's oldest son, joined him in Virginia for a brief period, perhaps during this illness. By the late spring of 1863, Smith had returned to Georgia with a medical discharge. Until the end of the war he held the rank of first lieutenant in the Forrest Artillery Company, a home guard unit.[16]

Smith was back in Rome in time to see the first Federal troops there in May 1863. Fortunately, Confederate general Nathan Bedford Forrest managed to trick a larger Union force into surrendering just a few miles outside the city. Following Forrest's surprise (but welcome) victory, Smith and others organized a celebration to honor him.[17] The city was not so lucky a year later when Gen. William T. Sherman threatened Rome on his march against Atlanta. In the middle of May 1864 Confederate military officials gave the orders to evacuate Rome. Many of the town's residents did not wait for orders; some had begun to move away as early as the spring of 1862, but after August 1863, when the Union threat became more severe, "emigration was almost a steady process." Smith's parents had already refugeed to Alabama in January 1864.[18]

On May 17, when the Confederate troops withdrew from Rome, the few remaining Romans in town went with them. Although Rome had been under threat of attack for some time, many of the May refugees seemed totally unprepared to evacuate; according to Reuben Norton, Smith's brother-in-law, people were in such a hurry that they left their homes and possessions "in the Same condition as they would if going to church." Smith had been more cautious. Before leaving, he shipped "a small fortune in salt and several valuable things he treasured," including his library and a huge hogshead of fine china, to Columbus, Georgia, thinking they would be safe there. Columbus fared badly during the war, however, and everything Smith had hoped to protect was burned (with the exception of a large white marble clock which he got back several years after the war). The same fate befell a piano he had shipped to Madison. Smith left a bale of yard-wide cotton sheeting with some friends outside of town; they put a valance and a mirror on it, and Union raiders left the bale alone, thinking it was a dresser.[19]

Despite these preparations, the Smiths still left in a hurry. According to their stories, they were having dinner when the news of the Federals' approach came. They quickly joined the other "runagees," as Smith called the Confederate refugees who had to keep running. At first they set out for Atlanta, burning the Etowah Bridge behind them in an effort to keep from being followed. When Atlanta proved unsafe, they went to Alabama, where they joined Smith's parents. Union troops forced them to take to the road again. This time they headed for the Hutchins plantation on the Chatta-hoochee.[20]

Life was hard for the runagees. There was always too little food, medicine, and sleep, and too much running, illness, and danger. At one point Octavia gave ten dollars for a tablespoon of castor oil and twenty dollars for a pound of sugar. Smith and the rest of his family became separated somewhere along the journey, and it was several days before he found them. When a marauding band of soldiers stole the party's mules and horses, hidden in a canebreak, Smith and another man armed themselves and stole the animals back.[21]

Once the family was safe at the Hutchins plantation, Smith went to Macon. Confederate president Jefferson Davis had appointed him to a special court to try southerners accused of treason. In one case he helped convict three brothers from Columbus for complicity with the enemy; they were sent to a Savannah jail, but the Union army soon freed them. When the Federals reached Macon, Smith gathered the official court papers, stuffed them into a carpetbag along with several large rocks, and threw it all into the river.[22]

Except for a twelve-day period (May 24–June 5, 1864), Union

troops occupied Rome until November, when Sherman began his march to the sea. There was some destruction by the soldiers; perhaps most unforgivable to Smith was the vandalism in the town cemetery. The occupying forces' evacuation orders included burning or destroying only those public properties, army supplies, and private industries that might prove useful to the Confederate war effort, but either by accident or malice, a number of houses were also burned.[23]

The Federals had used Rose Hill, the Smiths' home, as a headquarters. Union generals John M. Corse, Jacob D. Cox, Jefferson C. Davis, and William Vandever are said to have slept in the house, and on the night of October 28, Sherman himself entered Rome and stayed at Rose Hill.[24] Tip, the faithful slave, refugeed with the Smiths but returned once to Rome. He reported back that Union soldiers had built stables and shacks in the yard and telegraph poles with lines running into the house. Horse troughs, many made from pews taken from the Presbyterian Church, littered the grounds. Tip told his masters that the soldiers "just set and spit on yo' fine carpets en tare yore curtins en ruin evything."[25]

The Smiths returned to their home in December 1864, presumably at a more leisurely pace than they had left it the previous May. "We found our dwelling sacked and gutted of all its furniture," Smith later recalled. "We left it full and found it a skeleton." His young daughter remembered that "all the floors of the house were stained with tobacco juice and other things and the walls disfigured in every way." The only items left in the house were those that had been too heavy to move: a large table (on which Sherman had supposedly planned his march to the sea) and a bureau made of a sideboard with doors on the bottom and a bookcase with panes of leaded glass on the top.[26]

One of Octavia's prized possessions was a scrapbook she had kept since she was a girl. In it were notes from her childhood friends, love letters and poems that Charles had written to her in their courting days, and letters he had mailed home during the war. (Smith had hoped to use the letters to compile a written account of his experiences.) In their haste to leave Rome in May 1864, the Smiths left the album behind on the parlor table. When they returned it was gone, picked up by a Union soldier who thought it would make a nice gift for his sweetheart. Twenty years later, the woman (who had married another man) asked her old boyfriend to see if he could locate the original owner of the album so it could be returned. He sent a letter to Octavia Hutchins, Mitford Cottage, Lawrenceville, Georgia, the address in the album. The Lawrenceville postmaster forwarded the letter to the Smiths, who by this time lived in Cartersville, and also wrote back to the man to let him know that Octavia had married the famous Bill Arp. This bit of news gave the man second thoughts, and he decided to keep the album after all. Only after the Smiths threatened "The Law" did he return the album. The man had written sweet notes to his girlfriend on a page or two of the book; "Needless to say," remembered one daughter, "Mama cut the writing out and burned it." [27]

Another Union soldier, this one a telegraph operator from Indiana, had picked up an expensive workstand that Octavia had received as a birthday present. Years later, he wrote to the Smiths with an offer to return the table or, if they were willing, to buy it. Smith wrote back asking for the return of the table, but they never heard from him again. [28]

Union soldiers were not the only people who had looted the homes. Shortly after their return, the Smiths saw a woman sitting in a mahogany rocking chair in front of a house on the outskirts of Rome. They recognized the chair and a matching table beside it as theirs, and the woman finally confessed that she had found them in a vacant house in town. The Smiths had to buy back their own furniture. [29]

As the Union forces left Rome, various bands of stragglers and assorted local bad characters took virtual control of the city, preying on its few residents in a reign of anarchy that lasted for two or three months. There were many robberies and thefts, and at least one murder (a man was killed when he tried to prevent several others from robbing an older couple). This was the state of affairs when

Rome: 1851–1877

the Smiths returned. Smith described the situation in January 1865 to Samuel Gibbons, an old friend who had refugeed to Yorkville, South Carolina. "I hope you will return with your family and live among us," Smith wrote. "We want enough good citizens to put down the thieves and robbers." Smith went on to list several of the more atrocious crimes, including the murder. "We want help to do some hanging. We have now about 60 citizens, and I think the majority are in partnership with some gangs of robbers." Order returned slowly as people came back to Rome.[30]

There was little food available in Rome—the thirty "nice large hams" Smith had stored in his smokehouse had gone, with all the other food on the premises, to feed the Union soldiers—and Smith had a large family to feed. There was only one cow left in the county, he later reported (perhaps with some exaggeration), and he bought it for $3,000 in Confederate money, an IOU for $500, and thirty yards of shirting. The cow was to provide milk for the children; for food, Smith paid several hundred dollars for a few bushels of corn, which he hid and ground only as needed.[31]

Long before the end of the war, Confederate money began to decline in value. Smith owed $3,000 at the beginning of the war, but his creditors refused to take Confederate money for the debts. At the end of the war he had eighteen dollars in greenbacks, which he said made him "next to the richest man in town. Bob Hargrove had $19." Asahel wrote to a kinsman in Rome, "I expect Charles is with you by this time. How he will get a start again with his large family and everything gone seems hard to tell. But he is always hopeful and cheerful." Charles got along for a while by returning to his old trade; with Bob Hargrove he opened a small store in a building Smith owned in town. Their stock was small, but it offered just about all that was available to Rome residents. There was the bale of cloth that had been disguised as a dresser, plus a few bunches of factory yarn, two pounds of coffee, two pounds of sugar, and a half box of tobacco. While refugeeing in Alabama, Smith had successfully defended a man against a charge of embezzling. His fee was $10,000 in Confederate money. With half of this he bought cotton cards (used in the processing of raw cotton), and with the other half he bought a lump of opium. Smith and Hargrove sold the opium for $5 per ounce and the cotton cards for $200 per pair, or folks could bring in sorghum, chickens, potatoes, and so forth, for trade. In August 1865 Smith wrote Hutchins: "Business pretty good. We have just recd. a large stock and think we will sell them."[32]

Five years before, Smith had been a well-liked, witty, fairly prosperous lawyer. He came out of the war "a Southern institution, a kind of national jester for the Confederacy."[33] To pick up this part of his life, we must go back to April 1861. On the 12th of the month, Confederates opened fire on the small Union force in Fort Sumter in Charleston Harbor. Major Robert Anderson surrendered the fort on the fourteenth. On the following day, President Abraham Lincoln issued a proclamation calling on the loyal states to supply 75,000 militiamen to put down "combinations too powerful to be suppressed by the ordinary course of judicial proceedings." The document was also addressed to the rebelling states; Lincoln ordered the persons making up those combinations "to disperse and retire peaceably to their respective abodes within twenty days from this date." Smith thought the proclamation was "very absurd and ridiculous,"[34] so one day as he sat in his Rome law office he decided to write a satiric response. The letter, written as if the author were an almost illiterate backwoodsman, pretended to give the president some friendly, well-meaning advice.

As Smith read the letter to some friends from the steps of the Rome courthouse, a man named Bill Earp listened and joined in the laughter. Earp, a typical Georgia cracker, was one of the best-liked men in town, despite his fondness for drink and his occasional violent spells. When Smith finished reading the letter, Earp stepped forward and asked, "Squire, are you going to print that?" Smith said he might, and Earp asked him what name he would use. When Smith replied that he had not decided yet, Earp said, "Well, 'Squire, I wish you would put mine, for them's my sentiments."[35] Smith did have the letter published; it appeared a few days later in one of the local papers (or perhaps in Atlanta's *Southern Confederacy*) over the name of "Bill Arp."[36]

Two historians of Georgia journalism have noted that "although the South at war produced its own brand of comic relief, little found its way into the Georgia press. The few jokes and light articles published pursued the antebellum motifs, and were usually inserted as fillers." Smith's letter was therefore a welcome and refreshing sight to southerners, especially those in Smith's home state. Editors of other newspapers copied the letter freely, in both senses of the word; Smith probably received no pay for these reprintings. The letter to Lincoln was an immediate success with southern readers, both civilians at home and soldiers at camp. Readers and editors demanded more, and by the end of December 1862, three more letters to Lincoln appeared, all signed by Bill Arp.[37]

Smith did not restrict his wartime writings to satirical letters addressed to the president. In some of the letters—all written in the dialect that was so popular among mid-nineteenth-century humorists and all signed by Bill Arp—Smith described his family's refugeeing experiences or applauded the battle spirit shown by southerners in the war. In others, he censured those people whose actions hurt the Confederate war effort—the draft dodgers and the extortioners, for example, and the extreme states'-righters who refused to cooperate fully with the Confederate government. As the southern cause looked increasingly hopeless, he urged readers to remain strong. When the end finally came, he wrote that the South was "conquered, but not convinced,"[38] and he continued to write for the rights and honor of the South.

Smith brought most of these newspaper letters together a year after the war ended in *Bill Arp, So Called: A Side Show of the Southern Side of the War*. When he submitted the manuscript to the publisher, Smith requested that the misspelling be purged from the letters; "good taste," he wrote, "would not condemn one or two letters for murdering her Majesty's English, yet a frequent repetition of the offence can hardly be justified." The *Metropolitan Record*, a fiercely partisan Democratic paper published in New York, issued a thousand copies of the book, which sold out quickly. As a second printing was being readied, a Republican mob broke up the editor's office. Smith reportedly did not receive a penny from the venture, and it is said that the experience made him "disgusted with the book business" for several years.[39]

For a brief period during the war, Smith was an editor for Atlanta's *Southern Confederacy*. According to a historian of Georgia wartime journalism, the *Southern Confederacy* was "one of the most rabid of the secessionist papers in the South." Smith himself later described it as "fire and brimstone against the yankees," and elsewhere said he "wrote for it sometimes just to give our boys some comfort and our enemies some sass."[40]

When Smith resumed his political career after the war, his newspaper letters had made the name of Bill Arp a familiar one to many southerners. Following the election of 1865, in which Smith won a state senatorial seat, the *Rome Courier* joked: "We learn that at Kingston yesterday 79 votes were polled for 'Bill Arp' and only one vote for C. H. Smith. If Bill should beat Smith, wouldn't it be a joke?"[41]

During his term as senator, Smith once addressed his "feller citizens" in a Bill Arp letter: "My friends, our aim has onestly been to git you all back into the Union. . . . Up to this time it have been an uphill business. The teem was a good one, and the gear all sound, and the waggin greased, but the rode is perhaps the ruffest in the world." The road got rougher as the United States Congress, in the Reconstruction Act of March 1867, decreed that the existing governments in ten of the former Confederate states were unlawful. The act disbanded the legislatures in those states and set up military rule in the South. Smith, mayor of Rome at that time, occasionally had trouble with the local Federal commander, Capt. Charles de la Mesa. The young people of the town decided to put on a play, "The Officer's Funeral," in order to raise money to replace the church pews that had been destroyed during the Union occupation of the city. The stage they designed resembled a battle scene, complete with an old Confederate flag in the corner. De la Mesa was there on the night of the play, Smith later recalled in a Bill Arp letter. "When he saw the flag he left the hall in a tower of rage. Next morning he put all the prominent persons connected with the tableaux

under arrest." Smith wrote to Gen. George H. Thomas in Louisville, Kentucky, begging leniency for the town's citizens. (Since the
war's end, Thomas had been commander of the Military Division
of Tennessee, which included Georgia; for a brief time after passage
of the Reconstruction Act, he headed the Third Military District.)
"I told him that our people in Rome had in good faith accepted the
situation," Smith wrote, "and the boys intended no insult by the
display of the flag." The citizens were released with the warning
that it was treason "to glory in their shame, and flaunt the symbol
of their crime in the face of the country." [42]

As mayor, Smith did whatever he could to help his fellow citizens.
A problem involving a man named Buchanan, who had left Rome
early during the war with his family, arose a month after the incident with de la Mesa. Buchanan had failed to tell anyone, even his
friends, where he was going. Town officials therefore assumed his
property in Rome was deserted and sold it. Smith later learned that
Buchanan had joined a military company in South Carolina and
promised to do what he could to help recover the property. "Justice
shall be done," he wrote a friend, ". . . as I will not wrong a soldier." [43] Smith had had troubles of his own the previous year when
the Freedmen's Bureau (which oversaw labor contracts) charged
him with improperly dismissing a black nurse. Smith had said that
the nurse did not take proper care of the children. [44]

In 1867, the same year that Smith became mayor, he joined the
law practice of Joel Branham. Like his previous law associations, this
was a happy one. Smith and Branham kept no books, but divided
the fees as they came in, sharing profits and losses equally. The
lawyers put all their earnings into Smith's bank account, and each
drew on the account as he needed—"a most unwise arrangement,"
Branham later admitted, "but it showed my confidence in Major
Smith, and it was not abused." Smith did most of the office work,
while Branham handled the actual trials. "Major Smith was averse
to disputation," Branham recalled. "It was even difficult to get him
to go to the court house when he was a witness in a case." [45]

Smith also continued his involvement in the newspaper business in these years. For a while after the war he was on the staff of the *Rome Courier*, the local paper published in several editions that had printed a number of his Bill Arp letters, but he seemed to stay at odds with Melville Dwinell, the *Courier*'s editor. Perhaps as a result of these conflicts he briefly edited the *Rome Commercial*, a competing paper. "Our local Press is an affliction to us," he wrote to a friend a few years later, "no doubt sent by Providence to keep us humble." [46]

The source of the disagreements between Smith and the *Courier* was usually politics. In 1870, Smith and the *Courier* differed in their choices for candidates for a seat in the state legislature, with the *Courier* supporting the Democratic candidate, former Confederate general P. M. B. Young, and Smith, although himself a Democrat, supporting Republican George P. Burnett. Smith's support did not signal a sudden acceptance of the Radical line; rather, he supported Burnett "on personal grounds" [47] that he did not further explain.

Connected with this particular conflict with the *Courier* was the issue of railroads. Smith's interest in railroads went back to his youth. His father had purchased $5,000 in Georgia Railroad stock before the road was built and kept it until 1849, when he had to sell it (at twenty-seven cents on the dollar) in a period of financial difficulty. The buyer was none other than Nathan Louis Hutchins, Charles's future father-in-law, so the stock stayed in the family. Charles would later have connections with a number of railroads, as well as a steamboat company. [48]

At the same time that the Georgia Railroad was being built with private funds, the Western and Atlantic, an important line from Chattanooga to Atlanta, was being constructed with state money. Georgia invested almost $5,000,000 during the 1840s in building the line. The road was profitable, returning about $350,000 annually between 1865 and 1868, but mismanagement put the road heavily into debt in 1870. When Dunlap Scott, a leading Democrat, introduced a bill in the state legislature to lease the road to a private firm, many Georgians agreed with the proposal. A number of people, however, including several leading railroad men, thought that the state should get rid of the road completely, selling it rather than leasing it. [49]

In a letter to the *Rome Daily Courier,* written under the name of "Flat Woods," Smith denounced Scott's proposal. "Is thar any difference betwixt Skott's bill for leasing the State Rode and any other Legislative *swindle?*" he asked. An exchange of letters took place in the pages of the *Weekly Courier.* Smith predicted that "the lease will prove to be an enormous speculation to the lesees, and a like loss to the State." He said he had not intended an attack on Scott's character, but he resented Scott's assertion that anyone who would vote for Burnett—who was an official of the state road—had been "greased." [50] A decade later, when the lease was up for renewal, Smith wrote: "I dont believe the state ought to own railroads no how for they make a power of fuss and sow discord among brethren and demoralize our politicians so that you can't tell a saint from a sinner." Smith explained his philosophy of railroad ownership in greater detail in an 1869 letter to the *Courier* in which he urged citizens of Rome to invest in a line from Rome to Decatur. "It certainly is not right for a few men to have all the burden of developing and maintaining the commercial interests of our city and our county," he said. "In the past a few have done it—a few public spirited men who have ventured their means in every enterprise that has made us what we are. . . . It is always the same few in every community, and the rest come in and enjoy with them the benefits thereof." [51]

The *Courier* did not accept Smith's explanation for his support of Burnett—that he did it for "personal" reasons—and, like Scott, accused him of selling out. In one issue, the *Weekly Courier* printed a comment from another newspaper about Smith's actions: "This thing puzzles us. We don't understand it." A week later, in a piece titled "I'll 'ang My 'Arp on a Willer Tree," the paper waxed poetic in its criticism of Smith:

> By a personal friend I was caught by the 'and
> And was led to a mountain 'igh,
> And 'e showed me a beautiful prospect there,
> And the places was fair to my eye,
>
> So I'll 'ang my 'Arp on a willer tree,
> And never will toutch it agin,

And I'll vote for the man what greases me
Because 'e 'as plenty o' tin.

An office I saw in that prospect fair,
And the picture is 'aunting me yet,
For plenty good pickings lay scattered around,
And didn't I like it—you bet,

. . . .

Oh, General Young is a very nice man,
But 'e doesn't know 'ow to grease,
So I'll cling to the tail of my personal friend
'Till the waters of Tartarus freeze.

After the election—which Burnett lost—one of Smith's opponents apologized to him in the *Rome Courier* for his role in the controversy and urged readers not to make harsh judgments against Smith. Smith had acted out of patriotism and unselfish motives when he pushed for Burnett, the man said.[52]

Another disagreement between Smith and the *Courier* came about a year later in the municipal elections. "The discontents and malcontents who have long been jealous and envious of what they call the Smith Ring (meaning me and my friends) combined and confederated some three months ago to break it up," Smith wrote to his brother-in-law in December 1871. "I have known of their intentions for a long time and prepared my battery to meet the assault." Smith gave the particulars of the election—including his estimate of how much money changed hands as a result of gambling—and then related the dirty side of the campaign: "Rome never knew such excitement. The race was a bitter one and engendered much bad feeling. We were shamefully slandered by our enemies but we bore it meekly as long as we could. . . . A mean contemptible Editor . . . who edits Dwinell's paper wrote so many lies about us that Hines and Royal [Smith's sons] are watching for him on the street. Dwinell and his Editor keep close for they know it will not be healthy to pass the Ring on the street."[53]

In the summer and fall of 1871, a joint committee of Congress—the Joint Select Committee to Inquire into the Condition of Affairs in the Late Insurrectionary States—investigated the activities of the

Ku Klux Klan in the post-war South. The committee interviewed hundreds of witnesses whose testimony filled twelve large volumes of small print. Two of the dozen or so witnesses who testified on Klan activities in Rome were P. M. Sheibley and Z. B. Hargrove, two names that also show up among Smith's political "enemies" in his letter to his brother-in-law on that year's elections.

Sheibley, Rome's postmaster, described at length for the committee how "violence is done by disguised men, and generally toward the colored people, threatening them that they shall not vote; shall not interfere in elections; that they must not vote the radical ticket." Sheibley said that the intimidation had started in earnest during the 1870 elections.[54]

Hargrove, an attorney in Rome, told the committee that he had been a Democrat for most of his life and had served as an officer in the Confederate army. "I was a rebel, and a true one, I reckon, if there ever was one," he said, but added that he had later voiced support for Reconstruction, "though that was rather in antagonism to my party." In his testimony, Hargrove discussed the "non-reconstruction men, who were . . . engaged in open acts of violence toward many." "During the last election," he said, ". . . I came in direct conflict with these lawless men, more or less, because then I espoused the republican cause. . . . I, with some few other men who had been acting with the democratic party up to that time, concluded that we would act with it no longer if it was to be governed by men such as those." Later in his testimony, he was asked when he quit the Democratic party. "I expect it quit me about eighteen months ago," he replied.

> *Question.*: Oh, it quit you, did it?
> *Answer.*: Yes, sir.
> *Question.*: In what form did it quit you?
> *Answer.*: It went into the hands of violent men, and, as I thought, it undertook to live by means of violence.[55]

That these two names, Sheibley and Hargrove, appear both in a list of Smith's political opponents and in the report of the congressional committee investigating Klan outrages is probably more than simple coincidence. The Floyd County area was a "major theater of Klan operations in Georgia." Smith himself was a member of the Klan. In her memoirs, his daughter Marian described her discovery of this fact: "One evening late I went unexpectedly into the parlor. My father, mother, sister and two young men were talking in low, earnest tones. On the sofa were the strangest things, white and long and some holes in them that looked like eyes. I only had a glimpse for Mama saw me and quick I was put out of the room, Mama telling me that I must not speak of what I saw for it would get Papa into trouble." "I belonged to the infamous ku klux klan," Smith wrote in 1882. "It was the conservative views of the ku-klux that saved the state; leastways I will say that the ku-klux kept down lawless niggers and plundering carpet baggers, and there was no other power at the time that could save our wives and children from their outrages." [56]

When John B. Gordon, reputed Grand Dragon of the Georgia Klan in its early years, was summoned to testify before the committee, Smith rode to Washington with him and sent back a reassuring report of what Gordon planned to say:

> He says he will testify that there are organizations at the South for the defence and protection of the people—that in his opinion such organizations were necessary, and in some places are necessary now—that by reason of the sudden freedom of the slaves, and the influx of carpet-baggers, our people, our homes and our altars are in danger—that the power of the government was against us, or it was withheld from protecting us—that the organization was not a political one, nor was it designed to continue the rebellion or subvert the laws of the United States, but simply for protection against bad negroes and worse white men. He will further testify, that in his opinion, these organizations have done good—far more good than harm. They have prevented rather than promoted carnage and arson and rape and bloodshed—that the occasion for them is fast passing away and that when good men get into office and power at the South and the people feel safe under the protection of the Courts and the laws, these organizations will cease to exist. [57]

Smith's statement is written with such conviction that it is hard to believe that he did not share Gordon's sentiments.

We can do no better than to speculate about Smith's activities in the Klan. According to one historian, Gordon left the organization perhaps as early as 1868; if so, maybe his friend Smith left with him. This historian goes on to say that by 1871 "the 'respectable men' who had organized the Klan had largely fallen away, leaving it to younger poor whites who suffered more acutely from Negrophobia." Another scholar who studied the Klan in Georgia found that by July 1870 "the better educated and politically motivated were replaced with a group of lower intellect motivated by prejudice and personal gain."[58]

George P. Burnett, the Republican candidate for the state legislature Smith had supported in 1870, told the congressional committee that in Summerville during the campaign "some disguised men, known as Ku-Klux in that country," visited him and gave him a note telling him that he would not be allowed to speak there and that he must leave town by a certain time.[59] It is difficult to imagine Smith publicly supporting a Republican and privately threatening him, so perhaps Smith had left the Klan by that time. In any case, however, he certainly sympathized with the goals of the Klan, if not its methods, throughout its existence.

The end of the war had not meant the end of Bill Arp. Although Smith wrote relatively few Arp letters in the dozen years following the war, his fiery spirit remained. Arp's early letters of the era were hopeful. In the first week of September 1865, many southern newspapers printed a letter from Bill Arp that one editor said was "the first chirp of any bird after the surrender, and gave relief and hope to thousands of drooping hearts."[60] The letter was addressed to Artemus Ward (Charles Farrar Browne), a northern humorist known for his moderate political views. In this letter—one of his most famous—Arp demanded that southern patriotism and bravery be honored and that southerners be allowed to rejoin the Union on an equal footing with their northern brethren. Arp wrote that the South was not in a position to force the issue, but that the North could have a peaceful and easy reconciliation of the sections by meeting his conditions. Arp was not satisfied with the North's response, and for the next few years he vented his fury by writing letters—some hostile, some humorous—on a number of topics related to Reconstruction. (These letters are discussed in greater detail in chapter 4.)

Smith published his second book, *Bill Arp's Peace Papers*, in 1873. Like his first, this was a collection of items that had originally appeared in the newspapers. *Peace Papers* reprinted some of the pieces in *Bill Arp, So Called*, but also contained many of the letters Arp wrote during Reconstruction. Where Smith had asked the publisher to revise the orthography of the first book, *Peace Papers* reverted to the old misspelling.

The years in Rome following the war were not good ones, financially, for Smith. The large inheritance that Octavia received when her father died in 1870, perhaps as much as $25,000, was gone in a few years, lost to a bank failure, various railroad schemes, and a general economic slump. His law practice was slow in reviving, and many citizens of Rome who did need a lawyer found that they could not afford to pay for one. "Not enough money recd. to buy bread," he wrote to Nathan L. Hutchins, Jr., in 1867. "The prospect is really alarming." Toward the end of 1871, Smith wrote that his "business is very dull—collections poor—money scarce. I am like Micawber, waiting for something to turn up." A year and a half later, he wrote Hutchins again, saying that he would depend on the profits from *Bill Arp's Peace Papers* to help the financial situation, but that "Carleton [the publisher] is too slow—I must hurry him up."[61]

Perhaps it was these money matters, combined with his dislike for litigation, that persuaded Smith to move away from Rome and try a fresh start elsewhere. He had already sold a lot on his Rome property to a doctor, and had built a cottage for his son Hines on another piece of the land. Still, in 1877, he was able to sell the remainder for $6,000, enough to move his family to a two hundred acre farm just outside of Cartersville, Georgia. The Smiths christened their new home Fontainebleu, from Fontaine, the name of the previous owner, and the blue feelings of Mrs. Smith and the children on leaving Rome.[62]

Three

Cartersville:
1877–1903

Fontainebleu, the Smith's country home near Cartersville, was "a beautiful little farm," Smith later wrote, "where there were springs and branches, a meadow and a creek near by, with a canebrake border. Not far away was a mill and a pond, and there was a mountain in the background where small game abounded. There we raised Jersey cows and colts and sheep and chickens and peafowls, and lived well by day and feasted on music by night. . . . It was a lovely home, and all the younger children grew up there to manhood and womanhood, and were happy." In front of the house was a grove of Spanish oaks, with a couple of swings for the children. The house itself had two rooms when Smith bought it, but he added five more. One room was for guests, and Smith once jokingly wrote that one was enough, for "if you put up martin gourds, the martins are shore to cum." Actually, friends were always welcome, and they often came. The Smiths believed strongly in the sentence painted in gold above the mantle in the parlor: "The ornaments of this house are the friends who visit it."[1]

In his first year on the farm Smith planted, among other things, peanuts, watermelons, canteloupes, wheat, peas, potatoes, onions, oats, and corn. There was also a flower garden and grapevines in a long arbor he had built. In May 1878 he reported that "there was 54 chickens, 7 ducks, 5 goslins, 12 turkeys, and seven pigs, hatched out last week and Daisy had a calf and Mollie a colt besides." It was a fairly large farm, and since a half mile of the public road cut across the property, there had to be a lot of fence—four miles, he once estimated. Smith farmed only a portion of the land himself, renting most of it out to tenants. He was proud to be a scientific farmer; he read books and magazines on the subject, and was apparently successful in a few of his agricultural forays.[2]

But if Smith expected the farm to turn around the financial misfortunes his family had experienced in Rome after the war, he was mistaken. "Farming is a slow way to make money," he complained after a few years of trying. He noted that farming was a lot like fishing: "Every time you start out you can just see yourself catchin' 'em; but after tryin' every hole in the creek you go home sorrowfully, with a fisherman's luck." "We have lived harder and poorer the last 8 months than ever before in our lives," Smith wrote to his brother-in-law in June 1878. "It took all available means to pay for the farm and stock it. . . . I have a good farm and think we can make a good living on it but there will be nothing for extras." In that same letter, however, Smith indicated that things might be getting better: "For a month I have been earning 5 Dollars a week from the Constitution for my random letters. This has helped us out wonderfully."[3]

These "random letters" had begun on May 17, 1878. On that day, the *Atlanta Constitution* printed, on its first page, a letter from Bill Arp. Labeled "A Letter from the Georgia Humorist," the column extolled the joys of farming. "It's an honest, quiet life," Bill Arp wrote, "and it does me so much good to work and git all over in a swet of perspiration."[4] This was the first of a long series of letters that Smith would write for the *Constitution*. His column appeared weekly, with a few brief interruptions, until his death in August 1903.

Henry Woodfin Grady had joined the staff of the *Constitution* soon after Evan P. Howell acquired control of the paper in 1876, and it was probably Grady who introduced Bill Arp to a wider reading audience by making him a *Constitution* correspondent. Smith and Grady had been friends for several years. In September 1869, Grady, then a young "newspaper apprentice," went to Rome to edit Melville Dwinell's *Rome Courier.* The following year Grady purchased a competing paper, the *Rome Commercial* (which Smith had edited for a brief time). Raymond B. Nixon, Grady's biographer, stressed the importance of Grady's years in Rome in shaping his journalistic skills and allowing him to prove himself. But "the most significant influence upon Grady in Rome," Nixon added, ". . . was his contact with what he described as 'a nest of the raciest, keenest and pleasantest wits that ever chance threw together.' " The group would sit around the courthouse or visit the newspaper office, telling jokes and swapping tall tales. "Their fun-hunting was leisurely," Grady recalled, "but earnest and continuous. Many, many a golden green afternoon did they wear out with social converse." A number of the men were lawyers, but "a new joke was of more importance to them than a new case." Grady said that their laughter was contagious; a man listening to them "became humorous by absorption, just as the teetotaler was made drunk by sleeping with the toper." Some of Rome's leading citizens were a part of this "nest," but Grady was especially impressed with Smith, who by this time had been Bill Arp for almost a decade.[5]

On May 28, 1878, Grady officially welcomed Arp into the *Constitution* family. In a long article that praised Smith's early writings, Grady wrote that "Maj. Smith has commenced a new career, and the readers of *The Constitution* will be able to see what he can do, which is a great deal more interesting than what he has done."[6] And Arp's new career certainly was different. During the war and Reconstruction, Arp had written on Abraham Lincoln's policies, Confederate draft dodgers, refugeeing, the southern battle spirit, Radical Republicans, the Freedmen's Bureau, and other such subjects. In the first two years of his *Constitution* column, Arp treated his readers to weekly letters about farm superstitions, a Democratic barbecue, memories of his father's store, Georgia politician William Felton, kissing, poetry, the hardships of winter on the farm, the joys of spring, a journalists' convention, eating green corn, spiders and snakes in the house, music, suggestions that city folk move to the country, farm economy, watermelons, and a host of other topics.

On two occasions Arp stopped writing his column for a while. In a December 1881 letter, after discussing farming, industries, and the tariff, he wrote: "And now, Mr. Editor, let me say adieu to you and your readers. Adieu for a season. I don't know how long, but I have long suspected I was writing too much—keeping my pen before the people too long—wearying them with vagaries that were crude and ill digested, with thoughts that were not new and advice that was not needed." But he was back six weeks later, as if he had never left. "He could not resist the appeals of the public," read an editorial comment.[7]

Ten years later he did it again. "Friends—readers of *The Constitution*, this is my last letter to you," he announced at the end of 1891. "For many years I have made you a weekly visit, and have tried to cheer the fireside and give good counsel to the children, and comfort to the parents. It grieves me to say goodby, but my time is out, and I must give place to worthier pens. My occupation is gone, and henceforth I must seek some other whereby to provide for the few years that are to come."[8] This time his absence was longer; he stayed away from the *Constitution* until May 29, 1892.

With these two exceptions, Bill Arp's column was a fairly regular feature in the *Constitution* for a quarter of a century. The column usually appeared on Sundays, but sometimes it showed up on other days of the week. Smith missed a few weeks here and there, especially as he got older and illness sometimes kept him from his desk. Generally, though, he wrote whenever possible. When his son Ralph, who had been working on a railroad in Florida, became severely ill with fever in 1885, Smith and his wife stayed in Florida with him for more than two months. Smith missed only one week's column during that span.[9] By the time he died, he had contributed some 1,250 pieces to the *Constitution*. Beginning in November 1888, the Louisville *Home and Farm* had a contract with Smith and the *Constitution* to reprint some of the weekly letters.[10]

Other newspapers also copied the Bill Arp letters, occasionally without giving credit either to him or to the *Constitution*. Most papers, however, especially the small country weeklies, printed the column by arrangement with the Western Newspaper Union. Ansel Nash Kellogg, creator of the first newspaper syndicate in 1865, had popularized the use of readyprint—four-page newspaper sheets, undated and with no headings, that were preprinted on the inside two pages or the outside two with "evergreen matter" (stories, national advertisements, and miscellaneous matter that could be used at any time and in any place). The editors of country weekly papers who subscribed to this service could then print the name of their papers and the date and fill the two blank pages with local news and advertisements. Since country editors hardly had the time to set the type for four pages each week, much less gather and write that much news, they welcomed the weekly shipments of "patent insides" or "outsides," as they came to be known. In the mid-1870s, Kellogg developed the stereotype plate as a means of delivering material to newspapers. Editors could print their own newspaper from these plates, arranging the material to suit their needs, and then return the plates to the syndicate. By 1880, three thousand weeklies (two-fifths of those published) were supplied by these services.[11]

The Western Newspaper Union was one of the largest of the syndicates. Founded in 1880, by 1910 it "had a virtual monopoly on the syndicate business supplied through the medium of printed services." When it picked up Bill Arp's column, he became one of the syndicate's most popular writers. "For the ready-print editors, Bill Arp was a gold mine," wrote Thomas D. Clark. "His letters took up considerable space for them, were highly readable and thoroughly acceptable." One scholar estimated that as many as seven hundred newspapers occasionally reprinted Arp's letters, and another scholar found them regularly reprinted as far away from Atlanta as Chicago, New York, Detroit, and San Francisco. Arp's letters were most popular, not surprisingly, in the South. A survey of North Carolina newspapers from the turn of the century found Arp's column in one-third of them, from the *Chatham Observer* and the *Farmer's Friend* of Morganton to Raleigh's *News and Observer*. A more comprehensive examination would no doubt raise that figure.[12]

Arp's *Constitution* column was so popular that the editors of the

Southern Cultivator, a monthly journal aimed at farm families, asked Smith to write original essays for them. Arp's pieces in the *Southern Cultivator,* which were usually on agricultural topics, began appearing late in 1882 and continued for almost four years.

Just after Smith became a weekly contributor to the *Constitution,* he set out on a second new career. On June 26, 1878, the *Constitution* printed a review of Smith's "first appearance as a lecturer." Smith had delivered talks to groups before 1878, but this Atlanta lecture was the beginning of his first organized lecture tour. The reviewer noted that the audience had "never heard a more delightful lecture. It was rich, chaste and elegant, and dripping all through with quiet, unctious [*sic*] humor. . . . No audience was ever better pleased with an entertainment" [13]—a fine review, even allowing for the reviewer's pride in the *Constitution*'s newest star.

Smith was a part-time lecturer for the rest of his life. Annie May Christie reported that he delivered hundreds of lectures in at least thirteen states (all but one, New York, in the South). Several factors motivated Smith to leave his home and family, sometimes for weeks at a time, to lecture. First, he needed the money. Rents from his farm tenants brought in a little, but by themselves were never enough. As Smith wrote in one of his Bill Arp letters, the rents paid for the farm expenses "and not much else." "If I depended on my farm for a support," he wrote, "we wouldent exactly perish, but we would get awfully hungry sometimes." Smith received a regular income for the *Constitution* columns, and the sale of his books added a small amount to that, but during the Cartersville years the lectures probably accounted for as much of the family's income as did anything else.[14]

"Farming will support the family pretty well," Smith wrote in an 1880 Bill Arp letter, "but it won't send the children off to boarding school nor make up for a dead mule, nor the loss of a wheat crop, nor buy a new carpet, and paper the walls, and get new curtains for the parlor, and so fourth, and so fifth, and sixth, and so on. Therefore, I have to start out now and then and swap off a little nonsense for a little money, and it seems to work pretty well." In an 1891 letter, Arp told his readers that, just when his wife was complaining of the need for new clothes for the family and new sheets and blankets for the beds, "the next mail brought me letters from Arkansas, inviting me to visit Pine Bluff and a fair at Warren and offering me $300." Similarly, when Bill Arp was asked to lecture in North Carolina in 1897, "My wife said as the larder was getting low and the girls needed some more winter clothes, and the tax man was bobbing around and the grandchildren would be expecting something for Christmas, she thought I had better go." "My wife—thoughtful woman—told me I had better start out and see if I couldent talk the good people out of enough to make the grandchildren happy," he wrote a couple of years later.[15]

Smith charged according to local custom—generally a quarter in small towns, fifty cents in the cities. One of his lectures in Florida was sponsored by a group that thought the *Constitution* paid for his speaking tours, and he did not find out about the mistake until just before his talk was to begin. He described the incident in a Bill Arp letter:

> An old gentleman, who seemed to be master of ceremonies, came to me and with great dignity and kindliness of manner said, "Major, would it be at all improper for us to take up a little collection to remunerate you for your traveling expenses. We have conferred about it and think you ought to have that much if it is agreeable to you."
>
> My photograph ought to have been taken right then. I turned my face towards the door to see if it was possible that there was no doorkeeper. There was none and more people kept walking in just like they were coming to church. I looked at my venerable friend and said: "Have none of these people paid anything?"
>
> "Well, no," said he. "We didn't know that you charged anything, but we thought we ought to take up a little collection," and so the hats were passed and some few put in quarters. Many more put in dimes. Still more dropped in nickels and two put in coppers and the rest put in nothing. I've got the coppers yet as a memento of the lost cause.[16]

Aside from these financial considerations, Smith lectured for the instruction and amusement of his audiences. Unfortunately, no one recorded Smith's exact words when he lectured, but several pieces in his last three books appear to be slightly polished versions of his lectures. "Behind the Scenes," for example, was a speech on the Civil War, and the essay entitled "The Aristocracy and the Common People" dealt with differences in southern society before and after the war. After a year of lecturing, Smith told his brother-in-law that he had heard a talk by Josh Billings, another popular humorist of the time, and he considered himself to be the superior speaker.[17]

Smith also lectured to help charitable and patriotic groups. His talks were often sponsored by organizations such as libraries, colleges, and historical and memorial associations; and he frequently split the proceeds with these groups.[18]

Finally, Smith lectured because he enjoyed seeing old friends and making new ones. From his *Constitution* columns and elsewhere, one gets the sense that he genuinely liked people, and people who met Smith seemed to return the affection. One man, W. Lafayette Smith (no relation), heard Smith lecture in Fayetteville, North Carolina, in 1893. In a letter home to his mother, he described the experience:

> Last night I met Maj Chas. H. Smith, better known as "Bill Arp." He is a very easy social kind of fellow and talks just about like he writes . . . . He lectured at the opera house last night and it was a very good one as well as amusing. He told many of his "ups and downs" in his young days[,] how he used to court "Mrs. Arp," &c, &c. When I met him he said,—"and this is another one of the Smith's is it?" I told him "yes" and that I was glad to have the pleasure of shaking his hand. I also told him that many a time in days gone by I had read his letters to my mother by the fire light at home. He wanted to know if you were still living, and said he was glad you enjoyed his writings. He also said:—"Give your good mother my kindest regards." [19]

Arp once lectured at a small town in northeast Texas variously known as Jarvis Switch or Strawberry. Many people there were truck farmers, and they wanted a shorter name to put on their packing crates. They were so impressed with Bill Arp—both the man and the brevity of his name—that they changed the name of the town to honor him. Arp, Texas, is still there today.[20]

Smith's speaking engagements were generally successful, but he reported a few failures. "I lectured in LaGrange last night to the biggest house and the smallest audience I ever saw mixed up together," he wrote in 1880. "You can't fool this town with nonsense. They are too smart." The small size of an audience in Texas a few years later was due to other circumstances:

> At one town where I was advertised to lecture I found on my arrival that the streets were flooded with posters, viz. "The church will open tonight as usual for prayer. We see that the opera house will be opened for worldly fun. Choose ye this day whom ye will serve." Well, I was the opera house man and so the good people got alarmed and my house was much larger than my audience. But that was all right I reckon, for I have no complaint to make, though I am inclined to think that if the preacher had charged a half dollar I would have come out better and done no damage to good morals or Christianity.

But Smith's appearance in Birmingham in 1886 was probably more typical. "I did not expect to be welcomed by many to hear me lecture," he wrote, "for I thought they were too bright to indulge in such pastimes, but I never stood up before a larger audience nor one that appeared to better advantage in those manners that indicate culture and refinement. There was not a vacant seat in the hall and some few had to sit standing." [21]

Smith kept up with his Bill Arp letters while he was lecturing. The *Constitution* columns he wrote while on a lengthy tour of Texas in 1885 got him into hot water with the folks back home. In the first of these eight letters, Arp said that he had met many former Georgians in Texas and remarked how wonderful it was that people down on their luck in Georgia could do so well by moving southwest. His descriptions of the Lone Star State grew brighter each week. People wrote to the *Constitution* to complain about Arp's letters, or at least to question them, and the paper was forced to print a note saying that although Arp's letters "leave the impression that Georgians can better themselves by going to Texas, . . . this comes from our William's good humor, for it was his purpose to leave no such impression. If he had the opportunity tomorrow he would not give ten acres of his Bartow county farm for the best farm in Texas." [22]

Arp apparently did not learn a lesson from this, however, for in

August 1892, when he returned to Texas for a month, he wrote back about the bright prospects for men who moved there—"If I was a young man I'd come myself," he declared in one letter. A week later, he marveled at the profits Texas pecan growers made. "Oh, if I had only come out here fifteen years ago and planted even 200 acres in pecans; do you think that I would now be travelling a thousand miles from home to sell my talk for more than it is worth? No, sir; nary time." Again, there were some complaints back in Georgia, but they seemed to be fewer than seven years before.[23]

Arp was back home during September, but returned to Texas in October for about six weeks. This time he stopped potential critics by writing in his first letter: "I shall peruse the country all along the line and of course will see the bright and beautiful side and write about it; and your readers must take it with some allowance for I am an invited guest, and it would be very bad manners for me to find fault with the country or her people."[24] When he started writing rapturous accounts of his visits to the Gulf Coast of Florida a couple of years later, he was "admonished to let up on Clear Water." He never let up on Clearwater, though, and for the last ten years or so of his life he praised Florida's healthful climate and beautiful scenery and urged readers to buy winter homes there. He occasionally arranged deals for his readers to buy Florida land and collected a small commission.[25]

Smith published three more collections of newspaper columns in the Cartersville years: *Bill Arp's Scrap Book* (1884), *The Farm and the Fireside* (1891), and *Bill Arp: From the Uncivil War to Date* (1903). (A memorial edition of this last book, published shortly after Smith's death later that year, differed from the original only by the addition of a chapter "On the Home Life of Bill Arp," written by his daughter Marian, and a few photographs.) Like his first two books, each of these three reprinted some of the letters written during the war and Reconstruction, particularly the "runagee" accounts and the letter to Artemus Ward. There the similarity ends, however, for most of the pieces in these last three collections are delightful sketches of Smith's domestic life, his farm and friends, and his boy-

hood—sketches written for the *Constitution* and bearing such titles
as "Adventures on the Farm," "Mrs. Arp's Birthday," "The Beau-
tiful Snow," "New Year's Time," "Fodder Pulling," "Grandfather's
Days," "Making Sausage," "The House Where I Was Born," "A
Prosy Poem on Spring," "Rural Observations," "The Old Trunk,"
"Old Times," and "The Old School Days."

These books brought little wealth to Smith. When he published
The Farm and the Fireside in 1891, he wrote in a Bill Arp letter that
he expected "a little money, . . . a little fame and some fun" from the
book. He received twenty-five cents for each copy sold, and told his
wife that he hoped to "sell enough to keep you in missionary money.
One copy a week will do that, won't it?" Shortly after publication of
From the Uncivil War to Date, he wrote that he had sold five hundred
copies at $1.25 each, but that he would have to raise the price to
$1.50, as he was receiving only 2½ cents per book in royalties.[26]

In the summer of 1888, Arp wrote that he had wished "a thousand
times" to be, like his father, a schoolteacher—"not that I was vain
and thought that I could teach better than others," he explained, but
because of his love for the young people and his desire to help shape
them into useful and happy citizens. This desire to teach Georgia's
youth moved him, five years later, to write a history of Georgia to
be used as a school text. "It is a labor of love with me," he said,
"and my best ambition is to found it upon the truth." When asked
if the book would be sectional, he replied, "No, . . . but it will be
Georgian, and if that makes it southern I cannot help it." [27]

Smith wrote *A School History of Georgia* especially for "the young
people whose fathers and grandfathers fought in that war—fought
for something they believed to be right." [28] The history was divided
into two parts; following the text proper, written mainly in the form
of biographical sketches of famous Georgians, was a series of five
"Historical Readings" that dealt with such controversial topics as
slavery and Georgia's secession from the Union.

Despite the lectures and the books, it was the *Constitution* letters that brought the most fame to Arp and his creator. One way to
gauge Arp's popularity is to examine the mail he received from his

readers. He once noted that the thirty letters or so he wrote each week did not take care of all the people who wrote to him.[29] When he wrote a column on Mormonism, he received tracts and pamphlets from people trying to convert him; when he wrote on sectional reconciliation, he received letters from northerners saying that their section did not hate the South; when he wrote on race relations, he received from a black reader a letter "full of profane abuse and blasphemy for the views expressed"; when he wrote on labor unions he received letters condemning him from both sides of the issue.[30] "Numerous correspondents" wrote for information on a magazine he mentioned; a column on whippings at school brought "several letters from teachers"; his mail was "flooded" with responses to a column on textbooks, and he received "quite a flood" of letters again about a series of columns on the Cherokee Indians.[31] When Arp asked readers for a copy of a poem he could not find, he reported that he received 347 replies, including one from Minnesota and one from Washington; when he mentioned a speech by Henry Rootes Jackson on the African slave trade, he received "scores of letters from Massachusetts to California." [32]

Many people wrote to Bill Arp for help and advice. They asked him to critique their manuscripts, to secure teaching positions for their daughters, to send biographical information about famous Georgians, and even to help with a missing word contest that the *Constitution* sponsored. (One woman in this last category said that if Arp would provide the answers, she would split the winnings with him.) [33] Some of the requests were pathetic. People wrote for help proving a pension claim or finding lost children or friends. An especially sad example was a Confederate veteran who sent Arp his small collection of Confederate stamps and currency. Arp wrote that the man was old and crippled, and he gladly solicited bids on the items.[34] On a lighter note, children often wrote to Bill Arp requesting help with homework problems or asking him to write their essays for school. One boy had the nerve to ask Arp for two compositions, so he could choose the better.[35]

In the spring of 1903, Arp wrote a column that dealt with, among other topics, Thaddeus K. Oglesby's recent book, *Some Truths of History—The South Vindicated*. Arp's one-paragraph notice of the book appeared in the March 22, 1903, issue of the *Constitution* and was reprinted in other newspapers. Arp called the book "the best contribution to southern historical literature that has yet appeared" and urged readers to send $1.25 to Oglesby for a copy. Many readers did just that; Oglesby received orders mentioning Arp's recommendation from as far away as Washington, Minnesota, Pennsylvania, New York, and even Canada. Most of these simply mentioned Arp's name, but a few proved the affection that readers had for Arp. One reader wrote that the suggestion for the book came from "our friend 'Bill Arp.'" Arp's writings were even more personal for another man; he wrote that "Bill Arp told me to send you a dollar and a quarter and you would send me your book." [36]

People in Georgia were proud of their Bill Arp and, like the folks in Texas, named communities for him. There was at one time an Arp in Banks County (northeast Georgia) and an Arp in Irwin County (south central Georgia), but these are only memories now. There is still a Bill Arp community in Douglas County, a few miles west of Atlanta, complete with a Bill Arp Elementary School and a Bill Arp Grocery and Hardware. [37]

In 1887, when the children had left home, the Smiths moved from the farm into Cartersville. According to the family story, Charles and Octavia soon grew lonely by themselves, so one morning at the breakfast table he said, "Octavia, we can't stand this; I'm going to town and buy a house." The large, old-fashioned house that he chose was set atop a hill far back from the road (Erwin Street), just a few blocks from the middle of Cartersville. A grove of oak trees in front of the house moved son Victor to name it "The Shadows." With the exception of winter vacations in Florida, where he had built a cottage near his daughter Stella's home, and his lecture tours, which became less frequent with the years, Smith spent the rest of his life there. [38]

Moving from the farm into town did not mean retirement for Smith. He continued his weekly column for the *Constitution,* and correspondence with readers who wrote to him apparently took up a good bit of his time. He wrote his history of Georgia, an article on race relations for *Forum*, the introduction to a pamphlet containing speeches of Henry R. Jackson and Daniel Webster, a promotional pamphlet on Florida's west coast, and several original chapters for *Bill Arp: From the Uncivil War to Date*, among other items. In 1900 he wrote in his *Constitution* column that he was thinking of putting together a book of "poetic gems" that would sell for under a dollar and would be good for parents to buy for their children "to mold and refine their characters and give them pleasure and comfort all their lives." Smith asked "lovers of good, pure poetic literature" to send the names and authors of their favorite poems, and a month later he announced that work on the book was progressing smoothly. He never mentioned it again, however, and there is no evidence that the book was ever published.[39] Smith also spent more time reading. Readers of his *Constitution* column sometimes sent him books, which he would read and occasionally pass on to others. Near the end of his life, his personal library numbered over four hundred volumes.[40]

While on the farm, Smith had promoted the building of a country schoolhouse for the children who lived in the area. His concern for education continued after he moved into town. Smith was on the board of the public school system, established in 1888, and he occasionally mentioned the good work of the board in his Bill Arp letters. Another educational venture, begun a year or so later, was less successful. Sam Jones, the popular evangelist who lived in Cartersville, began soliciting contributions late in 1886 for a women's college. Soon he had received nearly ten thousand dollars for the project. The cornerstone for Sam Jones Female College was laid in September 1887, and listed Smith as a member of the board of directors. In 1889, however, a petition signed by certain stockholders alleged that the corporation set up to finance and build the school had never been legally organized. A receiver was appointed and the property was sold to the city for twenty-five hundred dollars.[41]

Smith also stayed busy tending his garden. David Freeman, who lived across the street and appeared in a number of Bill Arp's *Constitution* columns as "Nabor Freeman," described Smith as a creative "landscape artist": "A terrace of fine roses alternates with one of swift growing 'Kentucky Wonders,' and a bunch of lillies or tulips usually forms a head or tail piece for a lettuce bed." A granddaughter remembered how "he used to make bouquets of radishes, onions and roses and give them to visitors." Smith was especially proud of his strawberries and tomatoes, and often claimed to have the biggest and best in town. He gave vegetables away by the basketful to friends and neighbors, saving the best for people who were sick. He was also proud of his roses, and every morning in the spring and summer placed a rose or a small bouquet of other flowers by his wife's plate at the breakfast table. In 1901 he jokingly suggested a gardening motif for his epitaph:

> He was a man of words and deeds,
> He kept his garden clean of weeds;
> And when the weeds began to grow
> He slayed them with his garden hoe.

A year later, one of his sons promised to visit, but only if Smith agreed not to show off his strawberries more than seven times each day.[42]

Some three hundred "close friends" gathered at The Shadows in March 1899 to help the Smiths celebrate their golden wedding anniversary. Gifts included a number of gold items (a fountain pen, rings, ladles, an umbrella, a bookmark, toothpicks, and a gold-headed cane) and a cake cutter from Joel Chandler Harris inscribed "To Bill Arp from Uncle Remus." Newspapers across the South carried news of the celebration, and the *Constitution* printed two large articles on it.[43]

During the last ten years of his life, Smith suffered almost constantly from one illness or another. During 1893 he often wrote that a "neuralgia headache" had almost incapacitated him for several months. When he was working on his history of Georgia that year, doctors advised him not to read or write "or even to think very much," but after making him suffer "like a poor sinner ought to suffer," the headache left him.[44] At other times he complained about his kidneys, a persistent cough, the grippe, and "swollen extremities."[45] Throughout much of 1902 he suffered from angina pectoris, which left him confined to bed for several months and restricted to an almost totally liquid diet for most of the rest of his life.[46]

Despite the illness Smith remained cheerful. His grandchildren were a special joy for him, especially Jessie's daughters Caroline (born June 1895) and Marilu (born December 1896). They lived only two blocks away, so he was able to see them almost every day. Their father, Will Young, of Young Brothers Drug Store, had to work at night, so Smith often visited the girls after dinner to help put them to bed. (In September 1901, four months after he suggested a gardening epitaph, Smith changed his mind and wrote that his tombstone should read: "He was a faithful husband and father. He nursed the children and grandchildren as long as he lasted.") The girls returned his visits in the daytime. "Nabor" Freeman recalled seeing them often: "Mary Lou and Caroline pulling at grandpa's coattails in the home or on a pretty day on the lawn is a common sight." Smith's daughter wrote that, when he tired of reading or writing, "he would totter out to his chair on the porch and with his 'far-glasses' on wait patiently for the coming of his little grandchildren. His mind, grown child-like, craved their companionship." He mentioned the girls often in his Bill Arp letters. "I had rather look out my window and see two little girls coming up the walk hand in hand to see me than to write about anything," he wrote in March 1903, and two months later he ended one of his weekly letters by writing, "But I see my little children coming up the winding path, and the race problem must take a back seat."[47]

Bill Arp's last column apeared in the *Constitution* on August 9, 1903. The next week Smith became very ill, this time with gall bladder trouble, and a short note, which the *Constitution* reprinted in facsimile, took the place of his weekly letter: "I have been quite sick all the week. Can hardly write at all. You will have to excuse me this week."[48] He underwent an operation on August 21, at which time the doctors removed "three thousand gall stones, ranging in size from that of a mustard seed to that of a marble, the great obstructive mass being enough to fill the double hands." [49] Although the surgery was considered successful, enough of the secretions from the blocked gall bladder had escaped into his system to poison his body. The *Constitution* printed daily reports of his condition, and its readers waited as he fell lower and lower. He died on August 24, 1903, at the age of seventy-seven.

Two days later, merchants closed their stores in Smith's honor as the town of Cartersville buried its "First Citizen." The overflow crowd at the Presbyterian Church heard Sam Jones, one of the most famous evangelists of the day and a friend of Smith's, say that, "though we buried today Major Smith, 'Bill Arp' [will] live through future generations." Smith was laid to rest in the Cartersville Cemetery in a grave covered with flowers. On the day of the funeral, Sara, Ralph's eight-month-old daughter and Smith's youngest grandchild, also died, and her body was placed in the same grave with him. [50]

Part Two

Bill Arp

Four

War and Reconstruction

J ust after the Civil War, the people of Liberty, Missouri, read in their newspapers about the plight of the refugees along the line of Sherman's march and raised $6,000 to help feed them. At a town meeting, it was decided that Georgia's portion of the money would be $3,000. But to whom should the money be sent? Captain Tom McCarty, a crippled veteran, rose and said, "Gentlemen, I don't know but one man there, and his name is Arp, and I've been readin' of his letters for five years, and I be d——d if I wouldent trust him with all I've got." So the money went to Charles Henry Smith, and he used it to buy corn for the hungry.[1]

Captain McCarty was not the only person who had been reading Bill Arp's writings. According to one scholar, Arp "was the most popular Southern humorist during the Civil War." "Every soldier in the field knew Bill Arp's 'last'," wrote a contemporary observer. Of the pieces Arp wrote after fleeing Rome in 1864, a fellow Georgia refugee said: "He actually helped us bear our troubles by his different view of things." In a letter written shortly after the war, a former Confederate soldier asked his mother: "Have you ever seen any of Bill Arp's letters? They are splendid! 'Twould do your heart good to read them."[2]

Another clue to Arp's popularity can be found in the fascinating diary of Mary Boykin Chesnut. In the early summer of 1861, she reported that she met an acquaintance who "quoted a funny Georgia man who says we try our soldiers if they are hot enough before we enlist them. If when water is thrown on them, they do not sizz—they won't do—their patriotism is too cool." Although C. Vann Woodward, Chesnut's ablest and most recent editor, did not attribute this statement to him, the "funny Georgia man" was none other than Bill Arp, writing in his first letter to "Abe Linkhorn."[3]

Chesnut quoted Arp by name in an entry dated May 7, 1865: " 'Expect us to support niggers,' raves Bill Arp. 'What have we to support ourselves *on?*' " Woodward found this statement in Arp's open letter to Artemus Ward, but he failed to point out that Arp did not write this piece until September 1865, four months *after* Chesnut quoted from it. During the 1880s Chesnut added (with an eye toward publication) a good bit of new material to the journal she had kept in the 1860s, and this is one of the later embellishments; the reference to Arp does not appear in her original wartime journal. As it turns out, her earlier joke from the "funny Georgia man" on how the Confederacy chose its recruits was also an addition from the 1880s. According to Chesnut's biographer, "Foremost among [her reasons for revising the wartime diaries] was her conviction that her book should not be a record of daily domestic trifles, but rather a picture of an entire society." So even though there were no references to Arp in her original diaries, the fact that she added these two later when she was trying to portray the South during the war is itself likely evidence of Arp's wartime fame.[4]

Arp's writing style and the topics he treated during the war and Reconstruction years were different from those in his later *Atlanta Constitution* columns, but these early writings were, in their time, quite popular with a large number of southerners. The *Constitution* columns are discussed in later chapters; here we will examine Arp's writings from 1861, when he took his pen name, to 1873, the year of his second book's publication.

Mr. Linkhorn—Sur: These are to inform you that we are all well, and hope these lines may find you in *statue ko*."[5] So began Bill Arp's first letter to Abraham Lincoln. But all was not well in Georgia in 1861. With her six (soon to be ten) sister states in the Confederacy, Georgia faced a tremendous challenge in the fight for independence. Much can be said of the abilities of the South's military leaders and the valor of her soldiers and citizens, and it is true that a defensive war is in many ways much easier to fight than an offensive one. Still, at the time of the first real battle of the war, the Union had more than double the population of the Confederacy, and since slaves accounted for much of the southern population, the northern advantage in potential manpower was almost four to one. Northern farmers produced two and a half times as much as their southern counterparts, and the figures were even worse for industry: less than ten percent of the nation's industrial production was located in the South, and the North manufactured virtually all of the firearms and railroad equipment.

Furthermore, opinion on the war was sharply divided; terms such as "North" and "South" imply a unity of thought within each section that never really existed. "It was known that a majority of the people of Georgia favored secession," wrote I. W. Avery, "but the minority in favor of cooperation and delay was a very large and powerful body of public sentiment, ably and patriotically headed." Several of Georgia's leading statesmen, including Alexander H. Stephens, Benjamin H. Hill, and Herschel V. Johnson, were in this minority. When Georgians voted in January 1861 for delegates to a convention that would decide the question of the state's role in the Union, opponents of secession received about the same number of votes as proponents. In fact, many areas in northern Georgia, including Smith's Floyd County, voted heavily against disunion. Although many Unionists switched their allegiance to support the Confederacy after the secession ordinance passed or after the firing on Fort Sumter and Lincoln's call for troops, Georgia remained divided on the issues of secession and the war. Similar stories could be told for other southern states.[6]

With a good deal of initial dissension, the South had just entered into a war against a larger and stronger enemy, and so Bill Arp's first sentence—"we are all well"—was not quite true. But Arp did not write and publish this letter in order to give an accurate and complete account of the South's condition in the middle of April 1861; he did it instead to build morale, both in himself and in his friends, to unify support for the war, and to get in a few jabs at Lincoln's orders for the southern rebels to go home and quit causing trouble. "We received your proklamation," Arp wrote, "and as you have put us on very short notis, a few of us boys have conkluded to write you, and ax for a little more time. The fact is, we are most obleeged to have a few more days, for the way things are happening, it is utterly onpossible for us to disperse in twenty days. . . . I tried my darndest yisterday to disperse and retire, but it was no go."[7]

Since Arp was pretending in this letter to be the president's friend, he warned Lincoln about the fiery spirit of the Confederate soldiers. "The boys round here want watchin," he wrote, "or they'll take sumthin. A few days ago I heard they surrounded two of our best citizens, because they was named Fort and Sumter. Most of em are so hot that they fairly siz when you pour water on em, and thats the way they make up their military companies here now— when a man applies to jine the volunteers, they sprinkle him, and if he sizzes they take him, and if he don't they don't."[8]

Arp told the President that he was afraid his pro-Union sentiments might get him into trouble and asked if he could have the disguise that Lincoln, fearful for his life, had used (according to contemporary rumor) to sneak into Washington for his own inauguration. "I suppose you wouldn't be likely to use the same disgize agin, when you left, and therefore I propose to swap. I am five feet five, and could git my plow breeches and coat to you in eight or ten days if you can wait that long." The discussion of Lincoln's disguise was followed by another innocent comment concerning Lincoln's orders: "Your proklamation says somethin about takin possession of all the private property at 'All Hazards.' We can't find no such place on the map." A few more paragraphs in this vein, including a hopeful P.S. ("If you can possibly xtend that order to thirty days, do so"), and Arp closed.[9]

Arp wrote a second letter to Lincoln nine months after the first, in January 1862, while he was with the army in Virginia. "In the spring of the year I writ you a letter from my native sile [soil], axin for a little more time to disperse," he began. "I told you then that twenty days was not enuf—that the thing could not be did in that brief interval. You can look back and see I was right. . . . The spring hav shed its fragrance, the summer is over and gone, the yaller leaves of autum hav kivered the ground, old winter is slobberin his froth on the yearth, but we hav not been able to disperse as yet." [10]

Arp mentioned that he and some friends had gone to see the president to ask for an extension of the twenty days, "but we got on a bust in old Virginny, about the 21st of Jewly, and like to hav got run over by a passel of fellers runnin from Bull Run to your city." (Here he was poking fun at the Union retreat from the Battle of Manassas.) Arp then expressed concern about what the war might mean for northern textile production: "What are your faktories doin nowadays? I hearn you had quit runnin their masheens, owing to a thin crop of kotton. If you would put sweet ile on your faktories, they wouldn't rust while standin idle." [11]

In September 1862 Lincoln issued the Preliminary Emancipation Proclamation, announcing that he intended to proclaim the southern slaves free on January 1, 1863. This was too big a target for Arp to pass up, and in a third letter to Lincoln he asked, "Are it not possible that you are usin too much proklamation. More than 8teen months ago you published an edik, orderin the boys to retire and be peasable, but they disretired and went to fightin. The effek war bad, very bad. Now you have proklimated the niggers free after Ginerwary, and I am afeerd it will prove a fee simple for all time." [12]

"You are tryin to do too much at onst," Arp warned the president; "it are amazin to think what a big job you have undertook." Arp tried to help out with another bit of military advice: "Your Genruls don't travel the right road to Richmond, nohow. The way they hav been tryin to cum is through a mity Longstreet, over two powerful Hills, and across a tremendious Stonewall. It would be safer and cheaper for em to go round by the Rocky Mountings, if spendin time in military xcursions is their chief objek." [13] Arp continued the advice in a fourth letter to Lincoln, telling him to beware of "krossin them sikly rivers": "The Lee side of any shore are onhelthy to your populashun! Keep away from them Virginy water kourses. Go round em or under em, but for the sake of ekonomy don't try to kross em. It is too hard on your burryal squads and ambylance hosses." [14]

The emancipation of the slaves, due to take effect in a week, was Arp's biggest concern in this fourth and final letter to Lincoln:

> A poet hav sed that "Time ontied waiteth for no man." To my opinyun it are ontied now and hastenen on to that eventful period which you hav fixed, when Africa is to be unshakled, when Niggerdom ar to feel the power of your proklamation, when Uncle Tom are to change his base and evakuate his kabin, when all the emblems of darkness are to rush frantikally forth into the arms of their deliverers, and with perfumed and sented gratitude embrace your exsellency and Madam Harriet Beechers toe! What a galorious day that ar to be! What a sublime ery in history! What a proud kulmination and konsumation and koruskation of your politikul hoaps! After a few thousand hav clasped you in their ebony arms, it will be a fitten time, Mr. Linkhorn, for you to lay yourself down and die. Human ambition can hav no hier monument to klimb. After such a work you might komplete the immortal heroizm of your karacter by leapin from the topmost pinnakle of your glory upon the yearth below.
>
> But alas for human folly—alas for all subloonery things—our peepul will not believe, these krazy Rebels will not konsider! Christmas is already cum—only one more breef weak to slide away before we must part, forever part, with all our nigger heritage, and yet our stubborn peepul continue to buy em and sell em, and the shorter the lease, the hier the price they are payin. What infatyashun! I verily believe they will keep up their old ways until next Wednesday night, just as tho they dident have to giv em all up the next mornin afore breakfast. [15]

After these first four letters, written between April 1861 and December 1862 and all addressed to "Mr. Linkhorn," Arp never again wrote to the president. His later wartime letters, some fifteen in number, were usually addressed to newspaper editors and, like the Linkhorn letters, served the twin purposes of ridiculing Yankees and comforting southerners. Arp remained reassuring to the end of the war. In a letter dated February 1865, perhaps his last before the surrender, Arp told his readers that Sherman's march through Georgia had not necessarily meant the collapse of the Confederacy:

> My doktrin hav always bin that if we was to fite and fite and fite till our army was played out, the biggist part of the Yanky job would be just begun. Atter they hav whipped us, then they hav got to subjugate us. They hav got to hold us down, and they can't do it. . . .
>
> Besides, we ain't whipped yet—not by three or four jug fulls. Spose Sherman did walk rite thru the State. Spose he did. Was eny body whipped? Didn't the rebellyun just klose rite up behind him, like shettin a pair of waful irons? He parted the atmosphere as he went along, and it kollapsed agin in his reer immegitly. He'll have to go over that old ground sevrul times yet, and then sell out and move away.[16]

Arp wrote on a variety of topics during the war. In some letters he related his own experiences facing (and later running away from) the Yankee soldiers. One of the earliest and best of these described the so-called Battle of Rome. The "battle" took place when Union troops made their first appearance in the area during the first week of May 1863. General Nathan Bedford Forrest and his 410 Confederate troops met the Yankees just twenty miles outside the city, close to the Alabama border. Colonel Abel D. Streight, who commanded the 1,446 Union soldiers, did not realize how few Confederates faced his men; so when Forrest sent in a flag of truce and demanded surrender, Streight, his men tired from three all-night marches, agreed to discuss terms. As the two leaders talked, Forrest gave orders to one of his captains to move a large number of (imaginary) troops. According to one historian, Forrest's officers, "catching the spirit of the game, . . . marched portions of their commands around and around the conical hills of that section until the weary and worried Streight, after returning for further consultation with his officers, finally came to the conclusion that the hills and hollows must be filled with armed Confederates." Rather than risk his men, Streight surrendered.[17]

In a letter written less than a week later, Bill Arp described the event for his readers. Arp explained that the people of Rome were not sure what to do as they listened to rumors of approaching Yankee soldiers, but there was "one unyversal determinashun to *do sumthin.*" Men rushed to the tops of the hills with their rifles, young lookouts climbed the courthouse with their spyglasses, and women searched for hiding places for their silverware and their children. "Ah! then were the time to try men's soles," he wrote.[18]

Arp described the "Battle of Rome" as if it had been a card game:

> Now, Mistur Editur, while these valyant feets wer goin on hereabouts, Genrul Forrest had been fitin the boddy and tale of the rade away down at the Alabam line. Finally he proposed to the rade to stop fitin, and play a game or two of poker, under a seder tree, which they acksepted. But the Genrul wer not in luck, and had a pore hand, and had bet his last dollar. The Yankees had a *Strait,* which wood hav taken Forrest and raked down the pile, but he looked em rite in the eyes and sed "*he would see em and 4,000 better.*" The Rade looked at him, and he looked at the Rade and *never blinked.* The Rade trimbled all in his boots and giv it up. *The Genrul bluffed em,* and ever sence that game were plade, the little town klose by have been kalled "*Cedar Bluff.*" It were *flush* times in Alabam, that day, shore.[19]

A year later it was Sherman, not Streight, who threatened the city, and Confederate general Joseph E. Johnston could do little to stop his progress. In the middle of May 1864, Johnston gave the orders to evacuate Rome. "If Mr. Shakspeer wer correkt when he writ that 'sweet are the juices of adversity,' then it are resunable to supose that me and my foaks must hav sum sweetnin to spar," Bill Arp wrote in a letter to the *Southern Confederacy* a couple of weeks later.

> When a man is arowsed in the ded of night, and smells the approach of the fowl invader; when he feels konstraned to change his base and becum a runagee from his home, leavin behind him all those ususery things whitch hold body and sole together; when he looks, perhaps for the last time, upon his luvly home wher he has been for many delightful years raisin children and chickens, strawberries and pease, li soap and inguns, and all such luksuries of this sublunnerry life; when

he imagins evry onusual sound to be the crack of his earthly doom; when frum such influenses he begins a dignifide retreat, but soon is konstraned to leave the dignity behind, and git away without regard to the order of his goin,—if ther are eny sweet juice in the like of that, I have not bin able to see it. No, Mr. Editur, sich senes never happened in Bill Shakspear's day, or he would not have writ that line.[20]

Arp reported on his family's search for some sort of transportation out of the city. Finding none, they started out on foot, joining the rest of Rome's "runagees." One of their fellow travellers was "Big John" Underwood (no relation to Smith's Rome law partner), a large, good-hearted man who appeared in a number of Arp's writings. Big John's only means of escaping the Yankees were an old broken-down wagon and a cow; the two were attached, according to Arp's account, by the animal's tail, which John had tied to the wagon. One of Arp's refugee letters contained an ode to Big John:

> Farwell, Big John, Farwell!
> 'Twas paneful to my hart,
> To see thy chanses of eskape
> Was that old steer and kart.
>
> Methinks I see thee now,
> With axel trees all broak,
> And wheels with nary hub at all,
> And hubs with nary spoak.
>
> But tho the mud is deep
> Thy wits will never fale;
> That faithful steer will pull thee out,
> If thou wilt hold his tale.[21]

It might seem remarkable that Bill Arp could keep his sense of humor under these circumstances. But, as Arp said at the end of this letter, he and his fellow runagees had to look for the funny side of their situation:

Often, alas, how often, was the teer seen swimmin in the eye, and the lip quiver with emoshun, as memry lingurd aroun the deserted hoams, and thoughts dwelt upon past enjoymints and future desola-

shun. We plukked the wild flowers as we passed, sung songs of merry-
ment, xchanged our wit with children, smotherin by every meens the
sorrer of our fate. These things, together with the komik events that
okurred by the way, wer the safety valves that saved the poor hart from
bustin. But for these, our heads would have bin fountains, and our
harts a river of teers.[22]

Arp managed to keep smiling even when he and his family returned to Rome seven months later. He described the homecoming
in a letter written shortly after the end of the war:

We wer about as happy as we had been miserble, and when I
remarkd that Genrul Vandiver, who okkupide our haus, must be a
gentleman for not burnin it, Mrs. Arp replide—
"I wonder what he done with my sewing masheen?"
"He didn't cut down our shade trees," sed I.
"My buro and karpet and crokery is all gone," sed she.
"It may be possibul," sed I, "that the Genrul—"
"And my barrel of soap," sed she.
"It may be possibul," sed I, "that the Genrul moved off our things
to take kare of em for us. I reckon we'll git em all back atter while."
"*Atter while*," sed Mrs. Arp like an echo, and ever sinse then when
I alood to our Northern brethrin, she only replies, "*Atter while*."[23]

Arp wrote the above for the New York *Metropolitan Record*, a paper
with southern sympathies that published several of his early letters
as well as his first book. In another letter about their return home,
also published in his first book but originally written for a southern
paper, Arp's sense of humor was nowhere in sight. In part of the
letter, Arp surveyed the damage done to the city cemetery:

Could you stand upon the hills of this desolate city and see its wasted
and withered beauties—could you traverse our cemetery hill, that
once so beautifully hung its clustered shades over the banks of our
rivers, I know you would feel that there was no fitness in a union
with that people. The wanton destruction of all those ornaments with
which we had adorned the homes of our dead, has murdered our
Christian charity and stabbed our forgiveness to the quick. The digging of rifle-pits through the cemetery might possibly have been a

military necessity, but it was a brutal insult to our dead to undermine their graves. Their harmless bones might have been removed to some quiet spot. It was intensely fiendish to take our ornaments and tombstones and place them like rock and rubbish in their fortifications—to shatter the iron railing into a thousand fragments—to pitch their tents right over the ground where our loved ones were resting in hallowed peace—to beat their tatoo and reveille, and sing their rude songs, and chuckle their devilish merriment right over the homes of our dead— the sacred spots where we had planted the fairest flowers to sweeten their sad graves.[24]

This discussion of Union troops in the city cemetery is one of the few times during the war that Arp was pointedly critical of northern behavior. Far more often, he criticized his fellow southerners for not doing all they could to support the Confederate war effort. In what may have been the first letter he wrote after the four to "Mr. Linkhorn," Arp complained about southern extortioners, "vampires" who took advantage of wartime shortages to make huge profits at the expense of others. Arp described his experiences on a trip home from the army: "Having undertook to recruit my family supplies, my pocket book looked like an elephant had trod on it before I was half through. It took three months' pay to buy a pair of shoes and a fine-tooth comb. Shoeing and shirting and hatting the children was indefinitely postponed." [25]

Arp also complained about the Confederate cavalry, which he characterized as horse thieves afraid to face the enemy. "The Konfederit cavilry is ubikuitous and everlastin," he wrote. "I hav traveld a heep of late, and had okkashun to retire into sum very sequestered rejuns, but nary hill nor holler, nary vale or vally, nary mounting gorge or inaksessibel raveen hav I found, but what the cavilry had bin there, and *jest left*. And that is the reeson they can't be whipped, for they hav always *jest left*, and took a odd hoss or two with em." "Swappin hosses is a weakness to which they are subjek," he wrote in another letter, "but they give a man very little trubble that way, for they can swap with him when he ain't at home, or when he's asleep, just as well as if he was awake and was there." [26]

In several other letters, Arp condemned the men who evaded conscription into the Confederate military service. One of their tricks was to become prematurely old. The first Confederate conscription act, passed in April 1862, declared that all white males aged eighteen to thirty-five were in the army. The upper limit was raised to forty-five in September 1862, and in February 1864 a third act extended the draft to cover those between seventeen and fifty. "How rapidly some folks grow old in these trying times!" Arp wrote after the second act. "Such is the rapid progress of human events in these fighting times, that a man who was only forty last year, can be forty-six this." [27]

States were allowed to exempt from the draft certain officials and those with vital jobs. Probably every southern governor abused the privilege of making these exemptions to some degree, but Georgia's Governor Brown was one of "the chief offenders." Arp criticized not only Brown for making the exemptions, but also the many who sought and accepted them—"Joe Brown's Pets," as they were called. "There's the mail must be carried," he wrote, "the telegraph attended to, steamboats and cars must travel, shoes must be made, potash be burnt, and all mechanics must go ahead; and then there's the numerous holes and hiding-places around a depot, or hospital, or the Quartermaster's department, or the passport office, etc." In another letter, Arp poked fun at a character he called "Potash" who worked at a "niter buro" making gunpowder: "I'm told there is about twelve hundred of you fellers, skulkin behind a passel of ash hoppers, pretendin you are stewin down patriotism into powder. Blamed if I can't smell the *lie* on you." [28]

The ill and infirm, of course, were also exempt from the draft, and, according to Arp, "the bulk of the dodging is done in the chronic line. Before this developing war, it was not thought possible for so much rheumatics and chronics, so many sore legs and weak backs, to exist in a limestone country." Whatever excuse people used to avoid fighting, Arp could guess the result of all that draft dodging: "We will have a race of peepel atter a while that ain't worth a cuss. The good ones are gittin killed up, but these *skulkers* and *shirkers* and *dodgers* don't die. There ain't one died sinse the war broke out."[29]

Governor Brown was a constant source of irritation and frustration to Arp. An extreme states'-righter at a time when it was necessary for the southern states to work closely together, Brown opposed President Jefferson Davis and the Confederate Congress on matters such as conscription, finances, the suspension of the writ of habeas corpus, and the conduct of the war. Brown was a powerful leader; "until the end of the war," one historian wrote, "Brown towered over the legislature and dominated the state almost as though he was the sovereign of an independent republic."[30]

Late in 1863, Brown and the Stephens brothers, Alexander and Linton, began discussing plans for an all-out attack in the state legislature on what they viewed as Confederate usurpations of Georgia's rights. They decided that, at an appropriate time, the governor would call for a special meeting of the legislature, and at that meeting give a major address espousing the anti-Confederate position. Linton Stephens would then offer resolutions, which brother Alexander would endorse. The opportune time came in the middle of February 1864 when the Confederate Congress suspended the writ of habeas corpus for the third time (the first two times having been in April and October 1862). Brown called the legislature to meet in special session on March 10.

Brown began his lengthy speech by thanking the legislators for the "personal kindness and official courtesy" shown him. This was followed by a discussion of cotton planting, illegal distilleries, and aid for soldiers' families. Most of the rest of the message was a denunciation of the Confederate government and the acts it had recently passed. "Probably the history of the past furnishes few more striking instances of unsound policy combined with bad faith," Brown noted, than the recent currency act, one in a series of desperate measures designed to stabilize the South's economy and raise money for the war. He then condemned the Congress for debating the act in secret session, charging that "the *secret sessions* of Congress are becoming a blighting curse to the country." Concerning the conscription acts, Brown said that Georgia "will never cease to require that all her constitutional rights be respected and the liberties of her people preserved." On the suspension of the writ of habeas corpus, which President Davis had used sparingly to deal with dissenters, Brown asked, "What will we have gained when we have achieved our independence of the Northern States, if in our efforts to do so, we have permitted our form of Government to be subverted, and have lost *Constitutional Liberty* at home?" The governor then offered a lengthy and biased retelling of American history, his point being to prove that the South's "sole object from the beginning has been to defend, maintain, and preserve our ancient usages, customs, liberties, and institutions, as achieved and established by our ancestors in the revolution of 1776." Brown closed with a section on how to end the war. "The pen of the statesman, more potent than the sword of the warrior, must do what the latter failed to do," Brown asserted, and called for the South to offer the North the chance for a negotiated peace after every Confederate victory.[31]

Brown's speech received wide attention from the press, although few of the major newspapers supported him. Likewise, Linton Stephens's two resolutions were only a limited success. One, denouncing the suspension of habeas corpus, passed, and the agitation it raised rendered the suspension of the writ null in Georgia. The other, on making peace overtures to the North, stated that such a course would "be regretted by nobody, . . . except men whose importance and whose gains would be diminished by peace, and men whose ambitious designs would need cover under the ever-recurring plea of the necessities of war." This slap at the Richmond government was offset by a clause added by the legislature expressing "undiminished confidence in the integrity and patriotism of Jefferson Davis," and the resolution passed only after having been watered down beyond usefulness.[32]

Bill Arp's "Messig to All Foaks," which appeared in several southern newspapers shortly afterwards,[33] is a wonderful parody of Brown's speech. "Bein much gratified for your distinguished konsiderashun which hav bin showerd down upon me like an avylanch in times past, and heretofo, and befo now, and prevyous," Arp began, "I desire to atrakt your attenshun on this posthumous okkashun."[34] On the recent currency bill and the way in which it was passed, Arp said:

> [It] are beleeved to be that great and most monstrus maulstroom [maelstrom] which the geographers deskribe as aboundin on the koast of Norway, but which by sum jugglery or hokus pokus or sekret session hav resently bin brought and moved into the konfedersy, to swaller up all the money in cirkulashun. With a kind of whurly gig loko moshun it hav drawn the kurrensy into its orful and greedy vortex, leavin a man nuthin but a sikly skrap of yaller paper. . . . My opinyon is, that sum other Bill mite hav bin found that would hav done better or worse. . . . If they had applide to your distinguished and umble feller-sitizen, I would hav ondertook the job. But, alas! they didn't. On the kontrary, they barred the doors, and shot the winder blinds, and let down the kurtins, and stopped up the key holes, and went into a place kalled *sekret session*, which are perhaps a little the klosest communyon ever established in a well-waterd country. A Grand Jewry or a Masonic Lodge, or a kno-nothin konvention, ain't a sirkumstance to it.[35]

Moving on, Arp discussed "habeus korpus": "It is, perhaps, *when suspended,* the most savagerous beest that ever got after tories and trators. To all honest and patriotik foaks it is said to be perfekly harmless, but still, nevertheless, notwithstandin, howsumever, *it mout git loose,* and way lay our liberties, and tear the hind sites offen a man befo he could beller for help." "Sinse the diskovery of Ameriky by Pokahontas," Arp noted later in his message, "the *Habeus Korpus* hav never been suspended over enebody, xcept about three hundred thousin soljers in the Konfederit army. For nearly three years Genrul Lee and Genrul Johnston hav had it suspended over all the fitin boys in their kommands. With most astonishin pashens they bear up under this oppreshun, and kontinue to live on haf rashuns, and fite, and march, and toil, and struggle, and *never komplain about nothin.*"[36]

"And this brings me to konsider for your edifykashun," Arp continued, "the *konskripshun bill*, which has so long deprived you of the right to volunteer, and like a vampire gnawd away at your burnin and glowin patriotizm." (This was probably aimed more at Alexander Stephens, who had argued that the conscription bill "would tend to check the ardor of the people by appearing to slight their spontaneous patriotic service.") As for what brought on the war, "it wur kaused xklusively by Gen. States Rights goin to sleep one day, and old Kolonel Federlist cum along and tride to kut his hamstring." Finally, Arp introduced his plan for making "propersishuns for pease": "Atter every viktory over our enemies, let us holler at the top of our voises, pease! pease!! pease!!! In the langwage of Patrik Henry, let us cry, 'Pease when there is no pease.' "[37]

In another piece written about the same time—an open letter to Brown reminiscent of his earlier letters to Lincoln—Arp poked fun at the resolutions Brown and the Stephens brothers had put before the legislature by suggesting a few of his own. "You could pass 'em if you could pass yours," Arp said.

> First. *Be it enacted*, That I am a whale, and if there is any bigger fish a-swimming in the nasty deep, than I am *that*.
>
> Secondly. *Resolved*, That Richmond is Jonah, and will be swallowed up in a few days. . . .
>
> Thirdly. *Resolved*, That whereas some ignorant poet has asked, What constitutes a State? he is informed that *it's me;* I am the State myself.
>
> Fourthly. *Resolved*, That I am the centre of space—the Southern Confederacy—the solar system . . . in fact, if there is any other big thing, then I am that.[38]

There is no evidence that Joe Brown ever responded to Arp's "Messig to All Foaks," but, given the piece's wide circulation, there is little chance that he could have missed seeing it. A few years later, Arp would count Brown as one of his good friends, but during the war the two men were almost exactly opposite in their views of the southern war effort and the relationship between Georgia and the Confederacy.

Arp's opposition to Brown did not mean that he gladly accepted all points of Jefferson Davis's policies. Arp wrote a letter shortly after one of the currency bills was passed, for example, "to express my opinion about the way my finances have been managed by other people," and his opinion was less than positive. But while Arp complained occasionally about Confederate policies, he always maintained that the Confederacy had the right to take such steps as were necessary for the sake of military, economic, and political expediency. With his pen, Arp defended the Confederacy against Joe Brown and other southerners who attacked it.[39]

During the war Bill Arp "became the accepted mouthpiece of the Southern people"—at least some southern people—and he remained a spokesman for the South during the difficult days of Reconstruction. He addressed his first letter after the war to Artemus Ward, a politically moderate northern humorist, "bekaus you are about the only man I know in all 'God's kountry,' *so called.*" Arp began the letter, one of his most famous, by saying: "For sum sevrul years we Rebs, *so called,* but now late of said kountry deceased, hav been a tryin mity hard to do sumthin. We didn't quite do it, and now it is very paneful, I ashoor you, to dry up all of a sudden, and make out like we wasn't there." Southerners had to voice a few complaints before they could harmonize, Arp wrote. One such complaint concerned the way northern newspapers continued to abuse the South. "I'll be hornswoggled if the talkin, and the writin, and the slanderin hav got to be done all on one side eny longer," he wrote. "It's a blamed outrage, *so called.* Ain't your editors got nuthin else to do but to peck at us, skwib at us, and krow over us? Is evry man what can write a paragraf to konsider us as bars in a kage, and be always a jobbin at us to hear us growl?"[40]

The South had done nothing to be ashamed of, said Arp, and he demanded that the North recognize the South's bravery: "We made a bully fite, selah, and the whole Amerikan nation ought to feel proud of it. It shows what Amerikans can do when they think they are imposed on—'*so called.*'" Arp went on to complain about the changing patterns of race relations being forced on the South: "When I see a blakgard a goin roun the streets with a gun on his shoulder, why rite then, for a few minits, I hate the whole Yanky nashun. Jerusalem! how my blood biles! The institushun which wer handed down to us by the hevinly kingdom of Massychusetts, now put over us with powder and ball!"[41]

"With these few remarks I think I feel better," Arp closed, "and hope I hain't made nobody fitin mad, for I am not on that line at this time."[42] Arp's letter to Ward was dated September 1, 1865, and it appeared in a number of southern newspapers (its original place of publication is unknown) within a couple of weeks. On October 26, the *Rome Courier* printed a second postwar Arp letter; when reprinted in his books, it bore the title "Bill Arp on the State of the Country." "I'm much cammer and sereener than I was a few months ago," he wrote. "I begin to feel kindly towerds all peepul, except sum. I'm now endeverin to be a great nashunal man. I've taken up a motto of no North, no South, no East, no West; but let me tell you, my frend, I'll bet on Dixie as long as I've got a doller. . . . I'm a good Union Reb, and my battle cry is Dixie and the Union." Not surprisingly, Dixie came first, and Arp went on to explain how, although the state of the country had gotten better, there was still room for improvement. One problem was the continued military occupation of the South. "If the war is over," he asked, "what's the use of fillin up our towns and sittys with soljers any longer? Where's the libberty and freedum? The fakt is, Genrul Sherman and his katterpillers made such a clean sweep of evrything, that I don't see much to rekonstruk. They took so many libbertys aroun here that there's nary libberty left."[43]

Arp then discussed two issues he had brought up in his letter to Artemus Ward: blacks and northern newspapers. "Why don't they rekonstruct the niggers if they are ever goin to?" Arp asked concerning the first of these. "They've giv em a powerful site of freedum and devilish little else. Here's the big freedmen's buro, and the little buros all over the country, and the papers are full of grand orders and speshal orders, and paragrafs, but I'll bet a possum that sum of em steals my wood this winter or freezes to deth. Freedmen's buro! Freedmen's humbug, I say." On the second issue, Arp wrote about "them newspaper skribblers who slip down to the edge of Dixey evry twenty-four hours and peep over at us on tipto," and then go home and write stories that say "He ain't ded—he ain't ded—look out everybody! I'm jest from thar—seen his toe move—heern him grunt—he's a gwine to rise agin. Don't withdraw the soljers, but send down more troops immegeately." [44]

Late in 1865 the *Chattanooga Gazette* criticized Bill Arp for being disharmonious in his letters since the war. Arp's fairly indignant response, printed in the *Rome Courier* on November 9, noted that the Chattanooga paper "coppid from Yankee papers the meanest of their slander," but "we bore it silent and proud. . . . Now, when of late a umble indivijual makes bold to bust his biler, and xpress his sentiments in two breef letters, you git up like a sanktifide preecher and read him a publik lektur about *harmonizin*." [45]

These three letters make an interesting and instructive set. Gone was the feigned sympathy for Lincoln and Brown; this Arp was "proudly defiant." As he wrote to Artemus Ward, "If we ain't allowed to xpress our sentiments, we can take it out in *hatin;* and hatin runs hevy in my family, shore. I hated a man so bad onst that all the hare cum off my hed, and the man drowned himself in a hog waller that nite." All the South wanted, Arp said, was to have her patriotism and bravery recognized by the North and, even more important, to be allowed to give her side of things—"to xpress our sentiments." [46]

Bill Arp, So Called, which reprinted Arp's letters through the first part of 1866, appeared one year after the war's end. Published in New York, the book was intended for a northern audience, as Arp makes clear in his preface (titled "To the Publisher"). At one point Arp apologized to "the charitable reader" who might "find something to condemn in the following pages. It is not in my heart to offend a good man, whether he live North or South." More to the point, after noting that "it is not in human nature to smother resentment against those who would still play the tyrant and grind us into dust," Arp wrote: "But to you, kind reader, who can speak gently to the erring (if we have erred), who would pour oil upon the troubled waters, and prefer the hand of kindred love, let me say that, though proudly defiant of our enemies, the noble manliness of our people will meet you cordially at the first sincere effort toward an honorable reconciliation." [47]

It might seem odd that Arp would address this collection to northern readers, since so many of the letters themselves were addressed to southerners: those on Joe Brown, for instance, or on the cavalry or draft dodgers. Even the first four, written ostensibly to Abraham Lincoln, were obviously meant for a southern readership. It was not until after the war, with his letter to Artemus Ward, that Arp first addressed an audience outside the South, and only a handful of the thirty pieces in his first book were originally written to and for a northern audience.

The economic condition of the postwar South could account for at least part of this apparent contradiction. As one scholar described the situation, "War's end left the South with no major publishing firms equipped to produce and market books. Besides, Southerners were too poor to buy them." [48] These financial considerations— the lack of southern publishers and the relative number of northern book buyers—perhaps moved Arp to be sure that he did not offend his largest group of potential readers.

A more important reason for Arp to address the book to northern readers was the same one that motivated his letter to Artemus Ward, his report "On the State of the Country," and his reply to the *Chattanooga Gazette*. "For the sentiments that pervade these letters," Arp explained in his preface,

> I have no apology to make. At the time they appeared in the press of the South, these sentiments were the silent echoes of our people's thoughts, and this accounts in the main for the popularity with which they were received. Of course they contain exaggerations, and prophecies which were never fulfilled; but both sections were playing "brag" as well as "battle," and though we could not compete with our opponents in the former, yet some of us did try to hold our own. At both games we were whipped by overwhelming forces, and we have given it up. Conquered, but not convinced, we have accepted the situation, and have pledged ourselves to abide by it. [49]

For Arp, accepting the situation did not mean being happy about it; southerners were "conquered, but not convinced," and it was his intention to express his dissenting views from time to time and to fight for his right to do so. In other words, he addressed the book to northern readers because he was functioning as the South's spokesman, writing *for* southerners as much as *to* them. "It may be said that the character of these letters has no tendency to soften the animosities engendered by the late unhappy strife," he continued in the preface. "I can only answer, that it is not in rebel nature to be humble to those who would put the heel of tyranny upon us." Like the letter to Artemus Ward, the preface made a promise: if the northern people did not make a "sincere effort toward an honorable reconciliation," then "we will close up the avenues of our hearts, and, like the red man of the forest, transmit our bitterness and our wrongs as a heritage to our children." [50]

The "Prefase" of Arp's second book, *Bill Arp's Peace Papers* (1873), is similar in tone to that of his first. His hopes for an honorable reconciliation having gone unmet, Arp repeated his demands, beginning with a story:

> One day as I was goin along I heard a man gritin his teeth, and I saw his eyes flash fire, and he slapd his fist in his hand like poppin wagin whips, and he was a tellin another man about a fite he had had. His upper lip was all in a trimble, and the big vaines on his forrerd was swelled up like mackarony. He was powerful mad. Feelin an intrust in the like of that, I stopd and listend, and I looked all over him to see if there wasent blood or dirt, or hair on his cloathes. Well, as I dident see eny, ses I, "Mister, when did all this happen?" He pawsed—and shuttin one eye like he was a thinkin, ses he, "Well-its-now-been-nigh-onto-27 years ago."
>
> We aint that man. We hope nobdy will presoom to think we carry our war heat that long. The fakt is, it aint the war that our peepul is mad about no how. Its this confounded, everlastin, abominabul peace—this tail to the comet—this rubbin the skab off before the sore gets well.
>
> . . . Now, its useless and hipocritikal to cry pease, when there aint no pease. We may all mix and mingle, and trade, and joak, and carry

on together, but away down in our bowels there is a burnin goin on, and if our northern brethrin dont do sumthin to put the fire out, it will break loose sum of these days, and play the devil generully.[51]

Reading the preface to Arp's second book, one might imagine that the letters he had written since the end of the war had been bitter, demanding that southern rights be honored and threatening to hold up a peaceful reconciliation until the North met the South halfway. Some of Arp's Reconstruction letters were indeed of this type, prompting Wade Hall to call Arp "probably the most critical commentator on radical Reconstruction policy among the [southern] humorists."[52]

Arp often wrote of his frustrations with military reconstruction. Under the First Reconstruction Act, passed in March 1867, the South had been divided into five military districts, each under the command of a military officer empowered to maintain the peace and enforce the laws. Rome was one of seven cities chosen for military posts in the Third Military District, which included Georgia, Alabama, and Florida.[53] In three letters reprinted in *Peace Papers*, Arp complained about the situation, and particularly about the local commandant, Capt. Charles de la Mesa. When de la Mesa had several people jailed for putting on a play that featured, as a prop, a Confederate battle flag, Arp "was mity mad," he said later. "The Mayor of this town," he wrote, speaking of himself, "had a little korrespondense with Genrul Thomas the other day, and only cum out sekond best, tho it warn't an open field nor a fare fite."[54]

A second letter complained of the excesses of "the Rome Buro" (the Freedmen's Bureau): "It tries a poor farmer without givin him notis of time, place, or cirkumstances. Before he knows it, there's a judgment agin him for more than he's worth, and his property seezed, and his boddy put under gard, and his family terryfide, and all for nuthin—no writ—no charges—no kourts—no jury—no trial! . . . Is there no law; no libberty; no sekurity? Ain't there a scrap of the good old konstitushun which gives evry man the rite of trial by jury?"[55]

In another letter—when reprinted, it carried the title "Bill Arp on Nigger Equality"—Arp took a firm stand on the freedmen:

Now this nigger bisness is a sore that I thought would be allowed to cure up sum time. I don't want to speak disrespkful of Mr. [President Ulysses] Grant nor myself, but I'm obleeged to think that either him or me is a fool. He beleeves in nigger equality and I don't—that is to say, he beleeves a nigger is as good as a Southern man, tho not quite so good as a Yank. He won't shampoo in a nigger barber shop, but we must. He wouldn't swet by a nigger in a jewry box, but we shall. He wouldn't set by em in a car, or a hotel, or a meetin house, but we've got to. That's the law.

. . . There's as much difference in races of peepul as in dogs, or cats, or chickens, or bears, or sheep, or hosses, or elefants. One kind was made better at the start than another, and mixin em makes em worse instead of better. It's agin natur.

. . . The nigger wasent made to keep a post offis nor set on a jewry. He wasent made for intelektual persoots. He was made to dig, and ditch, and grub, and hoe, and plow a mule, and tote things about for white foaks, and nothin else don't soot him, and that don't soot him as well as doin nothin.

. . . But I ain't agin the nigger. I like him. I'm his frend, and I want him kept jest where he belongs. I don't want the radicals to be foolin him about his own natur, and puttin fool ideas in his hed.[56]

While some of Arp's Reconstruction letters were bitter in tone, others were marked by the same sense of humor that had distinguished his wartime writings. There was more humor than hostility, for example, in his description of "the Rekonstruktion Committee." This joint committee, proposed by Thaddeus Stevens in December 1865, had been set up to "inquire into the condition" of the former Confederate states. One of the committee's main tasks was to interview various witnesses. Arp's piece contains his (totally fictitious) testimony before the committee.

"Your name is Arp, I believe, sur?"
"So called," says I.
"You reside in the State of Georgy?"

"I can't say xactly," says I. "I liv in Rome, rite in the fork of the two Injun rivers."

"In the State of Georgy?" says he, feersly.

"I'm in a state of oncertainty about that," says I. "We don't know whether Georgy is a State or not. I would like for you to state yourself, if you know. The state of the kountry requires that this matter be settled, and I will proseed to state—"

"Never mind, sur," says he. "How old are you, Mr. Arp?"

"That depends on sirkumstances," says I. "I don't know whether to count the last five years or not."

Arp recounted his entire testimony, all in this vein, to the point where, "havin given genrul satisfacshun," he was dismissed by the committee.[57]

In another humorous letter, written in the winter of 1865–66 when he was a state senator, Arp described the momentous questions facing the legislature, such as "whether our poor innersent childern, born durin the war, wer all illegal, and had to be born over agin or not. This . . . pint are much unsettled, but our wimmen are advised to be cam and serene." Funny or not, Arp's letters during these years "enjoyed an unparalleled popularity throughout the South," as one scholar wrote, "performing a yeoman service by sustaining the morale of its people through the grievous days of Reconstruction."[58]

When Charles Henry Smith wrote his first letter to Abe Linkhorn in backwoods dialect, he used the comic misspelling that was so popular at the time, but he gave another reason for writing as he did: to honor Bill Earp, his cracker friend from Rome. "When I began writing under the signature of Bill Arp," he later explained, "I was honestly idealizing the language and humor of an unlettered country man who bears that name. I tried to write as he would, could he have written at all." He recalled Bill Earp as "an humble man and unlettered in books; never went to school but a month or two in his life, and could neither read nor write; but still he had more than his share of common sense, more than his share of ingenuity, and plan and contrivance, more than his share of good mother-wit and good humor, and was always welcome when he came about." Smith was quick to point out that he "did not rob Bill Arp of his good name, but took it on request." Smith always treasured the associations he had made with the common people of Georgia and sometimes bragged, "But for my town raising and old field school education, I, too, would have made a very respectable cracker."[59]

Several folklorists and linguistic scholars have commented on Bill Arp's use of the dialect of mid- and late-nineteenth-century northern Georgia. Some of the misspelling in his early letters was eye dialect, that is, misspelling simply for the sake of humor. This, of course, was the primary tool of the Phunny Phellows, who "violated conventions, not to achieve verisimilitude, but to amuse." But Arp's letters also present "a faithful reproduction of the American English of his time and place." In using words such as "allow" for "opine," "jine" for "join," "mout" for "might," "sot" for "sat," "tell" for "till," "tuk" for "taken," and "year" for "ear," Arp "preserved folk . . . dialect which otherwise might have been lost."[60]

The main reason Smith used dialect writing, however, was the effectiveness of the device as a tool for satire. Bill Arp might have been a fool character, but he was a "fool character with a deep understanding." Walter Blair described how "Smith used the ignorance of his creation to good purpose": Arp's "slips in writing made him say—apparently by accident—what southern readers were eager to have him say." In his letters to Lincoln, for example, Arp "accidentally" ridiculed the president's order for southern rebels to disperse and retire, the Union retreat from Manassas, the Emancipation Proclamation, and so forth.[61]

Furthermore, by taking on the comic persona, Smith could write more freely, saying things that might otherwise have gone unsaid. This was the key to Arp's popularity: he could "say with a grin what his neighbors were thinking with a scowl,"[62] whether he addressed Governor Brown's policies, the Confederate cavalry, refugeeing, the

Freedmen's Bureau, the Reconstruction Committee, or the northern press. Not all southerners agreed with Arp's sentiments, of course, but a large number did, and for them Arp's writings became, in a very real sense, their own voice. Bill Arp emerged from the Civil War and Reconstruction as a major spokesman for the South, and he would keep that position for the rest of his life.

Five

The New South

S hortly after the Civil War, Bill Earp, the man from whom Charles Henry Smith had borrowed his pen name, moved to Texas where, in 1877, a Fort Worth newspaper recorded his death: "He fell from a wagon loaded with corn; the wheels passing over his neck killed him instantly."[1] Back in Georgia, Earp's namesake also died, as Smith's cracker character, the writer of satiric, semiliterate letters to Abraham Lincoln, began writing on the pleasures of hard work in the fields. "Your farmin' colum is a great comfort to me," this new Bill Arp wrote to the editors of the *Atlanta Constitution*.

It makes me feel sorter independent of my nabors. They are mity clever and kind, but when I ax 'em about this thing and that thing, I can see a suppressed smile a playin' around as tho' it was amusin' how little I knowd. You see this is my fust year at the bisness, and all my late friends who kindly predicted that me and my folks would perish to death by the fust day of June, has been watchin' me afur off, and they are somewhat disappointed. We did run alarmingly short of vittels; that's a fact, and I reckon they heard of it, for we havent been afflicted with company to any extent. We've had a hard time of it this spring, shore. Sweet prospects, sweet birds and sweet flowers was all around us, but we couldent eat 'em. Sorter like that feller who writ about water—water everywhere, but not a drop to drink.

But I like farmin', nevertheless. Its an honest, quiet life, and it does me so much good to work and git all over in a swet of perspiration.

I enjoy my umble food and my repose, and get up every mornin' renewed and rejuvenated like an eagle in his flight, or words to that effect. I know I shall like it more and more, for we have already passed over the Rubycon and are beginnin' to reap the rewards of industry. Spring chickens have got ripe and the hens keep bloomin' on. Over 200 now respond to my old 'oman's call every mornin' as she totes around the bread tray singin' teheeky, teheeky, teheeky. I tell you she watches those birds close for she knows the value of 'em. She was raised a Methodist, she was, and many a time has watched through the crack of the door sadly, and seen the preachers helped to the last gizzard in the dish. There was 54 chickens, 7 ducks, 5 goslins, 12 turkeys and 7 pigs, hatched out last week, and Daisy had a calf and Molly a colt besides. This looks like bisness, don't it? This is what I call successful farmin'—multiplying and replenishing according to scripter. Then we have a plenty of peas and potatoes and other garden yerbs, which help a poor man out, and by the 4th of July will have wheat bread and bisket and blackberry pies and pass a regular declaration of independence.[2]

So began the first of Bill Arp's weekly letters to the *Constitution*. The differences between this and his earlier writings are obvious. Gone are the bitterness and frustration of the war and Reconstruction pieces, seemingly replaced with the gentle musings of a contented farmer. Some of the misspelling is still there, but that too would disappear within a couple of years. With this letter, a new Bill Arp was born.

Much of what Bill Arp wrote at the *Constitution* has been called "homely philosophy," a broad but vague term, hard to define with any precision. Variations include "country," "rustic," "homespun," "cheerful," "folksy," and "bucolic" philosophy. Generally, when Arp wrote on current social and political questions, he was not writing homely philosophy; when he wrote on almost anything else, he was. During his quarter-century at the *Constitution*, Arp covered many topics. In fact, sometimes he discussed many topics each week, writing as he did in a rambling style that more closely resembled a conversation between friends than a formal essay. In one column, for example, he first described the phases of the moon; then he discussed, in order, superstitions associated with the moon, superstitions in general, the rabbit's foot carried by a gubernatorial candidate, and the coming elections.[3] One topic flowed naturally into another, and probably few readers realized that Arp had moved, in a few paragraphs, from astronomy to state politics.

In another letter, even more discursive than the previous one, Arp began with a few mild complaints about how hot the summer had been. This reminded Arp of a sermon he once heard in which the preacher used what some considered to be bad language to show his congregation how hot hell would be for those who strayed from the right path. Then Arp talked about men and boys who say "damn," and followed this with a short history of cussing, including anecdotes on the subject. Arp had heard one of these anecdotes from a man who also told a story about a country boy who stole a kiss from a girl and was taken to court over it. This in turn reminded Arp of another interesting court case. "But," he concluded, "it is getting a little cooler now."[4] In this column Arp at least managed to get back to where he had started.

Most of what Arp wrote in the two columns mentioned above could be called homely philosophy, as could most of the *Constitution* letters he selected for his last three collections. Although his homely philosophy was applied to diverse topics, a few subjects showed up more often than others: his home and family, farming, the past, and the common people of Georgia.

When the Smiths moved to Cartersville from Rome in 1877, the oldest of their ten children was twenty-seven, the youngest three. This created a complicated family situation; as Bill Arp himself noted, "When folks that spring from a numerous family become numerous themselves and the first children marry off before the last are born, the children and grandchildren and uncles and nephews and cousins get all mixed up together so that a man can't tell tother from which, hardly."[5] With so many kinfolk around, it is not surprising that Arp wrote so often about them. In fact, Arp wrote more about his family and domestic life than any other topic during his years with the *Constitution*. Faithful readers became familiar with the whole Arp family, especially "Mrs. Arp" (never "Mrs. Smith") and Carl, Jessie, and Ralph, their youngest children.

Some weeks Arp devoted his entire column to one or two domestic episodes. He wrote of investigating sounds on the front porch at night; planning and enjoying a picnic in the sycamore grove; building a dam in the stream for the children; making sausage; preparing to receive city cousins; chasing snakes and bats from the house; cleaning up after a candy-pulling party; and hundreds of other incidents.[6] The following passage, as reprinted in *The Farm and the Fireside*, details one such episode:

> Last night Mrs. Arp, my wife, told the girls she didn't think their lightbread was quite as light and nice as she used to make it, and she would show them her way, so they could take pattern. She fixed up the yeast and made up the dough and put it down by the fire to rise, and this morning it had riz about a quarter of an inch, which she remarked was very curious, but reckoned it was too cold, and so she put it in the oven to bake and then it got sullen and riz downwards, and by the time it was done it was about as thick as a ginger cake, and weighed nigh unto a pound to the square inch. She never said anything, but hid it away on the top shelf of the cupboard. I saw the girls a blinking around, and when lunch time came I got it down and carried it along like it was a keg of nails and put it before her. "I thought you would like some lightbread," said I.
>
> She laid down her knife and fork, and for a moment was altogether unadequate to the occasion. Suddenly she seized the stubborn loaf, and as I ran out of the door it took me right in the small of my back, and I actually thought somebody had struck me on the spine with a maul. "Now, Mr. Impudence, take that," said she. "If a man asks for bread will you give him a stone," said I. Seeing that hostilities were about to be renewed, I retired prematurely to the piazzo to ruminate on the rise of cotton and wheat, and iron, and everything else but bread. She's got two little grandsons staying with her, and unbeknowing to me she hacked that bread into chunks and armed five little chaps with 'em, and she came forth as captain of the gang and suddenly they took me unawares in a riotous and tumultous manner. They banged

me up awfully before I could get out of the way. My head is sore all over, and take it all in all, I consider myself the injured person. I mention this circumstance as a warnin' to let all things alone when your wife hides 'em, especially bread that wouldent rise.[7]

Arp sometimes used a brief sketch of his family life to introduce a more general topic. In April 1880 he began a column with an account of his children's activities on April Fool's Day—how they had sewn his shirt sleeves together, hidden firecracker fuses in his cigars, and so on. He continued the theme of fools in the remainder of the letter with a discussion of Albion W. Tourgee's *A Fool's Errand*. Elsewhere he told readers that one of his children had just been married; that led naturally to a discussion of love and wedded life. In another column, a mention of the first money his son Carl earned was followed by a brief treatise on the proper method of raising children.[8] In the following passage, Arp talks about babies, moving with ease from the specific to the general:

The poet hath said that "a baby in the house is a well spring of pleasure." There is a bran new one here now, the first in eight years, and it has raised a powerful commotion. It's not our baby, exactly, but it's in the line of descent, and Mrs. Arp takes on over it all the same as she used to do when she was regularly in the business. I thought maybe she had forgotten how to nurse 'em and talk to 'em, but she is singing the same old familiar songs that have sweetened the dreams of half a score, and she blesses the little eyes and the little mouth and uses the same infantile language that nobody but babies understand. For she says, "tum here to its dandmudder," and "bess its 'ittle heart," and talks about its sweet little footsy-tootsies and holds it up to the window to see the wagons go by and the wheels going rouny-pouny, and now my liberty is curtailed, for as I go stamping around with my heavy farm shoes she shakes her ominous finger at me just like she used to and says, "Don't you see the baby is asleep?" And so I have to tip-toe around, and ever and anon she wants a little fire, or some hot water, or some catnip, for the baby is a-crying and shorely has got the colic. The doors have to be shut now for fear of a draft of air on the baby, and a little hole in the window pane about as big as a dime had to be patched, and I have to hunt up a passel of kindlings every night and put 'em where they will be handy, and they have sent me off to another room where the baby can't hear me snore, and all things considered, the baby is running the machine, and the well spring of pleasure is the center of space. A grandmother is a wonderful help and a great comfort at such a time as this, for what does a young mother, with her first child, know about colic and thrash, and hives and hiccups, and it takes a good deal of faith to dose 'em with sut tea and catnip, and lime water, and paregoric, and soothing syrup, and sometimes with all these the child gets worse, and if it gets better I've always had a curiosity to know which remedy it was that did the work. Children born of healthy parents can stand a power of medicine and get over it, for after the cry comes the sleep, and sleep is a wonderful restorer. Rock 'em awhile in the cradle, then take 'em up and jolt 'em a little on the knee and then turn 'em over and jolt 'em on the other side, and then give 'em some sugar in a rag and after awhile they will go to sleep and let the poor mother rest. There is no patent on this business, no way of raising 'em all the same way, but it is trouble, trouble from the start, and nobody but a mother knows how much trouble it is. A man ought to be mighty good just for his mother's sake, if nothing else, for there is no toil or trial like nursing and caring for a little child, and there is no grief so great as a mother's if all her care and anxiety is wasted on an ungrateful child.[9]

Arp's domestic sketches were probably the most popular of all his columns for the *Constitution;* they were certainly the most delightful to read. Many people could identify with the characters and situations of these sketches. One reader said, "Don't Bill Arp tell things the plainest? I have laughed till I cried over some of his letters; for the same things had happened in our own family, and it seemed that he must have been right here in the house when he wrote them."[10]

Before 1887, when Smith and his family moved from the countryside outside of Cartersville into town, he wrote frequently about his farm. Sometimes the letters were quite detailed, with instructions on how to build a fence or plant onions. More often, though, he simply spoke of his pleasures at toiling in the earth, laughing good-naturedly when the bugs got to his tomatoes before he did, or bragging about his successes. Arp's letters were a celebration of the rural life. "Farming is an ever-changing employment," he wrote. "There is something new turns up nearly every day, something unexpected and out of the general run. It aint so with storekeepers, nor carpentering, nor any mechanical business, for with those pursuits one day is pretty much like another, and that is why I like farming." Digging potatoes, pulling fodder, threshing wheat—things that many people might find as boring and tedious as Arp found keeping store or carpentering—had special virtue for Arp, because farming was hard but honest work that allowed a man to live close to nature. "A farmer's life is a pretty hard one in some respects," he wrote, ". . . but the law of compensation comes in and balances off all its troubles." [11]

Another subject of Arp's *Constitution* column was the past, especially his childhood experiences. Annie May Christie, his biographer, catalogued some of these: "He loved to tell of the good times he had on his two-mile walk to school, of making candles and quillpens, of going fishing on Saturday afternoon, of feeding mulberry leaves to his father's silkworms as one of his home chores, gathering 'chickapins,' chestnuts, and walnuts, going to mill, riding the mail fifty miles twice a week for his postmaster father at the age of twelve, watching the 'best man' of the Pinkneyville district and the 'best man' of the Ben Smith district fight in the Lawrenceville square to prove which was the 'best man' in the county." [12] In the published collections, his letters were given such titles as "Sticking to the Old," "The Old Trunk," "The Old School Days," "The Old Tavern," "Old Things Are Passing Away and All Things Have Become New," "The House Where I Was Born," and "Arp's Reminiscences of Fifty Years."

The Georgia folk were also much in evidence in Arp's letters to the *Constitution*. Since he had taken as his pseudonym the name of a Georgia cracker, this was especially appropriate. In an essay on Georgia crackers, Arp wrote that they were a "rough, rude people" who "were generally poor, but they enjoyed life more than they did money." They were "merry-hearted, unconcerned, [and] independent," and asked only "to be let alone by the laws and the outside world." Arp treasured the friendships he had made with these people, and treated them in his writings with respect and affection. He wrote about the original Bill Earp with "a sympathetic understanding not to be found in [the writings] of earlier Southern humorists," in the words of one scholar. Other crackers who frequently appeared in Arp's letters were Cobe Guyton, the jovial tenant on his farm, and "Big John" Underwood, who in many sketches represented the voice of common sense.[13]

Arp implicitly honored the Georgia folk in many of his letters. For example, he rarely used a common adage if a folk saying could take its place. Instead of writing, "The Lord will provide," he wrote, "The Lord never sent a 'possum into the world but what He planted a 'simmon tree close by." "As poor as gully dirt," "as limber as a greasy rag," "as lively and gay as a colt in a meadow," "sweatin' like a run-down filly," "blowin' worse than a tired steer," "like a sick frog watchin' for rain"—all of these provided realistic imagery based on Arp's rural environment and the folk around him. Arp also spiced his writings with bits of folk superstition. "To get rid of screech owls," he advised readers to "put the shovel in the fire when one of 'em was a screechin and he would leave forthwith." "Meat will shrink in the pot if the moon is on the wane when you kill it," he noted elsewhere, although he added that "I don't care anything about the moon myself." In addition, the *Constitution* letters contain folk tales, rhymes, games, and songs.[14]

What are we to make of this new Bill Arp? John Morris, writing in the *Library of Southern Literature* shortly after Charles Henry Smith's death, noted that "[Arp's] work falls naturally into two quite dissimilar parts: his letters of war and reconstruction and his farm and fireside sketches. The former group is chiefly controversial, frequently personal, and quite bitter in tone. The latter is mellower, patriarchal, humorously philosophical." Later scholars tended to agree with Morris's assessment of the post-1878 Arp. Napier Wilt described Arp as "a good humored, hard working, courageous Southern farmer" who "talks about farm life, his family and friends, and general social conditions." "Much of the bad grammar, awkward spellings, and passion of the earlier Bill Arp letters gave way to the philosophical farmer figure smoking at twilight," wrote Wade Hall. "The satire of the earlier letters has been replaced by a genial, homely philosophy, wistfully comic, dealing with family and farm life." [15]

Walter Blair and Hamlin Hill, who used the device of Roman numerals to distinguish the two Arps, wrote that "Bill Arp II . . . was the contented farmer, the happily married man, and the lover of his family, the community, the country (as opposed to the city), and mankind." "The character of Bill Arp somehow had been mislaid," Blair wrote elsewhere. "Not only most of the bad grammar and spelling but also much of the fire which had flamed in Bill's earlier political letters was missing" from his *Constitution* letters. According to another commentator, "Arp turned to a folksy, down-home style" in his letters, stressing among other things "the simple joys of country life." William Lenz perhaps put it most succinctly: "What concerns [Arp] after 1878 are the pleasures and comforts of hearth and home." [16]

The common theme that runs throughout the scholarship on Arp is that he was, after 1878, a contented man, cheerful and hopefully optimistic. He no longer wrote on the Union army, extortioners, Gov. Joseph E. Brown, and the Freedmen's Bureau; now he concerned himself with farming, children, superstitions, Georgia crackers, and other peaceful topics. According to these scholars, Arp had become reconciled to the Confederacy's defeat and was ready to accept, even to welcome, the coming of a new age in the South. Most of these scholars based their assessment of Arp's writings on the published collections of his newspaper columns, not on the newspaper columns themselves. Arp wrote roughly 1,250 columns for the *Atlanta Constitution* between 1878 and 1903. The exact number will probably never be known. Annie May Christie listed 1,348 Bill Arp pieces in her dissertation, but about a hundred of those were published either before 1878 (Arp's war and Reconstruction pieces) or outside the *Constitution*.[17] Christie missed a few of the *Constitution* letters, but since the paper's files are incomplete, my number, which is slightly higher than hers, is also inexact.

The situation is complicated by the question of just what constituted a Bill Arp letter. Some of his *Constitution* columns were reprinted from other sources, such as his history of Georgia or his essays in the *Southern Cultivator*. From the middle of 1885 to the end of the year, Arp wrote an additional column that appeared in the *Constitution* on Mondays. Usually titled "Home and Farm" or "The Farm," it was similar in style and subject matter to his regular Sunday column. Furthermore, at least one of Arp's pieces in the *Constitution* was published anonymously. "The Story of Centre," which told of a swindler who escaped the angry citizens of Rome, Georgia, by crossing over to the safety of Alabama, had no by-line when it appeared in the *Constitution* on January 20, 1884. A week later, an editor answered a reader's question by identifying the piece as being "from the pen of Bill Arp." The sketch was later published in one collection as if it had been a regular column.[18]

While an exact count of Arp's letters to the *Constitution* is impossible, the number 1,250 (an average of about 50 a year) probably does not miss the mark by much. Arp's last three collections contain only about 110 of these, however, which means that scholars have based their assessment of Arp's writings on less than one-tenth of his output for this period. Since the collections contain little besides homely philosophy, scholars who relied exclusively on the books could remain unaware that Arp often wrote on other topics.

When Arp was not writing homely philosophy, he was often writing about the "New South," a phrase that was ubiquitous among southerners in the 1880s and 1890s. The phrase in other contexts could have many meanings—chronological, geographical, ideological—but here it means a program of renewal and growth in the South, a program designed to make the South once again, like the rest of the nation, opulent, triumphant, and innocent. In the words of Paul M. Gaston, the movement's chief historian, the goals of the New South were "harmonious reconciliation of sectional differences, racial peace, and a new economic and social order based on industry and scientific, diversified agriculture." The greatest of these was industrialization, "the first plank of the New South program." Promoters of the New South realized that "wealth and power in the modern world flowed from machines and factories, not from unprocessed fields of white cotton"; so these New South prophets, as they came to be known, urged southerners to industrialize, mainly through the building of cotton mills, but also through iron production, lumbering, mining and other extractive industries, and so forth. Industrialization would bring wealth to the South and restore the region to a prominent place within the Union.[19]

The rest of the New South program was built on this "first plank." Agricultural reform would help farmers, of course, but it would also benefit industrialization by providing markets for the South's diversified products, by breaking down the animosity between agriculture and industry, and by ending the region's economic reliance on cotton. There was no place for large planters and King Cotton in the New South; the new agriculture emphasized diversified crops and scientific farming methods that would increase farmers' income and bring on a spirit of enterprise and self-sufficiency, which in turn would foster the move for industrialization.[20]

Sectional reconciliation and racial peace were also tied to industrialization—the first, to obtain northern investments that would provide the capital needed for industrialization; the second, to show that the South would satisfy the requirements of the Reconstruction amendments and give blacks at least the appearance of a chance to share in the South's prosperity. New South prophets hoped to lure northern money with speeches, industrial expositions, and pamphlets and magazine articles that showed the South's promising future. On the subject of race, promoters walked the thin line between friend of the Negro and white supremacy in their efforts to demonstrate that the South was a safe and deserving place for investment.[21]

The most famous and influential spokesman for the New South was Henry W. Grady. From the day he became editor of the *Atlanta Constitution* in 1876 until his death in 1889, Grady preached the creed of industrialization, diversified agriculture, and sectional and racial peace, making his paper "the major organ of the New South movement."[22] Grady's speech on "The New South," delivered on December 22, 1886, before the New England Society of New York, electrified the nation just as it did the 360 people who filled Delmonico's Restaurant that night. The speech stressed the theme of national unity more than industrialization,[23] but Grady later emphasized other aspects of the New South creed. Before the Bay State Club of Boston in 1889, Grady delivered one of his best-remembered calls to industrial action. Part of the speech described the funeral of a fellow Georgian:

> They buried him in the midst of a marble quarry: they cut through solid marble to make his grave; and yet a little tombstone they put above him was from Vermont. They buried him in the heart of a pine forest, and yet the pine coffin was imported from Cincinnati. They buried him within touch of an iron mine, and yet the nails in his coffin and the iron in the shovel that dug his grave were imported from Pittsburg [sic]. They buried him by the side of the best sheep-grazing country on the earth, and yet the wool in the coffin bands and the coffin bands themselves were brought from the North. The South didn't furnish a thing on earth for that funeral but the corpse and the hole in the ground. There they put him away and the clods rattled down on his coffin, and they buried him in a New York coat and a Boston pair of shoes and a pair of breeches from Chicago and a shirt from Cincinnati, leaving him nothing to carry into the next world with him to remind him of the country in which he lived, and for which he fought for four years, but the chill of blood in his veins and the marrow in his bones.[24]

Most of the other New South prophets were, like Grady, journalists. Francis W. Dawson, a transplanted Englishman who had fought for the Confederacy, preached the New South gospel as editor of the *News and Courier* of Charleston, South Carolina. Richard Hathaway Edmonds founded the *Manufacturers' Record* in Baltimore in the early 1880s. Soon recognized as the leading industrial journal of the South, Edmonds's paper featured weekly glowing (and at times exaggerated) accounts of new industries and investments in the South. Henry Watterson, who had been a Tennessee Unionist until the First Battle of Manassas, pressed the twin themes of reconciliation and industrialization on readers of his Louisville *Courier-Journal*. Daniel Augustus Tompkins, one of North Carolina's leading industrialists, purchased the *Charlotte Chronicle* (which he renamed the *Observer*) in order to "preach the doctrine of industrial development." Under the able editorial guidance of Joseph Pearson Caldwell, the *Observer* became an influential voice for the New South. Editors of smaller newspapers read Grady, Dawson, and the others and "echoed them with tiny peals in the local weeklies."[25]

In his weekly letters to the *Atlanta Constitution*, Bill Arp wrote with unflagging vigor, if not with Grady's eloquence, to promote the New South goals of industrialization and diversified farming. There is nothing to indicate that Grady and the *Constitution*'s editorial policy dictated Arp's position on these issues. The *Constitution* was actually fairly open on many questions. For example, while Grady favored a protective tariff, Arp was generally for free trade, and he said so often in his column. On the issue of the New South program, however, Arp was clearly in agreement with Grady. In an 1883 column he wrote:

> When I ruminate over the desolation that covered our land and our people fifteen years ago, it does look like we have been resurrected by magic. The south is on rising ground everywhere, but Georgia is in the lead. . . .
>
> Northern capital and English capital is quietly slipping around and investing in southern land and southern railroads, and southern business. Ever and anon, them rich fellers peek over the line and whisper, that's a good country, splendid country, and the folks look peaceful— Let's wedge in a little passel of money down there before everybody finds out what a good country it is. Let's buy some land or lend 'em some money and take a mortgage.
>
> Now, if we can get some capital invested in small enterprises and make our own buckets and tubs and washboards and axehandles and haims [hames] and plowhandles and hubs and axles and spokes

and horseshoes and trace chains and hatchets and hammers and window glass and ink and soda and starch and baking powders, and a
thousand other little things that we buy and use every day, we will be
all right. We want more variegated industry. Iron works and cotton
factories and big flour mills are big things and good things, but we
want a power of little things.

"The prosperity of the south will be assured," Arp wrote in another
column, if southerners would "reduce the cotton acreage to one-half
and manufacture one-half of what is made." [26]

"What the south wants is to be independent and self-sustaining,"
Arp once wrote, giving a tinge of sectional animosity to his rallying
cry for industrialization. "We have paid tribute and homage to the
north long enough. . . . Let us all work together and build up the
south." More often he based his argument on economic grounds.
"We want more industry and more opportunities for our boys and
girls," he wrote in 1881, "and we want our cotton worked up at
home and that will give us cheaper goods, for we won't have to pay
freight both ways." The economic motive also applied to industries
other than cotton mills. In 1880 Arp visited a manganese mining
company near Cartersville. In his next weekly letter, he bragged on
the mine's production, but noted that most of the manganese was
shipped to France where it was made into chemicals and then sold
back to Cartersville and other towns. "Our people must stop that
shipping business and work it up at home and save all the profits,"
Arp wrote. Fifteen years later Arp and his wife toured the Atlanta
Cotton States and International Exposition. They marvelled at the
aluminum wares on display there—all produced in the North—and
bought a pepper box for their table. "That aluminium clay is all
about in our hills and is being mined and shipped every day to Pitts-
burgh and there it is reduced and manufactured and the products
come back to us with two freights and big profits added," Arp wrote.
"Just so with our manganese and ochre and lumber and hides and
most of our cotton and wool. We have got to manufacture our own
materials or we will never catch up." [27]

Another reason Arp favored industrialization was that southern towns could improve their standards of living by building one or two factories. "It is most astonishing how much life and vigor these manufacturing industries instill into a community," he wrote in 1888. Arp saw ample evidence of this on his frequent lecture tours. "As I travel over the south, I can tell a prosperous town from a stagnant one by the wheels that are turning, the smoke stacks and the hum of the machinery, or the absence of all these," he explained. When Arp lectured in one South Carolina town, he noted that "the mill has brought good schools and artesian wells and new hotels and churches and many beautiful new residences"; in another, "new stores, new dwellings, new churches, parsonages and a fine public school building have gone up, a new courthouse is projected and all this comes from the cotton mill." [28]

Arp frequently returned from his lecture trips disappointed in the showing made by his home state. After seeing the huge Piedmont Wagon Company in Hickory, North Carolina, he wrote: "I can well imagine what Cartersville would be if she had a thousand mechanics at work and their families to feed, and she could have them if she had the nerve to invest in machinery." "Now why can't every town in Georgia do likewise[?]" he asked when he visited the mill in another North Carolina town. Arp was usually satisfied with the industrial achievements of Georgia and the rest of the South, however. In fact, he sometimes wrote (as did all good New South prophets) as if the New South goal of industrialization had already been accomplished. [29]

"Capital is coming south every day to be invested in manufactures," Arp wrote in 1883, ". . . and we want it to come." He often ended his columns on industrialization by inviting northern investors to send their money southward. "Now is a good time for those who are looking around for safe and substantial investments to come and see us," Arp said in 1888. "We have nothing to give away except a healthy climate and beautiful scenery, but our land and our minerals can be had at reasonable prices." Some of his descriptions of Cartersville, such as this one from an 1888 column, would have made a real estate agent jealous: "There is not a town in Georgia that has such beautiful suburbs for improvement. Situated on a high plateau with gently rolling surface and good drainage and beautiful views of the surrounding mountains and fast flowing streams on every side, she offers inviting homes and good business prospects to those who are seeking homes, no matter whether they come from the north or from the south." [30]

Related to Arp's promotion of southern industry was his push for railroads, which would benefit farmers and passengers as well as industrialists. "We want the railroads to prosper," he wrote in 1885. "They are of vital use to us. We cannot get along without them and we ought to encourage the building of more roads—the more the better." "Railroads have contributed more to the advancement of our state than all other causes combined," he wrote the following year, and elsewhere noted that "railroads are a necessity and they carry civilization wherever they go." [31]

In 1895 Arp had the chance to combine his admiration of railroads and his love for Florida's gulf coast when he was asked to write a promotional pamphlet for the Plant System. The handiwork of Connecticut-born Henry B. Plant, the Plant System was the result of the consolidation of many small roads between 1879 and 1899. By the latter year it had some two thousand miles of railroad connecting the towns on the west coast of Florida to points north, along with steamship lines and resort hotels in Tampa, Clearwater, and elsewhere, all controlled by Plant. Early in 1894, after lecturing to a full house at the music hall of the Tampa Bay Hotel, Arp wrote in his weekly *Constitution* letter that Plant "must be a wonderful man to plan such a system." Given Arp's views of Florida, railroads, and Henry Plant, he was a natural to write the promotional pamphlet. In *Leisure Hours in Florida on the West Coast Plant System,* Arp commended both the man and the system. Plant was, Arp noted, "an unselfish friend to the people of the South"; "if there's any bigger man in the line of public progress and public benefaction, I don't know it." Arp praised the convenience of the railroad and the comfort of the hotels, and gave a brief look at the history and attractions of each town along the way. [32]

"Georgia cannot favor manufacturers without benefiting the farmers," Arp wrote in 1887, and agricultural reform was for him, as for Grady and the other New South prophets, an important part of the New South program. As a farmer, Arp could speak from experience about the need for diversified crops and scientific agriculture. "The farmers in my neighborhood made a good crop of cotton last year, and sold it for a right good price," he wrote early in 1881, "but as shore as you are born, a good many of 'em are buying corn right now, and buying it on a credit, and paying 25 per cent more than they could buy it for cash. . . . It does look like our people ought to learn something from experience and make cotton the secondary crop instead of the first." Arp himself had grown cotton almost exclusively until 1881—"it took me three years to shake off the thing and quit being a fool," he wrote—but when he realized the merits of diversified farming, he used his column to convince other farmers to move away from King Cotton. "It would seem a great calamity for cotton to get down to 7 or 8 cents next fall," he said in June 1881, "but I reckon it would be the best thing for our people, for it's better to break all over at once than to be breaking little by little all the time. It would teach 'em a lesson that nothing else will." A month later, after discussing the advantages of growing clover, he wrote: "Excuse me for repeating things, but you see the most of our people are farmers, and if they prosper the state prospers, and it seems to me they are getting behind, and have got all their eggs in one basket, and the more cotton they make the less they will get for it." [33]

Arp was proud to be a scientific farmer. He told readers about the books and journals he used, and frequently repeated advice he got from them. He also promoted the state agricultural department. "I learn more when I go there than anywhere else," he wrote. "I believe that branch of the public service is doing more good than any other." In 1881, he happily reported (somewhat prematurely, as in the case of industrialization) that "our farmers [are] in dead earnest. They've got better stock and better implements, and are studying the science of farming more than they ever did before." [34]

Not surprisingly, Arp emphasized agricultural reform in his monthly essays in the *Southern Cultivator*. In one column he told farmers how and when to plant wheat, the proper ways of preparing the soil, and which seeds would do best in particular areas. In another he stressed the use of improved farm tools: "I wish that every farmer was able to buy a disc roller harrow, the best implement I have yet found to pulverize the land and put in the wheat and oats. . . . The disc harrow to pulverize and sow, and the free use of a roller afterwards to pack the surface, will ensure a good crop." A couple of months later, the *Southern Cultivator* printed a letter from a Florida reader who said he had seen Arp's description of the disc harrow and wanted to know where he could get one. The answer appeared further on in that issue in an advertisement for the Corbin Disc Harrow. The half-page ad contained testimonials from a number of people, including "Maj. C. H. Smith (Bill Arp)": "I am well pleased with the C. D. Harrow and recommend it as the best labor-saving implement ever introduced in the South." Readers apparently appreciated Arp's agricultural advice. One, W. D. Lidell, a Missouri farmer, said in a letter to the *Southern Cultivator* that "my favorite writer in your paper is 'Bill Arp,' for sound advice given in a cheerful way." [35]

In the *Southern Cultivator*, Arp occasionally noted (as he did in the *Constitution*) that one of the biggest problems facing agricultural reform was ignorance: "Unfortunately the old prejudice against 'book larnin'' still exists among the poorer and uneducated farmers." Arp therefore urged farmers to read more, and especially to read the *Southern Cultivator* regularly. In turn, the *Southern Cultivator* told readers to pay close attention to Arp's column in order to become not only "a more generous and whole-soul man," but also a "wiser, more experienced farmer." [36]

It should perhaps be noted that while Arp certainly believed that farmers should read agricultural books and magazines (including the *Southern Cultivator*) to learn the new scientific ways of farming, he had a special relationship with that journal. J. P. Harrison, the firm that published the *Southern Cultivator*, also published *Bill*

Arp's Scrap Book, his third collection. Frequent advertisements in the *Southern Cultivator* urged readers to send for a free sample of the paper, a premium list, and specimen pages of Arp's *Scrap Book.* The book would be sent free to anyone ordering a "club subscription" (at least eight copies mailed to one address), and regular subscribers could get the book at reduced rates. The *Southern Cultivator* also advertised the book by itself, sometimes with premiums of its own (the *Scrap Book* with "an elegant nickel-plated alarm clock" for four dollars, or with "an elegant stem-winding watch" for six).[37]

In one of the first scholarly studies of Arp's writings, Louella Landrum commented on his views of industrialization. "Though there is no evidence that [Arp] was an active champion in this cause," she wrote, "there is a general tone in his letters and essays which indicates that he was in accord with such progressive movements." [38] She was half right, for Arp *was* an active champion in the cause of industrialization. In fact, Arp's columns on this subject appear to bear out the common assumption that his homely philosophy writings signaled an implicit acceptance of a new age in the South. But as we shall see in the next chapter, this idea—that Arp, in his cheerfulness and bright optimism, epitomized the spirit of the New South—is wrong.

Six

The Old South

I t was a group of hopeful and ambitious young men that led the movement for southern industrialization. Henry Grady, youthful editor of the *Atlanta Constitution* and the quintessential spokesman for the New South, died in 1889 at the age of thirty-nine. *Charlotte Observer* publisher Daniel A. Tompkins was born in 1851, one year after Grady, and Joseph Caldwell, the *Observer*'s editor, was two years younger still. Richard H. Edmonds, of the *Manufacturers' Record,* turned four the year the Civil War began. Editors Francis Dawson and Henry Watterson, both born in 1840, were a bit older, but Paul Gaston's assessment of the New South spokesmen still generally holds true: "Too young to serve in the war, they passed through childhood and adolescence under its influence and reached maturity during the Reconstruction era. Thus their formative years coincided with the period of their region's greatest failure." As Gaston noted, "The years in which they matured had a sobering effect on them but, unlike the older generation—veterans of secession and defeat—they were full of youthful optimism about the future." [1]

These young spokesmen of the new order had little attachment to the antebellum South—their program looked to the future, not to the past—but they had to be careful not to offend their followers by making disparaging references to the romantic, idealized view of the Old South. Instead, they looked to the history of the Old South for something that would provide a foundation for the New, something that would make the one seem a natural and desirable continuation of the other. The Old South was dead, and that made it safe; as Wayne Mixon observed, "The magic of the Lost Cause, the source of its appeal to . . . New South spokesmen, was that it was so irrevocably and satisfyingly lost." The New South spokesmen therefore "fashioned an interpretation of the region's past that was congenial to the New South mentality; that is, they discovered in their history a heritage of nationalism and industrialism which . . . linked past, present, and future inseparably and harmoniously." [2]

On the face of it, there was little in this rewriting of the Old South's history that would have bothered Charles Henry Smith. As Bill Arp, he occasionally wrote on the theme of the South's heritage of nationalism and industrialism himself.[3] But Smith was older than most of the New South prophets. Born in 1826, he had reached maturity in the glory of the Old South, not in the defeat of the war and Reconstruction. By the time the Old South finally gave up the ghost in 1865, Smith was almost forty years old, the father of eight and an established and respected civic and business leader. When he began his weekly column in the *Atlanta Constitution* in 1878, he was nearly twice as old as his youthful editor, Henry Grady. So although Bill Arp could promote industrialization along with the best of them, he had little use for the New South prophets' self-serving view of the past. For Arp, the Old South was more than a justification for the New.

The 'Old South' is not dead by a long shot, and I am proud of it," Arp wrote in one of his weekly letters in 1887. This assertion was in response to an article printed the previous month in *Century* that had tried to show that "the South is morally better than it was before the war," that southerners were "building a New South that will be far grander than ever the Old South was or could have been." Arp's reaction to the *Century* article was harsh; he called it "a foul slander upon the old south" and shared with his readers the "elaborate and admirable reply" of a Mississippi newspaper. "'There is no new south,'" Arp quoted. "'The term is a misnomer and a myth. It is simply a phrase costume in which old prejudices masquerade through modern prints seeking to pervert the education of southern children into the conviction that their ancestors, if not criminal, were little more than a race of idlers, blunderers, blockheads and failures.'" "That's it," Arp wrote, "that's it exactly, that's what I've been thinking for lo these many years. . . . I affirm this humbly, conscientiously and with faith—reluctant faith—that our present methods will not and cannot produce as grand and noble men as the last half century before the war produced."[4]

As much as he promoted the industrialization favored by New South prophets, Arp himself hardly ever used the phrase "New South" in any but a disparaging sense. "Money rules the roost and the south is beginning to ape the north in bowing down to mammon, and therefore it's called 'The New South,'" he wrote in 1881. "I don't think the new south is as good as the old either in honesty or simplicity."[5] In a column sixteen years later, recounting a conversation he had recently had with several friends, Arp extended his criticism:

> We were talking about the old south and the new south and some said there was no new south; that we were the same people and have the same principles, the same religion and the same politics that our fathers had, but like the rest of the civilized world, we had advanced in education and general intelligence and in the enjoyment of the comforts of life.
>
> Well, I am no pessimist, but I am grieved to say that in many things we have advanced backward. We have more books and more newspapers and more schools, but that crime is on the increase is known and admitted by all who study the records of the courts. There are more idle young men than there need to be—yes, five times as many, according to population, and Ben Franklin said that idleness is the parent of vice. I can pick out a score of young men in every town who are doing nothing—young men of good families—and they are living on the old man or the old woman and seem to be content. Fifty years ago we had no vagabonds; every young man worked at something, and it was considered disreputable to lie around in idleness. . . .

Then we got to talking about the new woman—the female doctors
and lawyers and editors and preachers and teachers and bookkeepers
and saleswomen, and how women were forging ahead and taking the
places and occupations of the men, and my friend, Mr. Williams, of
California, surprised us by saying that there was a tribe of Indians in
the northwest who were already far in advance on this line. . . . In
this tribe the women dominate the men in the family and the field
and forest. They rule them absolutely. . . . So it seems that our new
woman has a savage precedent. Have we got to come to this?[6]

The above quotations show something of Arp's discontent with
the New South. Arp was not always complaining, of course. His
complaints were more humorous than real in an 1885 column, for
example, when he described a trip to the big city of Atlanta and his
puzzlement over such modern contrivances as elevators, telephones,
huge banks, and store detectives. Arp was perhaps unintentionally
funny when he expressed his dissatisfaction with the new age in
another column. After telling a few lawyer stories from his days on
the circuit, he wrote: "I don't believe we have as good anecdotes
now as we used to have." In 1897 he said, "I am grateful that my life
has been allotted to the last three quarters of this century—seven
decades that have witnessed more progress in science, art, invention and Christian civilization than in any previous thousand years
in the world's history." But as he noted later in that same column,
"Progress always brings a train of evil things along with it." Among
the evil things that Arp saw accompanying the progress of the postwar South were some that sound familiar a century later: cigarettes,
"promiscuous bathing," cocaine, an overemphasis on intercollegiate
athletics, "hip pocket pistols," and young people staying out late
at night.[7]

Where the New South prophets had judged the Old South by
the New, Arp turned the process around; everything he saw in the
New South, he saw through the eyes of the Old. "How can an old
man help comparing the present with the past?" he asked in 1901.
"Memory is his capital stock. . . . If I was now in my teens I would
be better reconciled to things as they are—to modern manners and

customs and to the sin and crime of this fast and reckless age. Our young people cannot realize that there ever was a better time and a better people. Therefore they give the morality of the past no thought and the crime of the present no great concern. They look upon the fearful catalogue in the daily papers as our normal condition and many join in it to keep up with the procession." Arp often complained that the principles and virtues of the Old South no longer seemed to have a place in society. Gone in the New South was the virtue of hard work, replaced by habits of laziness and easy living. Gone too, Arp insisted, were the domestic virtues of home and family; infidelity to the marriage vows and new roles for women had taken their place. Gone as well was the self-reliant spirit of the Old South, which had given way to dependence on others and on society. "I don't care what you call it," Arp wrote, "the new south or the old south rehabilitated, it is the south, our south, and it is a goodly heritage." But as Arp told his readers week after week, that goodly heritage was fast disappearing.[8]

One virtue of the Old South that Arp saw missing in the New was hard work. Industry (here meaning diligent labor, not manufacturing) might not have been the panacea for all the South's ills, but Arp claimed that it could work wonders. "A young man who will work diligently . . . will make character and good health, and . . . will keep out of temptation," he once wrote. In another column he advised parents of boys to "put em to work and keep em at it for idleness is the parent of all vice." Arp suggested once that "hard work in the field . . . would prevent suicides and restore lunatics to their proper senses." "There is no security except in honest industry," he said in another essay.[9]

Despite all these benefits of hard work, most men of the New South worked hard to avoid it, Arp observed. "This rising generation are powerful shifty," he wrote in 1881. "They can invent more ways to dodge work than any of their predecessors." "There seems to be . . . no inclination to work—to begin at the bottom and work up, but rather to get something for nothing and get it quick," Arp complained elsewhere. "Lottery tickets, cotton futures, gaming, or to marry rich is the idea." In an 1890 essay Arp condemned the Louisiana Lottery, which had been chartered by a special clause in the state constitution and was the nation's largest during this era. "Lotteries are a mark of low civilization," he said in that column, a sentiment he repeated a year later when he lectured at a chautauqua in Louisiana on "the widespread and alarming desire of our young men to find a shortroad to fortune—to get something for nothing." The speculator, who made tremendous profits without adding anything to the value of the product or the good of society, was no better; Arp called him "a blood sucker, a vampire, a buzzard, a public cuss."[10]

"About one man in eight or maybe ten is at work—that is, doing something to maintain his race—making something useful or growing something," Arp once wrote. "The balance are suckers. They suck the juice out of industry and live off of other people's labor." When the senior class from a nearby college came to Atlanta to have its picture made in the spring of 1886, a reporter asked the thirty-nine young men about their future vocations. More than half indicated that they would go into law or medicine, and most of the rest intended to enter into various other professions. One student said he would be a mechanic, and one other a farmer. "Can this be true?" Arp asked. "Only two out of thirty-nine who intend to produce anything to add to the common stock. Will the rest be consumers?"[11]

Arp's views on hard work shaped his attitudes toward education. Children "should be raised to habits of industry," he wrote. "The old fashioned boys had to work," he remembered, thinking back perhaps to his days at the Gwinnett Manual Labor Institute. "But school boys don't do anything now but study, and not overly much of that." Young people needed to be taught industry as well as the academic subjects—"Brains and muscle mixed make the best men I know and the most useful to the state," Arp noted in 1883—but the schools were failing in this, and their failure was creating a generation of southerners unsuited to carry on the Old South's virtues. This was a theme Arp addressed time and time again in his *Con-*

stitution column. "College habits are habits of physical indolence," he wrote. "A college boy has no education to work anything but his brains when he comes away. . . . His physical nature abhors work— he can't stand it." College is "a risk, a peril, a hazard," he said in 1887; "work, toil, industry is a bigger thing than books," he noted a dozen years later. As he wrote in another column, "Any kind of work that is honest is honorable. Don't spoil a natural mechanic by trying to make a poor lawyer of him. An industrial man in overalls is much more respectable than a lazy gas bag in broad cloth." [12]

The schools also failed to provide moral training for their students. "Moral training, good habits, good principles are of more importance than maps and figures," Arp wrote in 1890. These things "are not included in any school curriculum, and yet are the very foundation of society and good government, and of far more importance than trigonometry or Greek or rhetoric." Public schools of the New South were "run like machinery," Arp said, turning out students overeducated in academic subjects and undereducated in moral ones.[13]

In March 1889 the *Constitution* printed a letter from G. P. Webb, of Sherman, Texas. Webb had read "another attack on education from the charming pen of our great and good Bill Arp," and in his letter he went on to defend the schools. Arp's reply a week later nicely summarized his views on education:

> I am not opposed to collegiate education. I have never written a line from which you could draw such an inference. I have a very fair education myself and would not exchange it for all the wealth in the world, nor would I write anything or do anything that would deprive others of the same blessing. . . . But what I do maintain is that constant, earnest moral training should go along with it in every family and school and college. I maintain that it is more important to teach the youth of our country morality than algebra or chemistry. . . . How many professors deem it a duty to impress upon their pupils obedience to parents, obedience to law, honesty, truth, temperance, chastity, industry, and to do unto others as they would have others do unto them? If you say that these things should be taught at home, the answer is they are not taught at home. . . .

My friend Webb asks me if education contributes to the increase of crime. I answer, yes; emphatically yes. The statistics prove it beyond all question. The more education the more crime, in proportion to population. It is natural that there should be. . . . The more knowledge the more capacity, and as capacity is increased restraint must be increased. Moral restraint, legal restraint, all kinds of restraint. Line upon line and precept upon precept. It should come from the fireside and the school and the pulpit and especially from the school. . . . Moral training should go along with schooling, side by side, or a little ahead. . . . Let the three "R's" move on, but the three "H's" are better still—"Head, Heart and Hands." [14]

Like the decline of the virtue of hard work, the increase in immorality was a feature of the New South that bothered Arp. In his column for January 13, 1901—his second in the new century—Arp gave one of his lengthy lists of statistics on crime and immorality. "The nineteenth century leaves us this record as a legacy," he said. "Our concern is what are we going to do about it. Our lamentation is that the people have gotten used to it and reconciled to its continuance. It is looked upon as the normal condition of public morals and human affairs. Old men, old editors and old preachers cry aloud and spare not, but the young generation do not seem to be greatly concerned." [15]

This immorality took many forms. Sometimes it meant a higher crime rate; in 1895, for example, Arp noted that "the race between crime and morality is neck and neck, especially in our cities." Much more often immorality was whatever attacked the integrity of the family: "a father's bad habits, a mother's discontent, a son's dissipation or a daughter's frailty," Arp once wrote, a list of euphemisms vague enough to cover a multitude of sins, from inebriety, gambling, and neglect to promiscuity, infidelity, and divorce. "A happy home is the only paradise upon the earth," Arp said, "and whoever makes it unhappy is as guilty as was the serpent that destroyed the peace of Eden." [16]

Divorce was a special concern of Arp's. "Only the old people who married half a century ago can appreciate the contrast between now and then and the change for the worse is alarming," he wrote in 1899. "The marriage relation has lost much of its seriousness, its solemnity, its dignity, and consequently separations and divorces have increased far more rapidly than population." A dozen years earlier, in a column concerning the recent increase in the number of divorces, Arp noted that his figures represented less than half of the "unhappy marriages or broken marriage vows, cases that do not get into the courts, and hence it can be safely estimated that not more than eight families in ten have preserved the purity and honor of the family relation."[17]

The family was so important to Arp because, in an age of declining principles and morality, it represented the final protector of traditional values and virtues, the ultimate guardian of "good morals, good principles, obedience, self-denial, industry, kindness and good manners," as Arp enumerated them in one column. The family, Arp said, was "the mightiest bulwark of the state"; on it depended "not only the welfare of society, but the perpetuity of the nation." "The family is the most important institution upon the earth," he wrote. "It is the hope of the world. Its influence is greater than that of kings, emperors or cabinets."[18]

Closely connected to Arp's view of the family was his attitude toward women. Where men provided for the economic well-being of the family, it was up to women to protect the morality fostered by the home and fireside. This was the basis for Arp's criticism of "the new woman" who ignored this essential duty and found work outside the home, not out of economic necessity, but presumably to satisfy her own ego. "There is no greater contrast between the old south and the new south than in the advancement and humiliation of woman," Arp once wrote. On the one hand there was the aggressive new woman, and on the other, the "poor and pitiful" woman created by the new age. "A sad and serious change has come over the condition of woman," Arp wrote in June 1895. "There are thousands who cannot marry and have neither support nor protection and hence they have to become bread winners and support themselves." Arp noted a month later that most young men were either too lazy or too dissipated to support a wife, and said: "The time is past for confin-

ing women to the fireside when there is no support for them there."
Economic conditions might force even a married woman to work.
"She must be a helpmate," Arp wrote, "or, as the Scriptures say,
a 'helpmeet,' that is, she must help meet the expenses." Arp wrote
that women who had to work should receive wages equal to men's.[19]

Arp's complaint was that this new woman threatened the stability
of the family; he never pushed the idea that women were not qualified to be doctors, lawyers, editors, and so forth. In fact, he at least
mildly supported women's rights. Donald J. Fay pointed out that
Arp, in his homely philosophy sketches, "creat[ed] a husband who
would grant women virtual equality with men." Early in 1901, as
Arp looked back on the achievements of the nineteenth century,
he praised "the great advance in the social condition of woman
and the general recognition of her equality with man in most all
civil rights. . . . In every calling she has proved herself as intelli-
gent and as progressive as man and infinitely his superior in public
morals and private virtue." This view must not be pushed too far,
however. After Arp's only recorded meeting with a militant femi-
nist—a northern woman proselytizing in Atlanta—he wrote: "What
a comfort it is that we have not got such women down south."[20]

These twin themes of women's rights and women as protectors
of traditional values can be seen in Arp's writings on the subject of
female suffrage. "I used to think it was a horrible idea," he wrote in
1886, "but the older I grow the more willing I am to trust them with
the ballot." "One thing is certain, they would improve the manners of mankind, and would improve their morals, too," he added
in a column later that year. When a Mississippi convention considered giving women the vote in 1890, Arp asked: "What objection
can there be to such a law? We need just such a power in this
land. . . . [Women are] always on the side of good morals, and always
will be."[21]

"Our children are exposed to dangerous influences all the time
and need all the help they can get," Arp wrote, and he stressed the
roles of both men and women—fathers and mothers—in shaping
the morals and behavior of children. "The fireside is a better school

than the school room," he wrote. "The highest and holiest duty of a parent is to educate his children at all times and in every way that he can." "A close, loving companionship of a father with his children is their best safeguard," he wrote in one column, and in another, "It is the mothers who are the hope of the world—the saviors of the children." [22]

But New South parents were failing their children. One of "the chief causes" of the crime and immorality of the New South, Arp wrote in 1893, was "the lack of parental restraint. . . . The most striking difference between parents of the present day and those of fifty years ago is in the way they control their children." Parents used to spank their children, Arp said; now they "talk" to them. "Instead of children fearing their parents, most parents fear their children," he wrote in one column; and in another, after noting that the legislature was considering "a reformatory for young criminals," he suggested that "the parents of the rising generation should start a little one in each family and the big one wouldent be needed." [23]

The family was more than the source of guidance for children, however; its benefits were broader, and extended to all its members. In the words of one scholar, Arp "idealize[d] the family as central to maintaining the best of man's virtues." "Domestic pleasures have a tendency to calm the mind and keep it well balanced," Arp wrote in one column, and he noted in another that "it is the want of a home that makes tramps and vagabonds and desperate men." His most direct statement on the subject came in 1893: "The domestic fireside is the most sacred place upon the earth." For Arp, home and family represented the best principles of the Old South and the best hope of salvation for the New. [24]

Self-reliance was another virtue that Arp saw as missing in the New South. The new age, he said, was characterized by dependence on the state, on others, and on society. "Paternalism is the curse of a state or a nation," Arp wrote in one column, "the foundation of indolence and communism and anarchy," he said in another. It was this view that at least partly motivated Arp's dislike of the Farmers' Alliance and the Populist party. "The [Populist] platform is dead and buried, and all the vain hopes that inspired it have vanished away," Arp wrote, somewhat over-optimistically, in 1893. "It is at last an admitted fact that the farmers must depend on themselves and not on the government." Arp's dislike of paternalism also shaped his opinions on the tariff ("Protection for protection's sake must go"), the federal military pension (an "outrage [that] must be reformed, for it grows bigger as the years roll on"), and public education ("The old-fashioned school, where the teacher was directly responsible to the patrons, has never been excelled"). "Paternalism has run mad in this country," Arp wrote, and with its degeneration came a perilous decline in the traditional virtue of self-reliance.[25]

Arp also decried the growing dependency of working people. "I have great respect and admiration for the workingmen of this land," he wrote in 1885. "They are the backbone of government and will be its best protection when trouble comes." "Labor is just as good as money . . . , and is entitled to just as much consideration," Arp said five years later, but this entitlement had not resulted in equality for workers. In this column Arp spoke of "the tyranny of capital over labor" and lamented, "Woe unto the man who has to depend upon the rich for his living! His manhood is crushed, and he feels that he is helpless." Speculators also reduced the independence of workers. Arp wrote of "the common laborer [who] can barely live on his wages, and suddenly finds that bread and meat have gone up fifty per cent, and that the rich, heartless speculators have combined against him." The consequences of labor's unfortunate condition could be dreadful; "poverty and oppression are the nurses of nihilism and agrarianism and strikes for higher wages, and many a good man is drawn into them for lack of bread and clothing for his wife and children."[26]

Wealthy capitalists got richer while the workers got poorer—"Vanderbilt's gain is their loss," as Arp said early in his tenure at the *Constitution*—and this increased concentration of wealth made the whole nation, like the individual laborers, more dependent and therefore vulnerable. Arp disliked the capitalist who had several million dollars, "not because I am envious of his wealth," he said, "but because I am afraid of his power." "These colossal fortunes are becoming alarming," Arp said. "They endanger good government." Elsewhere Arp called them "the curses of a republican government," and warned that "something has got to be done or the plutocracy will sink this government down to the realms of Pluto before we are thinking about it." Arp therefore called for "a limitation of some sort" on these fortunes, usually in the form of a progressive income tax.[27]

Just as people surrendered some of their self-reliance to a paternalistic government and an increased concentration of wealth, so too did they give up a large measure of their independence to the fashions of the time—"the strain of society to keep up with society," Arp once called it. "Everybody is in a hurry now—a dreadful hurry—for there is a pressure upon us all, a pressure to keep up with the crowd, and the times, and with society," Arp wrote in an essay reprinted in *The Farm and the Fireside*. "Push ahead, keep moving, is the watchword now, and we must push or we will get run over, and be crushed and forgotten."[28]

Because Arp treasured the Old South's heritage of self-reliance, he praised farming, country life in general, and the common people, all of which represented to him the independence of days gone by. "I like independence, and that's why I like farmin'—nobody to look to for a livin' but Providence," Arp wrote in one of his first letters to the *Constitution*. The farmer "is the freeest man upon earth and the most independent," Arp said, and elsewhere noted that this made him "more secure against the ills of life than any other class." "The farmers are in the main the bulwarks of liberty and good government. Simple in habits, industrious, humble, dependent more upon God than man; their sons grow up manly and vigorous and their daughters modest and virtuous and are not carried away with the fashions and temptations of life."[29]

Small towns and country life in general had a similar attraction to Arp, and for the same reasons. "These small, unpretending towns," Arp said, were "the hope of the nation and its salvation." Young people there, like their counterparts in the country, "marry and go to work and live happily and humbly and do not strain to keep up with society, society!" "I am more and more convinced that the country is the place to find virtue and peace and simple habits and limited desire," he said in another column. "The fashion and follies and general devilment of the gay and giddy world do not reach these people." The "great big bloated cities" were just the opposite. "I can't see what makes folks want to crowd together so close for," Arp wrote. "It is not healthy, and it brings poverty and suffering and crime." Arp noted that "Jefferson spoke a truth when he said that great cities were pestilential to good health and good morals." [30]

The importance Arp placed on the traditional virtue of self-reliance led him to appreciate the common folk of Georgia. "The backwoodsmen of the south thirty and forty years ago were rude and rough," Arp said in 1886, "but they were thinkers and they were the shiftiest and most self-reliant people upon the earth." Arp's love for the independence and self-reliance of these people was especially evident in the columns he wrote while on his lecture tours. In 1884, for example, he visited a small community in northwest Georgia. "Good people live there," he noted. "Plain people, hospitable and kind and of simple habits and limited ambition. Hemmed in by the mountains, they have not yet been demoralized by the follies and fashions that modern civilization brings." "The common people will be as they ever have been," Arp wrote in 1891, "the safety of the republic." [31]

To say that Bill Arp lived in the past would be to distort his views, for just as he had one foot planted in the Old South, he had another in the New. His writings on Populism offer an instructive example of this ambivalence. Arp understood the problems facing southern farmers in the late 1880s and 1890s, but he complained that farmers who joined the Farmers' Alliance and later the Populist party expected the government to take care of them. His criticism went beyond the issue of paternalism, however. "The discontent and ingratitude of these political farmers is a sin against heaven," he wrote in one column. "Shrewd and unprincipled ambitious politicians sowed the seed of discontent among them, and from the stump and in their newspapers are everlastingly preaching the riches of Vanderbilt and the Goulds and Astors instead of the blessings of a peaceful home among the hills or in the villages where the sun shines and the rain falls and there is nothing between them and a kind providence except their own discontent." The Populists were among the harshest critics of the New South, and Arp agreed with many points of their critique. Still, their actions threatened the political order of the New South, and so, while Arp sympathized with the farmers, he attacked their political actions, just as he had attacked the independent movements in Georgia politics in the late 1870s. But if Arp did not live in the past—if he supported the New South's dominant political structure and its program for economic rejuvenation—his attitude toward the society of the New South (as well as other subjects, such as race relations and sectional reconciliation) was nevertheless heavily influenced by his adherence to the traditional values and virtues of the Old South.[32]

In the previous chapter we saw a Bill Arp who vigorously promoted industrialization and agricultural reform. That view tended to support the traditional scholarly interpretation of Arp's homely philosophy writings—that they were the expressions of a contented man looking optimistically to the future rather than mournfully to the past. As we have seen in this chapter, however, Bill Arp was far from contented. At the same time that he proselytized on the standard New South line concerning industries and farming, he also sharply criticized the spirit and society of the new age as he praised the old. In fact, Bill Arp fits quite well into Fred Hobson's portrait of the apologist who "felt he had to state his case persuasively and absolutely for the civilization of the Old South before that civilization slipped from memory."[33]

When Arp spoke of the days of his boyhood, the plain people of Georgia, and his farm and family, he was not expressing contentment with the new age; rather, he was stressing those features of his life that represented values and virtues he saw missing in the New South. Arp's writings on the past were more than the reminiscences of an old man; the Old South was a time and place of morals and manners, order and tranquillity. "Simplicity was the marked characteristic of the past age—simplicity in habits, manners and customs," Arp once wrote. In that same column he also explained his affection for the Georgia folk: they "were honest; they were faithful and true in their domestic relations; they earned their daily bread, and had no respect for money gained by trick or hazzard or speculation."[34] Similarly, the farm represented traditional values. Farming was hard work, but it was honest and independent work, and it allowed a man to see the fruits of his labor.

Arp enjoyed his family and home life, and that is certainly one reason he wrote so often on these topics, the most popular of his homely philosophy. "Home and sweet content and loving children bring us as near to heaven as we can get in this sublunary world," he wrote in 1897. "The time was when I had ambition and wanted to be a great man, but all that is nothing now. Domestic love is worth everything else." A few years later, Arp described his grand-children's excitement at watching the bantam hen's eggs hatch and concluded with one of his best aphorisms: "There are little things in our domestic life and there are big things, but I believe the little things are the biggest." But Arp's family was more than just a source of joy; at a time when society seemed pervaded by idle young men and aggressive new women, the family represented the best hope for the values and virtues of a better age.[35]

Bill Arp once wrote, "What is to be, will be, whether it happens or not." This has been true for studies of Arp himself. Early scholars declared him to be a contented and optimistic homely philosopher who cheerfully accepted the demise of the Old South and with open arms welcomed the New, and later scholars accepted this view without serious questioning. But when Arp stressed in his homely philosophy the days of his youth, traditional family ties, and the simple and pristine life of the farm and the Georgia folk, he implicitly condemned the New South society that had taken it all away. The homely philosopher can no longer be seen as a contented observer of the New South; he has become instead one of its most popular critics.[36]

Seven

The Negro
and Race Relations

As a slaveowner, Charles Henry Smith held what Annie May Christie characterized as "the typical patriarchal attitude" toward blacks: "the negro, in his place, was . . . child-like in his limited capacities and in his laziness and carelessness, innocent of criminal intent, sunny-natured and trusting as a child is, and therefore loveable." Blacks could be good workers, but they had to be supervised in the fields as well as out. "Just like so many children to watch and feed and clothe" is the way Octavia described Smith's sentiments toward his slaves. He genuinely liked some of them—Tip is the most prominent example—but held that racial traits bestowed by God constrained blacks to a lower social and intellectual level and made them forever dependent on whites.[1]

Smith believed the Negro to be "a distinct creation of the Almighty" with "original traits and instincts."[2] He outlined his view of the basic traits of the Negro in an 1882 column:

> He is nothing but a child, as long as he lives and has to lean upon the white man for protection and advice, just as a child leans upon his father. I don't believe there are ten negroes in a hundred who are capable of making a living without some sort of help from the white man. . . . He has many good traits of character and can make himself useful to the state when under the pressure of influence and close contact with the white race. He is naturally lazy and wasteful. He

never thinks about laying up money for old age and riches or for his children or his grandchildren, but is contented if he has enough for today and perhaps tomorrow. His contentment with life and its blessings is amazing and deserves imitation to some extent by our race. . . . The white man will sometimes cheat and swindle in a trade but the negro has no capacity for that. He would rather steal something from a man than try to swindle him out of it. But he wouldent steal much. Small pilfering is the extent of his capacity and his inclination. . . . The niggers steal ten times as often as white folks, but the white folks steal ten times as much when they do steal, so I reckon the account between the races is about evenly balanced.

"The negro is a good natured, contented, friendly creature, with but little conscience and no nerves—not enough conscience to pursue him or annoy him," Arp said elsewhere. "I like the darkeys, I do," he wrote in an essay reprinted in his *Scrap Book*, "but I haven't got much hope of 'em ever being anything but the same old careless, contented, thoughtless creatures they always was." [3]

Smith's perceptions of the Negro's "original traits and instincts" remained virtually the same through the days of slavery, the Civil War and Reconstruction, on down through the age of Jim Crow and lynching at the turn of the century. The way he wrote about blacks as Bill Arp, however, occasionally changed. During Reconstruction, for example, frustration and bitterness from the South's defeat and the forced changes in racial practices led Arp to write harshly at times. In his letter to Artemus Ward in September 1865, for instance, he described the mass migration of emancipated blacks from the countryside to the city: "The whole of Afriky have cum to town, wimmin and childern, and boys and baboons, and all. A man can tell how far it ar to the sitty better by the smell than the milepost." Despite the offensiveness of these sentences, Smith had not changed his mind about the Negroes' nature. "They wont work for us, and they wont work for themselves, and they'll perish to deth this winter," he went on in his letter to Ward, explaining the former slaves' need for white supervision. "They are now baskin in the summer's sun, a livin on roastin ears and freedom, with nary idee that winter will cum agin, or that Caster Ile and Salts cost munny." [4]

Following the end of Reconstruction, in the first decade or so of his tenure at the *Constitution,* Arp's writings on race relations reflected the gentle tone of his professed paternalism. But around 1890 another change came over Arp's writings. He still believed in the same racial characteristics, as this chapter will show, but fear and estrangement replaced the calm and affability of his early *Constitution* letters.

In a column written four months after he joined the *Constitution* staff, Arp wrote: "Well, I don't see much difference in the darkeys between now and then," "then" being the antebellum days of slavery. "Most all the race are the same niggers they used to be— they can't get along without a master, and they don't. They have to be managed just like little children." "I have been raised to look upon negroes as children, children in youth and in manhood and old age," he wrote in an essay reprinted as "Races and Human Nature." This childlike quality was the blacks' most important racial trait, for it, along with the white man's love for "dominion," justified the paternalism that, given the racial characteristics or traits of blacks and whites, offered the only possibility for successful race relations. "One loves to command and the other to obey," he wrote, speaking of the white and black races, "one to govern and the other to be governed. . . . It is dependence and independence. It is the guardian and the ward, and this relation is as agreeable as it is natural, so long as the one is humane and patriarchal and the other is obedient and industrious." 5

This relationship between the two races—the governor and the governed, the independent and the dependent, the guardian and the ward—emphasized the importance of place or rank in society. "Social equality is not a fixed, universal privilege in any race or people," Arp wrote in one column. "I would step aside and give the sidewalk to a king or a president or any great man. . . . I recognize the fact that I am in a humbler walk of life and must not intrude." In an essay reprinted as "The Negro," Arp applied this general social theory to race relations: "The white man was born to command,

and the negro knows it. The white man ranks him, and rank is a thing recognized and submitted to everywhere, and has been in all ages, and it is right. Rank is the safeguard of the social circle. I rank some folks and some folks rank me, and we are all happier and feel more at ease in our own circles than in those above us."[6]

The well-being of society depended on the consistent maintenance of this "rank." In 1880, Arp wrote that attempts to raise the "level" of blacks "was agin the order of natur. . . . One of the two races has got to play second fiddle to the other." The "natural relation [of blacks] to the white race is not one of equality but of inferiority and subordination," he wrote in one letter. When the Supreme Court struck down the Civil Rights Act of 1875 (which had prohibited discrimination on account of race in public accommodations and on juries), Arp commented: "Well, it doesn't take very much mind to settle the question. Nature settles more things than theory." Arp expressed his determination on this point in an 1889 column: "The negro was given a back seat by the god who made him and he will keep it."[7]

Arp was quick to point out that blacks were content with their place. "The masses of the negro race are never so happy as when in the cornfield or the cotton patch and being dependent upon the white man for protection and advice," he wrote in one column, and in another added that "they have no respect for white folks who put themselves on an equality with them." "The negroes never did want social equality," he said in response to the Supreme Court's decision concerning the 1875 Civil Rights Act. "They wouldent have it if we were to tender it." As Arp observed a few years later, "The negro when let alone to pursue the natural instincts and inclination of his race are content to live and labor in a subordinate condition."[8]

The word "place" has two meanings relevant to a discussion of race relations. In the previous paragraphs, "place" means "a proper or designated niche," and blacks, like women, children, and other groups, had their "place" in society. But the word can also mean "physical environment" or "physical surroundings."[9] (Arp used both senses of the word when he wrote, "A female darkey is a very useful institution in her place, and if her place ain't in the kitchen or at the wash-tub I don't know where it is. I've never seen any other place that fits em as well and looks so accordin to nature.") [10] When the second meaning is intended in a discussion of race relations, the phrase generally used is "race mixing," which was something to be avoided at all costs; blacks had to keep to their physical place just as they had to keep to their social station.

In 1880 Arp told of a man visiting Boston who heard a "splendid soprano voice" in a church choir. The singer turned out to be "a big black wench with lips like a pair of raw beefstakes." Arp's reaction was a combination of incredulity, disgust, and determination: "I wonder if our people will ever come to the like of that. I hope not. It shocks my emotions. The church choir! . . . Oh, horrible! What desecration! . . . I know they can sing and I always enjoy them in their places with the banjo and the bones, or at a minstrel show, but I don't believe they sing in the white folks' choirs in heaven and it's agin natur to mix em here." Three years later, when Henry Ward Beecher said that there was nothing wrong with interracial marriage ("amalgamation," as southerners often called it), Arp wrote: "We object, and we object so earnestly that it will not be tolerated. We know that it is against the order of nature—against the fitness of things, and we denounce it." When Theodore Roosevelt invited Booker T. Washington to dinner at the White House, Arp joined other southern journalists in denouncing the president's actions. "It is no longer the White house, but like the chameleon takes any color that comes," he wrote, and noted that Roosevelt's son would now probably marry Washington's daughter. [11]

The physical mixing of the races was, like the issue of social rank, a theme to which Arp returned throughout his career as a *Constitution* columnist. "Nothing is more surely settled than that the races don't want to mix," he wrote in 1887. "It is disagreeable all around. . . . It is against nature and we can't help it." "Some call this prejudice, but it is not prejudice," he wrote a few years later. "It is the law of natural repulsion and affects all classes." The mixing of races, he asserted, "will never be done. It is against nature and shocks the sentiment of our civilization."[12]

"The negro knows how it is and would be content if the fools and fanatics of the north would let him alone," Arp wrote in 1889. The problem of northern interference in the race question was one that greatly bothered Arp. Southern whites, he said, were better qualified to care for the South's blacks. "We raised em and raised their fathers and mothers and if we don't know how to manage em nobody does," he wrote in 1882. "Our native born people like the negro," he said elsewhere. "We know his kind nature and we know his manner." Northerners were simply too unfamiliar with the Negro to try to regulate southern race relations. "I would not give a farthing for any man's judgment about darkies who hadn't been born and raised with 'em and owned 'em," Arp wrote. "It takes a long time to learn the traits and instincts of a race of people." Arp also distrusted the would-be reformers of the North because of their motivations, which were based, as he saw it, on a hatred of the South (a topic covered in the following chapter).[13]

Arp demanded time and time again that southern race relations be left to southerners. Negroes, he wrote, "are not the nation's wards; they are ours, and we will look after them according to our own notions of the fitness of things." "All we ask," Arp said, "is that the race problem be let alone, and it will work out its own salvation. Providence is overseeing the business." In 1901 he was even more insistent: "The race problem belongs to us and will be settled on a wise and humane basis if the fool yankee editors and preachers will let us alone." He maintained that southern whites "are the best friends the negro has got," and to hear Arp tell it the Negro agreed: "He has today more respect for the old masters than for his so called northern friends," Arp wrote, and once he reported that a black man had told him, "I tell you what, boss, I will take a white man before a yankee eberytime."[14]

The Negro was, in his place, "a good institution," Arp wrote in 1882, and he repeated variations on this theme often during his quarter-century at the *Constitution*. "The darkies around here are a well-behaved, industrious set and give us no trouble. I never knew 'em to work as well," he wrote in one column. "I like these niggers and they like me," he said in another. "I'd rather have 'em than not have 'em. . . . I think a heap of 'em, and I'm going to stand by 'em and protect 'em. They are a good, kind-hearted, faithful race, and I love 'em." "They are doing very well in our part of the country," he wrote in 1890. "There is no friction. We are all calm and serene upon this question." "I know lots of negroes that I can get along with, and so does every white man," he wrote in 1899, and two years later, "There are lots of them in every community whom we have respect for and who are good, useful, law-abiding citizens. We can pick out scores in our town who are useful and industrious and pay respect to the respectable white people."[15]

The blacks that Arp liked were the ones who kept to the place to which white society had assigned them in society. Years before, the institution of slavery had educated blacks in the proper relations between the races. "The old-time negroes had a very good education—not in book learning, but by contact and association with their masters and their masters' families and neighbors," Arp wrote in 1901. "Our old-time slaves were better educated for usefulness and happiness than are the college graduates of today. They had more common sense and far more morality." Arp expressed the same idea in another column: "The negroes owe to the white people all the blessings they enjoy. It was slavery that civilized them and trained them to good habits."[16]

Blacks who had been born and raised in slavery had learned the proper relations of the races, and that education stayed with them in freedom. "If there is any better invention than a good old fashioned home-made darkey I don't know it," Arp once wrote, and his weekly letters to the *Constitution* are full of references to the "old fashioned darkey." "I think a heap of these old-fashioned negroes," he wrote in one. "Uncle Remus and his sort have gone into history as a lost race, and we ne'er shall see their like again." There were, in addition to "our friend" Tip, Sicily Mims, the Smiths' cook, who "came from the old fashioned stock"; Mamma Heyward, of whom Arp said, "If there is a true Christian in Cartersville we all believe she is one"; Mack Richardson, "the king of the draymen"; Dougherty Hutchins, "a clever old darkey who was raised in the family"; Uncle Sam, "who works in my garden and chops my wood and goes after ice on Sunday"; Will Carter, who will "do most everything and more too that an old fashioned nigger used to do before the war"; and Sanford Bell, a railroad conductor and an "honest, faithful, and serene man." Arp told how he occasionally passed Uncle Jordan, an old ex-slave who "was happy until freedom came," on the streets of Cartersville. "Sometimes I drop a dime in his trembling hand, and he always says 'God bless you, massa; you is a gemman, sir.' His gratitude and his compliment always reward me." "I do love these good old time niggers," Arp wrote.[17]

In a 1900 column, Arp told readers that he had been talking to old Uncle Lewis, one of his workers. He had reminded the former slave of the good old days "when there wasn't a chaingang in the south, nor a heinous crime nor a brutal outrage, committed by your people. . . . Now there are in Georgia alone over 4,000 of your people in the chaingangs." Arp recorded the end of the conversation: "Uncle Lewis had stopped cutting and was leaning on his ax helve. 'Dat's all so,' said he, 'and boss I knows it, and boss what I wants to know is dis: What must we poor niggers do about it?' There is the rub. I couldn't tell him, but I did say, 'Uncle Lewis, your race has got some mighty good traits, and I like having you about us.' "[18]

More and more, the increase in black crime that he had discussed with Uncle Lewis bothered Arp. "I was ruminating about this yesterday as our train passed a lot of convicts who were working the road between Atlanta and Decatur," he wrote in an 1891 column. "They were all negroes." In this column, as in many of his others, Arp recited figures, derived from the census and other sources, concerning crime rates and the racial composition of prison populations. He noted, for example, that "there are 30 per cent more whites than blacks in this state, and yet the negroes commit nine times more crime." "What is the matter with the negroes?"

Arp asked. "When will they do better? Nearly all of these convicts are between sixteen and forty, and but a very few were ever in slavery. They have been to school most of them, and most of them are from the cities and towns. The old-time negroes are not in the chaingang. . . . What is to become of the negro?"[19]

One reason for the decline of the Negro was education. "The negro is a good invention; he will continue to be good as long as he is a negro," Arp wrote in one essay. "When they try to set him up with a hifalutin education and make a white man of him, he becomes a new creature and a public nuisance." He noted that the Negro "is physically ordained for labor, muscular labor, and he likes it. A college life is his utter ruin as a man and a citizen." Education was of no "advantage to the colored race"; it was "a humbug" that "ruined the negro as a laborer." (Arp's opposition centered on "high classical education"; "If they had an agricultural college with a technological school attached the result might be different.") Furthermore, education excited "false hopes" in blacks. Arp reported that a Negro teacher was on trial in Cartersville charged with "telling his pupils that they ought to rise above doing the menial work for the white folks."[20]

When a newspaper ran an editorial in 1889 saying that the "experiment" of Negro education must go on, Arp disagreed:

The truth is, the negro has been in training for a century. Thousands of them were the confidential trusted household servants, . . . and absorbed knowledge by contact. And hence these good old negroes are good citizens now, but just as soon as freedom came and severed their companionship, and the young negroes were sent to school, their race instincts returned, and they degenerated in morals and became educated vagabonds. Thousands of them have graduated in the colleges and are no account. They are not doing anything that is honest or reputable. The muscle the Creator gave them as an endowment is wasted.

"Right here in Georgia," Arp wrote, "the uneducated negro before the war and for a few years after was moral and law-abiding and now there are 4,000 in the state and county chaingangs, 75 per cent of whom can read and write."[21] The cities were also responsible for the deterioration of the black race, Arp said. "Whoever heard of a Cartersville negro abusing the white people or complaining of oppression?" he asked. "There is no trouble here nor in the country." "The country darkies are behaving very well," he wrote in another letter. "The chaingang has to rely on the cities now." The criminals "are the scurf of the towns and cities—the overflow—for cities breed crime and corruption among both whites and blacks." In this column, Arp used statistics to show not only that most black convicts came from the cities, but also that the farther one goes from the city, the fewer the black convicts, even in predominantly black counties. "It is not the country negroes who are making mischief now," Arp wrote. "It is the town and city vagabonds who carry pistols and put on airs and impudence and go sporting around. Town is a bad place to raise niggers and children."[22]

Arp came to blame the North as well for the Negro's behavior. "Mistaken philanthropy and unmistaken malignity," he said, referring to the misguided attempts of the North to educate the Negro and the efforts of northern newspapers and politicians to urge blacks to stand up to the white race. "Our enemies at the north are exciting the negroes," he wrote, and said in 1900 that "every black scoundrel who has been lynched down south was the victim of their false teachings."[23]

The main reason for the increase in black crime, however, was that younger blacks did not know or practice the necessary proper relations with the white race because they had not had the proper roles instilled in them during slavery or through later close contact with whites. As Arp wrote in one column, "Close contact with the white man and dependence upon him is an absolute necessity for the prosperity and happiness of the negro." This association had educated and civilized the slaves; without it, blacks "would relapse into their original nature and become barbarians." (Arp had said the same thing some fifteen years before, just after the war: "A blak Alabama nigger is jest the same as his great gran daddy was in Afriky two thousan years ago. He's got sivilized and behaves sorter decent, but it's bekaus he lived with white foaks, and is obleeged to. If you turn him loos on an iland by himself, he'll relaps into a vagabon in ten years. He'd quit wearin close and go to beatin tin pans and eat lizzards before you git out of site.") Arp often noted that younger blacks seemed headed in this direction.[24]

These factors—education, the corrupting influence of cities, northern agitation, decreased dependence on the white race, and, above all else, the rejection of what Arp saw as the proper race relations—led to what he called "the alarming degeneracy of the negro." "The old set are good yet," Arp wrote, "but the new ones are going to the dogs." For one thing, the younger blacks seemed lazier than their parents. "The rising generation are no good to nurse, or to cook, or to wash, and what else they are fit for I have not discovered, for they dont work in these parts," he wrote. Elsewhere he discussed "this new generation that loaf around town and curse and drink, and carry pistols, and bluster around at all the elections," adding that these young blacks were "a curse to the country." He was harsher and more explicit in another column: "Dirty, oderiferous negro men and boys [do] not give the sidewalks to white ladies on one of our business streets. There is a regular den on another street that leads to two churches and all the negro vagrants of the town gather there and as many as possible stick their feet or their posteriors on the railing of the piazza and spit tobacco juice on the sidewalk to the disgust and annoyance of the ladies who have to pass there." In one of his frequent discussions of black criminals, Arp noted that "most of them are of the new issue who were never in slavery and a majority have advanced under freedom from simple larceny to burglary. Chickens are too small game for the modern darkey. . . . They had rather snatch a lady's pocketbook and run."[25]

More alarming to Arp, though, was the Negroes' "utter disregard for chastity and their conjugal obligations." Arp said that the race was "utterly devoid of those family virtues that are the safeguards of all good government," and he complained that "there are more bastard negroes in and around this city than those born in wedlock. They are not mulattoes, but they are negroes of full blood. The moral degeneracy of the race is alarming." "They have no conception of domestic virtue and morality," he wrote in 1901, and two years later made the same point: "They have almost ceased to marry, but take up and cohabit at pleasure and change when they feel like it. . . . In sight of my house is a woman with three sets of children—six in all—by three fathers, but she has no husband and has never been married." "This degradation of the negro has come along so gradually that our people have gotten used to it," Arp continued, but elsewhere he warned that blacks "are the most thievish, unchaste race upon the face of the earth, and they are infinitely worse now than they were when in slavery."[26]

"What is wanted," Arp wrote in 1901, "is good moral training and the fear of punishment for crime. The negroes got none of this from their parents or their teachers or preachers." "Good moral training" was a problem, since the old patriarchal model of race relations, where blacks learned from close association with whites, was fast disappearing, and black leaders refused to promote morality within the race. "Fear of punishment," however, was something else again, and Arp devoted many columns to this topic. "The idea of reforming a vicious, bad negro is nothing but fancy," he wrote. "There is not a solitary case in all history. It is not their nature." In 1887 Arp criticized the state legislature for planning "a reformatory that is to cost much money and do no good as far as the negroes are concerned." Arp's solution was simple: "Why not call back the whipping post? It will cure the negro of small crimes and idleness quicker than anything in the world." "Whipping," he said, "is the best punishment in the world for a malicious boy or a mean nigger. The old time darkies who were brought up under the fear of the lash are not in the chain-gang now."[27]

Uncle Sam, a former slave who had spent just over half his life in freedom, died in 1900. Uncle Sam was one of Arp's favorite "old time darkies." He "dident talk much," Arp said, "but sometimes he would lean on his hoe or his axe and spress his feelins. It did him good." Arp passed on one of Uncle Sam's speeches shortly after the ex-slave's death. The speech (which probably gives more of Arp's "feelins" than Uncle Sam's) is a good summary of Arp's views on the younger generation of blacks:

> My old master was a good man. . . . Dar was good people den and bad people jes' like dar is now—black and white, but de black has got wusser and wusser since dey got free. Effen a black man had a good master he was mighty well off, fer he didn't have no sponsibility. Effen I bin sho of a good master and my wife and children been sho of one and we all live togedder ontill we die I wouldent keer anything bout freedom. Niggers got too much freedom anyhow. My old master used to make de nigger gals get married and take a man and stick to him, but nowadays dey dont marry at all hardly. I got a lot of grandchildren what haint got no daddy to speak of and I dont know my sons in law. Dey dont come about in daytime. Dats what killed my old woman. She jes' so mortified and so shamed she never got over it. So many spurious children all round callin' her granny. Effen a white woman do dat way she is disgraced, but a black woman dont keer; she shine as big as ever and dey dont turn her outen de church. In der old times she got a whippin and dey ort to have it yet. White folks dun quit whippin bad niggers; dey send em to chaingang, and dey dont keer for dat. I hear dat dar is four or five thousand in dar from Georgy. How's dat—dident have nary one before de war. Gwine to school too much I spek and work too little. Don't know what is gwine to come of all dese growin' up niggers. Dar is a dozen or more round de depot or trampin' around town doin' nuthin all de time—livin' offen dey mammies and smokin' dese little paper seegars.[28]

"There are some of the new set who are clever, but not many," Arp wrote in 1886, "but take them all in all, we are getting along pretty well together." But within a few years the confidence and contentment Arp expressed in his early letters to the *Constitution* disappeared. "The race problem is assuming an alarming aspect," he reported in 1890. "The alienation between the two races at the south is spreading and intensifying. In some localities it would even now take but a spark to set a community on fire and the flames would spread far and wide and convulse the nation." Less than a year later he wrote that the old ties that slavery had provided were gone, and therefore

> the two races are living together merely by force of circumstances over which neither has any control. How long they can live together depends upon their good sense and forbearance. I feel sure that I can live with them and keep their respect and their friendship, but perhaps it is because I used to own slaves and still feel and maintain my love and superiority. Our class will soon pass away, and so will the old slaves who love to do us honor. How the coming generations will harmonize I cannot forsee nor fortell, but from the signs I fear there will be less forbearance from the one and less humility from the other.

On a lecture trip to Texas in 1892, Arp visited a county where all the blacks had been evicted. Arp said he thought it would "come to that in Georgia"; the "growing alienation between the races" made future coexistence uncertain. "There is friction between the races," he wrote a year later, "and it may be that the only solution is their removal to the public land in the west." "The conflict between them and us is irrepressible. It is widening and deepening as the years roll on." [29]

As the above quotations illustrate, Bill Arp's writings on blacks and race relations changed around 1890. Prior to that time, the races had been "getting along pretty well together." By 1893, however, the chasm between the races was "widening and deepening" and conflict seemed "irrepressible." Nowhere is this change in Arp's views more evident than in his writings on black "outrages" (the rape of white women) and lynching, the solution he came to embrace with great vigor.

Arp had not always endorsed lynching. "Nobody feels safe like they used to," he wrote in 1883. "It is getting to be a dread and a fear, for they are worse than brutes when their passions are aroused." But at that time the whipping post that he so often promoted seemed to be the only remedy. "They are hung and they are lynched," he said, but "this seems to have no effect on the race." Two years later Arp condemned mob law as "the very counterpart of that civil law which is called the perfection of reason. It is hasty vindication, uncertain and unreasonable." But Arp added that there was "one crime that would justify such summary vengeance." The problem was "the law's delay"; "If justice was surely and speedily administered these mobs would cease." [30]

Prior to 1890, Arp advocated lynching blacks who committed these outrages only when there was "proof beyond all moral question" and then only because of the slowness and uncertainty of the judicial system. But this changed. Early in 1890, John Newsome, an Iowa resident, wrote a complimentary letter that Arp passed along to his readers. The letter ended with a suggestion. "When it comes to the negro, or the nigger, as you call him, you seem to be entirely unable to see a man under a dark skin," Newsome had written. "Do try for the sake of your influence with your people to rise above your inherited prejudices." Arp responded that "Mr. Newsome is at heart a good man," but not familiar with the Negro. "He never had to send his children to school where there were negroes working in the fields near by where his daughters had to pass along. He knows nothing of the apprehension that parents feel who live in the country and have to send their girls to school or on errands to their nabors, or who sometimes have to leave wife and daughters unprotected at home." He told Newsome of a black man who had killed a twelve-year-old girl "in a deep ditch where he had outraged her" and noted that similar cases, "always brutal and fiendish," appeared in southern papers almost every week. "Mr. Newsome asks why it is that I can't see a man under a black skin. Yes, I see a man, a negro man—a nigger, if you please." [31]

The black man seemed suddenly to frighten Arp. "What security has a poor, humble woman living in the country if these outrages are passed over in silence?" he asked later in 1890. He was soon wholeheartedly advocating lynching as a means to that security. "Such negroes are brutes and deserve no more consideration," he wrote. "If his crime affected anyone who was near and dear to me I could see him burned and feel no regret." Lynchings were no longer caused by the law's delay; they were "the outblast of human indignation," "evidence of minds charged, perhaps overcharged, with love and respect for wives and daughters," occurring when "pent-up emotions break loose" in response to an outrage by these "devils incarnate—fiends in human form." "To my mind the sum of the whole matter is that neither the law's delay nor its uncertainty has anything to do with the impulses and emotions that control men when they pursue and overtake and identify and execute a negro for his crime against helpless innocence," he wrote in a column titled "In Defense of Lynching." "Every parent and husband and brother in the neighborhood immediately becomes an avenger of blood." [32]

Arp never renounced his stand on the "old fashioned darkies." In 1902 a reader solicited Arp's opinion of Charles Carroll's book *The Negro a Beast* and asked, "Do you believe the nigger is a beast?" "Which nigger?" was Arp's reply. "There are many good negroes, negroes whom we respect and love to befriend," he wrote elsewhere. "There are some in every community that I would trust," he wrote in 1900. "There are a dozen or more in Cartersville, and every community has a few." [33]

Arp's apparently ambiguous views of blacks—the "brute" and the "good negro"—can be seen in his writings on blacks and the franchise, a subject he addressed frequently in the 1890s when many southern states began making systematic efforts to take the vote away from their black citizens. Arp was surprisingly liberal in many of his discussions of black voting. The franchise, he said, should be based not "on race or color," but on "conduct and intelligence, and if it cut off many of the white race, let it cut." Voting should be based on "a good moral character," he wrote a few months later. "We all know many good negroes who should be allowed to vote and some bad white men who should not." He repeated this again the following year: "I do not feel satisfied with the sweeping exclusion of the present white primary law. I know a dozen negroes in this town who are morally, intelligently and industriously qualified to vote and I know two dozen white men who are not." "Don't shut the door forever on good negroes," he pleaded in 1901. [34]

At the same time that he urged the enfranchising of qualified

Negroes, however, Arp advocated the lynching of black brutes. "Outrage and murder combined removes the brute at once from the human code and places him along with the wild beasts, with mad dogs and hyenas." "Lynching for that crime is the law of nature, and will go on. When juries are organized to try hyenas and wolves and gorillas, maybe then these brutes in human form will be tried, but not before. The argument is exhausted, and we stand by our wives and children." "Ten years ago I wrote my first philippic against the brutes and advocated a summary vengeance and I stand by it and rejoice whenever a lynching occurs for an outrage upon a defense-less woman. If there is anything worse than lynching I'm for that." "That's my faith and part of my religion, and I've been on that line ever since these outrages began." "Whether it be orthodoxy or het-erodoxy, it is my doxy. . . . I would lynch every brute who assaulted a white woman. I could see him massacred or burned or hanged, drawn and quartered." And in a column written less than a year before his death, Arp was even more fanatical on the subject: "As for lynching, I repeat what I have said before, 'Let the good work go on. Lynch 'em! Hang 'em! Shoot 'em! Burn 'em!' " [35]

Throughout his twenty-five year career as a columnist for the *Atlanta Constitution*—and, from all available evidence, throughout his entire life—Bill Arp's basic ideas on the Negro remained the same. Blacks, he thought, were an inferior race, endowed by God with certain traits and needing at all times close contact with whites, not only for supervision but for moral guidance as well. Paternalism, his formula for successful race relations, rested on this idea. Blacks provided happy companionship and a willing workforce, and whites reciprocated with protection and guidance. The two races must be kept apart, with blacks keeping to their physical and social places, but if each race fulfilled its obligations in the bargain of paternalism, Arp saw no reason why blacks and whites could not live together (though separately) in a mutually beneficial biracial society.

Around 1890, Arp began advocating the lynching of black rapists, and he soon became one of the practice's major proponents. Arp was not the only southern white man who felt this way. According to statistics compiled by the National Association for the Advancement of Colored People, 2,834 people were lynched in the South during the thirty-year period from 1889 to 1918. Most of them (over 2,400) were black. More people were lynched in Georgia than in any other state during this period: 386, of whom 360 were black. The worst single year for lynching was 1892, when 155 blacks were so killed nationwide, but through the 1890s there were only three years when the number was less than a hundred. In that bloody decade, an average of nearly 140 people (about three-fourths of them black) were lynched yearly in the South.[36]

Historians of southern race relations have offered a number of political, economic, social, and psychological interpretations of the motivations for the segregation and disfranchisement of blacks at the end of the nineteenth century and for the racial violence that accompanied these trends.[37] If Bill Arp could address the historians on this issue, he might say that his writings on the subject changed around 1890 because the pattern of race relations itself changed. Blacks no longer played the role of dependent ward to the whites' independent guardian. Some blacks, of course, did—the "old time darkies," born and raised in slavery and educated there in the "proper" relations of the races. But others, especially the younger blacks born to freedom and therefore deprived of the vital education that slavery had given their parents, refused to go along. As this new generation reached adulthood, Arp saw more and more evidence of "the alarming degeneracy of the negro."

Arp's criticisms of the changed race relations of the 1890s were the same ones he made against New South society as a whole. The pernicious influence of large cities, education, improper guidance, and similar factors led the younger generation of southerners, black as well as white, to an increase in crime, a decline in morality, and a general unwillingness to work at honest and honorable labor. (In both instances, Arp's emphasis on the immorality of the younger generation is especially striking.) As historians have suggested, Arp perhaps had other and more complex reasons for the change in his attitude toward race relations. Still, it is interesting to note that he chose to describe his reasons for the change in terms of the values and virtues of the Old South.

Scholars have either missed or misread much of what Bill Arp wrote on the subjects of blacks and race relations. In his monumental study *The Black Image in the White Mind*, George M. Fredrickson used Charles Henry Smith's article in *Forum* ("Have American Negroes Too Much Liberty?") as an example of "Southern Negrophobia," but he made no mention of Smith's more virulent writings as Bill Arp. James C. Austin wrote that Arp believed the Negro to be "an inferior creature who needed the white man's protection and control," but took his analysis no further. Annie May Christie mentioned in one sentence that Arp occasionally wrote about the chain gang and lynching, "both of which [he] deplored." And Louella Landrum actually saw "a decided softening of feeling toward the negro problem" in Arp's writings after 1884.[38]

Despite what these scholars have said, the subject of race relations was of great importance to Arp, especially after 1890. Indeed, that subject became one of the most frequently mentioned in his *Constitution* column during those years. Arp's writings offer a detailed look at one southerner's views of race relations, views that in many ways were shared by a large number of white southerners. What is more important for the present study, these writings dramatically show Arp's discontent with the society of the New South and his attachment to the virtues of the Old.

Eight

The North and
Sectional Reconciliation

I n his "New South" speech, Henry Grady asked: "What does [the ex-Confederate soldier] do—this hero in gray with a heart of gold? Does he sit down in sullenness and despair? Not for a day. . . . 'Bill Arp' struck the keynote when he said, 'Well, I killed as many of them as they did of me, and now I am going to work.'"[1] But Arp's hopeful statement, even more optimistic in the context of Grady's speech, was hardly characteristic of his writings on sectional reconciliation in the *Atlanta Constitution.* Instead Arp wrote time and time again of lingering animosities, picturing for his readers the northern politicians, newspaper editors, and others who kept up the sectional strife. In many of his columns Arp moved from observer to participant, aggressively defending the South, even attacking the North for its moral laxity, its religious fanaticism, and its high divorce and crime rates.

There were times, Arp said, when it appeared that the sections would be able to live together in harmony. One such time was in 1878, when northerners quickly reacted to a yellow fever epidemic that was sweeping much of the South. "The way our calculatin brethren up north have been sendin money down to Mississippi makes me feel ashamed that I ever abused them," Arp wrote. "I shant do it anymore." Arp returned the favor a few years later when he asked readers to help the victims of the Johnstown flood in Pennsylvania. He urged southerners to "forget the past and remember that we are brethren."[2]

"Old Father Time is a good doctor," Arp wrote in 1879, an example of the hopefulness he occasionally expressed during his years at the *Constitution*. "The skies are brightening—the clouds are clearing away," he said in 1890. "If we can make peace with the north it will beat everything else. I won't care a cent about party if we can have peace and be friends. I would be willing to sleep two in a bed with a republican if he was friendly to us." Grover Cleveland's presidential victory in 1892 was in Arp's mind "the harbinger of peace and good will between the sections." In an 1895 column Arp noted that "our enemies are harmonizing of late more than at any time since the war," and he repeated that observation a week later: "The backbone of our alienation is broken and hereafter the north and south will fully harmonize." "Time has diluted the bitterness of those who were our most malignant enemies," he wrote in 1896. "Reflection has tempered the prejudices of our northern brethren."[3]

Early in 1886 a northern society honored Charles Henry Smith. The name of the organization and the nature of the honor remain unknown. Smith's acceptance letter to the secretary of the society survives, however, a somewhat sheepish note that, like the above-quoted passages from his *Constitution* columns, suggests a narrowing of the chasm separating the sections:

It is an honor not only unexpected but undeserved for I am conscious of having at times manifested something of that sectional prejudice which has for so long alienated our people. I sincerely wish that I could blot out my part in the sad drama of the past and have nothing with which to reproach myself. But human nature is the same everywhere and we all fight back when aggrieved. Like David of old we keep on sinning and repenting—sinning in haste and repenting in leisure. The comfort is that David went to Heaven and so we too have a chance by precedent.[4]

Still, for all his apologies and promises not to abuse the North, for all the signs of a peaceful reconciliation that he happily pointed out to his readers, Bill Arp could not hold back. "I'm powerful mad with the whole yanky nation,"[5] he wrote in 1879, and this early statement set the tone for many of his later columns in the *Constitution*.

In 1879 the *Constitution* printed a letter from William T. Sherman in which the former Union general discussed the industrial and agricultural resources of the South and encouraged northern emigration to Georgia. An editorialist in the *Constitution* praised the letter, saying that Sherman "writes . . . with the earnestness and presses his points with the vigor of one thoroughly interested in the progress and prosperity of Georgia." Bill Arp commented on Sherman's letter a few days later. He began by telling the story of Dixy, a neighbor's dog that had "sense and memory and resentment just like human people" and who "never molested anybody without provocation." Dixy had been attacked and seriously beaten by a stranger with a stick. Several years later, the stranger passed by the neighbor's home again. He saw the dog and started whistling and talking friendly, but Dixy remembered and got his revenge. "There's many a dixy dog who havent forgot," Arp wrote, "and all this muchin [mooching] up dont reconcile em worth a cent."[6]

Arp was one "dixy dog" who never forgot. Several times a year he remembered in his *Constitution* column the arrival of Sherman's troops in Rome, his family's refugeeing experiences, and their homecoming a few months later to an empty house. In the above column, for instance, Arp wrote that his wife complained that she "never had any peace or comfort since the night we had to get up out of bed and run away with nothing but a few clothes." Two years later, he told of Sherman "tearing our cemetery all to pieces at Rome where my children were buried, and taking the tombstones and monuments for his fortification when there was thousands of rock close by." In 1888 he compared the current "pestilence" in Florida (probably yellow fever) to the Union troops. "The difference," he noted, "was that the yankee followed you and kept you trotting, but the pestilence is kind enough to stay in one place."[7]

One evening in the late spring of 1890 Arp and his family had just finished a dinner topped off with strawberries and cream when they noticed a pounding on the roof. The pounding, it turned out, was only hail, but Arp reported to his readers that it had had him worried: "I thought it was Sherman," he said. "I always think of him in May when the strawberries come. Just twenty-six years ago we had a strawberry feast one night at our house, . . . and a little later old Sherman began to scatter his unfeeling shells right over the house. . . . All night long we hustled from the foul invader and left our beautiful home to his mercy and our strawberries and cow to his appetite." In June 1892, on the occasion of his wife's sixty-first birthday, he remembered how troubled her life had been, especially during the war. "It was nip and tuck then and she was dodging the yankees a good part of the time," he wrote. "The good book says, 'Love your enemies,' but that is such a hard thing to do. . . . The sanctified folks never had to run from the foul invader."[8]

Arp's written attacks on "the foul invader" continued until the month of his death. His last letter to the *Constitution*, on August 9, 1903, told again how the Yankees had chased his family from their beautiful home; how, as he and his fellow runagees had climbed the first hill outside of town, they looked back and saw the "vandals" break into the cemetery, where monuments and tombstones "were broken into pieces and tumbled down the hill"; how, when he and his family returned home, "we found darkness and desolation—not a bed or bedstead or mattress or bureau or chair or cooking vessel—nothing but the naked floor."[9]

"The experience was never forgotten—nor forgiven," one Bill Arp scholar commented, but the memory of the war was just one item in a long list of things that kept sectional animosities strong in Arp's mind. His most picturesque metaphor for the situation between the sections appeared in an 1882 column and involved an innocent youth, a bully, and a snow-covered hill: "Twenty-one years ago we slid out of the union, . . . but it has taken hard work and a long time to get back. Sorter like a boy coasting down a long hill on the snow. It is splendid fun going down, but mighty hard work to pull the sled up again, especially where there is a bigger boy to trip you up at every step and chuck you with snow balls." In his years at the *Constitution,* Arp suggested that there were many bigger boys on that snow-covered hill—northern politicians, for example, along with northern newspaper editors and book publishers, even northern preachers and poets.[10]

"We all trade and traffic and joke together," Arp wrote in 1879, "we buy their goods and they buy ours and our commercial relations are all pleasant and if it wasent for the politicians nobody would know that there was a split up in the family." Throughout his quarter-century at the *Constitution,* Arp identified northern politicians as a primary source of conflict between the sections. These politicians were, almost without exception, Republicans—members of the party, Arp wrote in 1898, that "still seeks to humiliate us . . . and to keep up the strife." "There's no compromising with the republican party," Arp wrote in 1880. "For fifteen years we have been hoisting the flag—begging for peace and good will, declaring our loyalty, tendering the olive branch, and the more we do it the more they abuse us." A few years later, Arp reported that he had received "a very good letter yesterday from a man who says that we mistake the northern republicans; that he knows them, and lived among them for twenty years, and they are the very best people up north." "I've heard that before," Arp replied in his column. "They are good to everybody but us."[11]

Northern politicians seemed to abuse the South at every opportunity. "I was thinkin' that nobody out of jail could with reason be unhappy today," Arp wrote in one column, but then he read an account of a speech delivered by Roscoe Conkling, a Republican senator from New York. This speech, Arp said, "was so full of lies and slanders upon the south and her heroes, I forgot all about the butiful day, and biled over with indignation." A few years later, Arp wrote of a speech by Senator James G. Blaine, a Republican from Maine, on Andersonville, the infamous Confederate prison. Arp described Blaine's address as "a bloody shirt dipped in slime, and it was delivered by him, not for a principle, or to illustrate truth, but to make political capital for himself."[12]

According to Arp, political gain was behind much of the northern hatred and abuse. He wrote in 1887 that he had thought the tariff would be the next big campaign issue, "but no," he said, "they cant unite the party on that. Fighting the south is the last resort. . . . Every four years the south gets awful ugly and don't know it." "Hating the south seems to be the stock in trade of most of the northern members [of Congress]," he wrote elsewhere.[13]

As president, Benjamin Harrison had had the chance to help harmonize the sections, Arp wrote, but he decided to seek renomination and hence was going after the southern black vote. His strategy included appointing blacks as postmasters in a number of southern cities, a policy Arp denounced. "Of all the offices in the gift of government," Arp later wrote, "there are none about which the people have such moral, social and political rights as the post offices." "No greater insult, no greater outrage upon our rights, could be perpetrated by a tyrant than to appoint a negro as postmaster in a white community," he explained in 1903, and noted that "nobody but an unprincipled politician" would seek to do such a thing. "It is an insult to our people and there is no excuse for it—no palliation." Republican president William McKinley also used the strategy of black patronage in "a deliberate party policy" designed "to raise hell between us and the negroes." When McKinley's successor Theodore Roosevelt continued the policy, Arp said: "We have no use for presidents who . . . love the negro better than the southern white folks."[14]

In 1890 Congress considered a bill sponsored by Henry Cabot Lodge to authorize federal supervisors to check on the qualifications of excluded voters in order to protect blacks' political rights. The measure, known in the South as the Force Bill, "means republican power without end, and southern degradation to the extreme," Arp said. The Senate voted down the bill, but Arp wrote that "the animus, the malice, the venom that inspired it is not dead."[15]

The actions of the northern politicians—abusing the South for political gain, putting blacks in the South's post offices, threatening interference in elections—led Arp to question the relationship between the federal government and the South. "I have been raised to think that those who rule should try to court the love of their subjects and make them love the government," he wrote in an 1883 column, "but for twenty years these rulers have put on their most winning ways to make us hate them and hate the government we live under." Seven years later he expressed the same idea with the question, "How can a government expect to prosper when it purposefully provokes the hate of one-third of its subjects?"[16]

Arp said that for most of his life he "dident have but one politics, and that was defending the south against the north." Northern politicians forced the rest of the South into the same position, he said; "The north wonders that there is a solid south. There always will be as long as the north has a solid hate." "It is their infernal, never-ending hate that keeps us solid," he repeated in another column. "As long as they elect our slanderers to office[,] just so long will there be no peace."[17]

Northern politicians were not the only ones who stood in the way of sectional reconciliation. There was also the northern press. "Their newspapers crow over us and bullrag us and tell lies on us," Arp complained early in his tenure at the *Constitution*. Northern newspapers abused the South largely for the same reason that northern politicians did. "The editors want some scandal to feed their readers on and the abuse of the south is like regular stock in trade and is always in demand," Arp wrote in 1899, and two years later added that "it grieves me to realize that the more malignant an editor is against us the more subscribers his paper gets." "I get awfully mad when I read the vile slanders of the northern papers," Arp wrote in an 1897 column. "The scriptures tell us to love our neighbors, but those fellows up there are not our neighbors."[18]

Like his criticism of northern politicians, Arp's attacks on the northern press continued through his years at the *Constitution*. "What the south wants more than anything else, is a stop to this everlasting abuse—this bloody shirt business—this slander by northern liars in the northern press to feed a northern appetite," he wrote in 1884, and two years later noted, "I never try to feel friendly and kind and forgiving but what some of their infernal papers write up something to make me hate them again." In another column he listed several newspaper and magazine articles from the northern press and asked, "What is the use of temporizing with such a people?" "It fatigues my indignation to read some of these northern republican newspapers," he wrote in February 1899, and three months later said that "these Boston papers make me so tired."[19]

The North's book publishers were just as guilty as its newspapers. "For more than half a century the partisan and sectional literature of the north has overshadowed and humiliated us with unfair, untrue and slanderous statements," Arp wrote. The writing of southern history was particularly troubling. "The south lost all but her honor in the war, and that we must preserve," he wrote in 1889, and elsewhere spoke of the need "to perpetuate southern history and defend our fathers and grandfathers from the slanders of northern foes." "Justice has not been done us," Arp said, and he often wrote in the *Constitution* of the need to protect "this generation against the malignant and slanderous productions" of the northern publishers that "have already poisoned the minds of thousands of our young people."[20]

Arp often used his weekly column to praise other books for their fair treatment of the South. (Fair treatment usually meant a southern bias rather than a northern one.) Thaddeus K. Oglesby's *The Britannica Answered and the South Vindicated* (1891) was a "masterful vindication of the south" that Arp asked parents to attach to the *Encyclopaedia Britannica* to counteract the damage done by the *Britannica*'s disparaging remarks on the South's literary and intellectual achievements. In another column Arp commended Percy Greg's *History of the United States* (first published in 1887), saying "at last the south has been vindicated by a master mind," and he urged readers to study Benjamin Franklin Grady's *The Case of the South against the North* (1899). Carlyle McKinley's *An Appeal to*

Pharaoh (1889) was "by far the best and most grateful statement of the race problem that has ever been written"; Mildred Lewis Rutherford's *American Authors* (1894) was "a treasure in the house"; and John Cussons's *A Glance at Current History* (1899, published a year later as *United States "History" as the Yankees Make and Take It*) "has impressed me profoundly and has proved a real comfort in my old age." Arp praised *Appleton's Cyclopaedia of American Biography* for "the prominence given to the southern people," and elsewhere said that anything published by that firm should be acceptable to southerners.[21]

As a member of the school board in Cartersville, Arp had the chance to examine and evaluate a number of textbooks. Books used in southern schools, he said, "should not be sectarian nor sectional, but they should certainly be in sympathy with our Christian civilization and they should be as liberal towards southern sentiment and southern patriotism as towards that of our northern brethren. . . . The south must be recognized as the equal of the north in morals and patriotism." This was a matter in which the South had been "shamefully careless," Arp wrote. "It is a well-known fact that there are teachers who are secretly paid by northern publishers to get their books into our schools." "Northern histories have crept stealthily into our schools and colleges," Arp warned in one column, "and even the histories of our own southern men have only timidly and tenderly defended [the South] for fear of giving offense." School children had been so misinformed that they "have to be told over and over again how we used to live and what was the true relation of southern masters to their negroes." "Let us stand on the watch towers and guard our own citadels," he wrote in 1891. "Let us receive no book . . . that does not do the south justice."[22]

In *A School History of Georgia*—written, Arp told readers of the *Constitution*, "to hand down to our children, pure and untarnished, the honor and integrity of our fathers"—Charles Henry Smith addressed many of the same issues about which he wrote as Bill Arp. The history harshly condemned northern conduct during the war and Reconstruction. "The track of Sherman's troops," he said, "was one broad trail of fire, plunder, robbery and destruction. Nothing was left. If a cyclone of fire had rushed along the country the ruin and desolation could not have been more complete. The rules of civilized warfare were utterly disregarded." Later, "peace was declared, but it was not the peace that a generous foe should give to a thoroughly conquered enemy." "The people were oppressed and made to feel that they were conquered and at the mercy of the conquerors," Smith wrote, ". . . and bitterness and hatred on both sides were the natural fruits. . . . The people were so galled and oppressed by these overbearing tyrants that to this day the 'Reconstruction Period' is regarded with almost as much horror as the war itself." [23]

Of the five "Historical Readings" that made up the second part of the book, three were defenses of the morality of the Old South: "The Condition of the Negro as a Slave" (which said that "there were no happier race of people upon earth than the negroes of the South"); "Why Georgia Withdrew from the Union" (because of the fanaticism of the Republican party, "the first sectional party in the history of the Union"); and "The African Slave Trade—Its Origin and Growth." In this last reading, Smith explained "that neither Georgia nor the South was responsible for slavery, nor for the traffic in slaves across the seas." The Boston firm that published Smith's history refused at first to take it as written because one of its readers "denied and contested" Smith's statements on slavery and the slave trade. "I had to prove my assertions," Smith told a correspondent, and the critic "finally yielded and the history was published as I wrote it." [24]

As Bill Arp, Smith wrote several *Constitution* letters that dealt with the broad topic of slavery and the slave trade. "There is no taint upon your ancestry," he told young readers in one column. "There was no curse in slavery." In other columns, Arp said not only that there had been nothing shameful in slavery, but that the North had been responsible for it and the slave trade. Of the *Britannica*'s discussion of the latter topic, Arp said that "a more infamous slander on the south was never uttered." "More than a century ago," Arp wrote in 1882, "[northerners] thought it was right to steal niggers from Africa, and so they stole 'em, and after while they found out the darkey didn't thrive in New England and they concluded it was a sin to own 'em, and so they sold 'em off to Virginia and down south, and then commenced to abuse the south for buying 'em." A decade later, Arp applauded an address delivered by former Confederate general Henry Rootes Jackson on the New England origin of slavery and the slave trade. Arp detailed some of Jackson's evidence and said that he was "charmed and comforted" when he read the speech. "Had I the authority," he wrote, "I would insist that every professor in every southern college . . . should read this to his class and teach it and linger and dwell upon it until the truth it contains was established in the minds of the pupils." In 1902, having lost his copy of the speech, he asked readers to supply him with a copy of that "most notable, instructive and eloquent address," and when the speech was reprinted in pamphlet form, Arp wrote the introduction.[25]

In 1902 Arp reported a letter he had received the week before from an Iowa man. "It is certainly a great curse," the letter read, "to have so many illiterate, low-lived negroes in your State. . . . To my mind, the 'forefathers' of Georgia sinned in purchasing and owning slaves, and now their children's children suffer the consequences." The letter's author, Arp said, was a "good man," but "lamentably ignorant" of the truth. "If slavery was a sin at all, which I deny, it was not our sin, nor that of our fathers. . . . The sin of slavery began in New England among his forefathers—not ours." Two weeks later, he finished the argument begun in response to the Iowan's letter: "No, there was no sin in slavery as instituted in the South by our fathers and forefathers, and that is why I write this letter—perhaps the last I shall ever write on the subject. I wish to impress it upon our boys and girls so that they may be ready and willing to defend their Southern ancestors." (Arp revived the argument one last time three months later.) Arp also addressed a number of other historical questions in his *Constitution* column, among them the myth that Jefferson Davis had been captured at the end of the Civil War wearing a disguise of woman's clothing, the outrages at the Andersonville Confederate prison, Gen. Ulysses S. Grant's role as a slaveholder, and the story of Nancy Hart, unsung southern heroine of the Revolution.[26]

In 1892 Arp mentioned "a feature connected with our relations to the northern people that should give us great concern, and that is the malignant attitude of the northern preachers." He complained that the Presbyterian press "is outspoken in condemning our methods of lynching negroes for certain crimes"; a Baptist paper "boldly advocated miscegenation as the only and best remedy for the antagonism between the races"; and a Methodist convention voted for a resolution against "the lawlessness and violence of the southern people towards the colored race." When Henry Ward Beecher said that modern religion was based on love rather than the hate and fanaticism of older theology, Arp wrote that this would mean a big change for the former abolitionist preacher: "How long has it been since the reverend gentleman was willing to see the southern people butchered, their towns and cities burned and their land made desolate. . . . I wonder if he never considers how much he contributed to this war of hate and death and arson and rape and robbery and desolation. It is time the preacher was discovering that true religion is love; but it is late; very late for him." In response to an Ohio minister's sermon in 1880 on southern race relations, Arp wrote: "The whole sermon is an incendiary document. It makes our people mad with them, and makes them afraid of us."[27]

According to Arp, northern preachers had the same motivation for abusing the South as did the other groups. "My candid opinion is that the majority of them have no more real religion than did Henry Ward Beecher," he wrote in 1899. "Like the editors, they rely on sensation to fill their pews and their pockets." Arp's distrust of northern preachers ran deep; when one admitted that giving total freedom to blacks had been a disaster, Arp wrote: "I don't know what to make of it and I am afraid of anything that comes from a yankee preacher. . . . We will have to watch them fellows, for they are always up to some devilment."[28]

Arp complained about northern politicians, the press and book publishers, preachers, and even poets. "The old crank," Arp wrote in 1891, referring to John Greenleaf Whittier. "Nearly half of [his] poetry . . . is sentimental slush about the downtrodden, crushed, manacled, bleeding slaves of the south." "There was no crazier fanatic in New England than Whittier," Arp wrote three years later. He described the poems in one of Whittier's collections as "pitiful appeals for the poor slave and invoking heaven's curse upon his master. . . . He fed the young people of New England upon poetic lies for thirty years and instilled into their hearts that hatred from which they have never recovered." When Arp was gathering poems for an anthology, he wrote that none of Whittier's "slanderous effusions" would be included.[29]

Whittier died in 1892, "but his poetic license and slanders still live," Arp wrote eight years later. Specifically, he complained about the poet's "Barbara Frietchie," the poem that portrays Stonewall Jackson as leading his troops through the streets of Frederick, Maryland, and ordering them to shoot down a United States flag that Barbara Frietchie had placed outside her attic window. According to Whittier, ninety-year-old Barbara snatched the flag before it could fall and, in the poem's most famous couplet, rebuked the Confederates: " 'Shoot, if you must, this old gray head, / But spare your country's flag,' she said." In a column that described the poem as a "miserable thing," a "wanton malignant myth," and a "vile slander," Arp demonstrated that the story in the poem never happened, but was the product of Whittier's misinformation, imagination, and hatred. "[Whittier] may get to heaven," Arp admitted, "for the grace of God is very great, but if I get there I'll not hunt him up to say howdy." A month later, he reported that a Boston paper had printed an article telling the truth of the Barbara Frietchie myth, "but that is only one thing settled. One slander nailed and it has taken thirty years to do that," he wrote.[30]

In the sectional war of politics, the pen, and the pulpit, Arp did not always simply defend the South; at times he turned the tables on the North. "New York has 12000 [white] prisoners, and not quite four times the population of Georgia with her 231 prisoners," he wrote in 1883, "and yet the northern papers are always abusing us about our lawlessness." Elsewhere he noted that "we have nearly a million whites in Georgia and only 148 white convicts, whereas in Massachusetts and New York there are thirteen hundred white convicts to a million of people." Arp's use of statistics to evaluate northern crime was similar to his discussion of black crime. "Only one white woman in the jails or chaingangs of Georgia and 748 in the puritan state of [Massachusetts]," he wrote in 1897. "What shall we do about it? What can we do?" He observed that "it is high time our southern churches were organizing boards of missions and sending misionaries up there."[31]

The statistics of northern crime showed a "difference in the moral training of the two sections," Arp wrote. "There is up there a growing looseness of morals in the relation of man and wife." "Divorce increases there twice as fast as population, and not more than eight families in ten have preserved the purity and honor of the marriage relation." "Their condition is amazing, pathetic, helpless," he wrote in one column, and in another remarked, "Alas for cultured, classic, critical, exacting New England. The seed that her fanatics sowed is bearing fruit."[32]

"Now I am not arraigning any northern state for its sad condition," Arp wrote in 1893, "but I am defending the south from slanderous assertions concerning its morals." Whatever his reasons, Arp wrote more and more frequently about the North's high crime rate and declining morality. When a Boston newspaper said in 1899 that southerners were "'a generation behind the times, in fact several New England generations behind it,'" Arp was quick to respond. "How is that?" he asked. "It hasent been 200 years since New England was burning innocent, harmless women for being witches. It hasent been fifty years since Boston merchants were shipping rum to Africa to buy negroes to sell again to slave countries. . . . We are behind that sort of business several generations." He went on to discuss the high crime and divorce rates in the North and the correspondingly low rates in the South. "How is that for living in glass houses? Yes, I reckon we are behind them several generations. I hope so."[33]

Paul Buck, writing half a century ago, asserted that "thirty years after Appomattox there remained no fundamental conflict between the aspirations of North and South. . . . The reunited nation was a fact." But Bill Arp was never reconciled with the North. He had tried, he often said, but when he died in 1903 he was no closer than he had been four decades before. "No," he wrote two years before his death, "I am still the same old rebel—unreconstructed [and] unrepentent."[34]

In her study of Bill Arp, Annie May Christie assessed his writings on sectional reconciliation. Arp, she said, "had plenty of courage and his indignation was strong when aroused, but his spirit, though continually rasped by Northern attacks, held little bitterness and would not allow him to lend himself to vituperation. . . . He called by name the Northern agitators and Southern betrayers of their section and spiritedly and openly took them to task for their sins. His fists were hard and he had an uncanny way of aiming them straight, but he disdained to hit below the belt." Similarly, Wade Hall's study of southern humor characterized Arp as a man who as late as 1902 "could still get his Rebel dander up" when defending the South.[35]

Other scholars, however, have missed this important aspect of Arp's post-1878 writings. In her study, Louella Landrum wrote that Arp's "wartime satires show a decided sectionalism, but as the war became more remote his satire is directed only against the human family as a whole." Jay B. Hubbell, in *The South in American Literature*, described Arp as "an advocate of reconciliation between North and South." Paul Richard Hilty, Jr., called Arp "a staunch advocate of reconciliation" "with a forgiving, hopeful, and unifying smile." Jennette Tandy, an early scholar of American humor whose influential *Crackerbox Philosophers in American Humor and Satire* was published in 1925, noted that "as his sectional pride simmers down, Bill Arp's letters become more idyllic." More recently, William

Lenz wrote that in Arp's writings for the *Constitution*, "the unity of family, state, and nation is now more important than keeping fresh memories of regionalism and secession." In the clearest statement of this misreading of Arp's writings, Walter Blair wrote that Arp, "in time, left behind his hate-filled assaults on the Yankees and became a commentator on nonpolitical matters." These scholars misread Arp's writings on the North and sectional reconciliation for the same reason they misread his writings on race relations: they read only the published collections of his letters, and few of his many essays on these topics were ever reprinted.[36]

There were several reasons why Arp wrote so often on the North and sectional reconciliation. First, of course, was the memory of the war, evident in the large number of columns he wrote on Sherman's destructiveness and his own family's refugeeing experiences. Another spur was northern criticism of southern actions, especially in the area of race relations, which forced Arp and other southern white spokesmen to articulate a defense or justification for southern practices and to argue that the northern critics were wrong. As his son-in-law said, Arp "never failed to lift his pen in defense of his native land and people."[37]

But there were other reasons. Arp criticized the North because he perceived it (just as he perceived the new generation of southerners, white and black) to be lazy, dishonest, and, above all else, immoral. Arp summed up many of his views on northern society in an 1889 column in the *Constitution*:

> The trouble with New England is that she has too much transcendental, sublimated refinement. There are a great many folks who have too much education. When it is properly mixed with work and moral training a man can't have too much, but without these it is the curse of a nation. The very latest statistics prove that crime is increasing much faster than population: all sorts of crime—murder, theft, forgery, drunkeness, debauchery and general cussedness. Honesty, industry, truth and morality are at a discount in the great cities, especially among the rich and the politicians. These virtues flourish only in the country among the respectable working classes—not among

the graduates of colleges, but among the common school people who have enough learning to make them enjoy their leisure in reading and not enough to destroy their fitness for the honest toil of human life. Most of our race have got to work for a living, and this high college training, somehow or other, breeds an inclination to dodge it.

Except for the first sentence, Arp could be discussing blacks or the society of the New South; he made the same criticisms in each case.[38]

At the same time that Bill Arp attacked the North for its immorality, he corrected misrepresentations of southern history to show that the South *was* moral. The sectional comparison led Arp to conclude in 1890 that the South was "the hope of the country, the salvation of the government. Here is conservatism and peace, and law and order. Here are good morals and good principles." "I believe in my heart that the south will have to save this government from a wreck," Arp wrote a few years later. "The morality and conservatism of the southern people are right now the safeguards of the nation." Elsewhere Arp noted that "the dear old south is long suffering and patient, but she still . . . loves to preserve the faith of the fathers and the morals of the nation. That is her destiny. I believe it as strongly as I believe that I live. The time will come when the mighty north will look to us for help, for protection against anarchy and revolution." Two years before his death, Arp spoke again of "the conservative spirit of the south" that would save the government. That spirit—the values and virtues of the Old South's heritage— "is yet alive with us and will be transmitted to our children," he said hopefully.[39]

Nine

The Meaning of
Bill Arp

Celestine Sibley, the *Atlanta Constitution* columnist who learned about Bill Arp when a student wrote to her in 1969, has done much since then to keep the memory of the homely philosopher alive. As mentioned in the Introduction, she frequently writes about Arp and included a number of quotations from him in her *Day by Day with Celestine Sibley*. On December 23, 1985, Sibley told her readers about the Christmas Arp described in one of his books. I wrote her shortly after that to compliment her on the essay, and also to tell her of my own study of Arp and ask a few questions about the paper's archives. Without my knowledge, she wrote a column on me and my research and urged her readers to send me any information they might have on Arp. Within two or three weeks of that column's appearance, I received more than fifty letters. Sibley later wrote that she herself had "received about 30 phone calls the day the column ran, and the mail on the subject is still coming in." The tremendous response indicated (as Sibley had learned almost two decades before) that many people still remember and revere Bill Arp.[1]

One admirer is William L. Brown, a native of Cartersville and an Atlanta businessman. In the mid-1970s, Brown, then a student at Berry College (near Rome, Georgia), read one of Arp's homely philosophy letters in the prose interpretation event at the Dixie

Invitational Speech Festival. His success there led him to create a one-man Bill Arp show as part of the Bartow County bicentennial celebration. In the show, Brown quoted extensively from Arp's works (concentrating on his early writings) and provided "original introductory and transitional material" to create a presentation "designed," according to the program, "to resemble a lecture as Major Smith might have given it." Brown could deliver the presentation either as a simple oral reading or as a dramatic monologue, in full make-up and costume. Either way, he said, "the wit and humor of Bill Arp himself never fails to take the show." [2]

Along with Sibley and Brown, a handful of others have resurrected Arp for an occasional article in a newspaper or local magazine. They remember Bill Arp because he was a famous Georgian, now almost forgotten, who defended his state and region during the Civil War and Reconstruction and who later wrote delightful sketches of his family life and other pleasant topics.

Scholars have also devoted considerable attention to Arp in the last few decades, often approaching his work from a literary, linguistic, or folkloric perspective. The scholars have not always been so admiring of Arp's work, however. Margaret Gillis Figh offered a mild criticism of Arp's writings in an article on his description of life in nineteenth-century Georgia. "Unfortunately," she said, "this material is interspersed among masses of somewhat [sic] dull expository matter." The author of the preface in a recent reprint of *Bill Arp's Peace Papers* was much harsher: "This is a rancid book which casts light upon the most disgraceful era in American history, an effusion of parochial ignorance barely concealed by a pretense of yokel humor." Scholars generally note that Arp was very popular in his time, and many cite as evidence for this the introduction he received before giving a lecture in Mississippi: "I can not say that Bill Arp is the greatest man, nor the best man, nor the most eloquent man, but I truthfully say that he is the best loved man in all the Southland." Few scholars have attempted to go beyond such statements to explain Arp's popularity, however, and none has adequately explained Arp's relationship to his readers. [3]

During the years of the Civil War and Reconstruction, Arp's role as spokesman for the South was relatively clear. While it is true that a number of southerners did not agree with his views, many did, at least in general terms, and for these people Arp's occasional letters offered a firm, straightforward, and welcome statement on the "Southern Side" of things. During the war, Arp cheered on the soldiers and civilians, criticized those whose actions hurt the Confederate war effort, and urged readers to keep the faith, even in the dark final days of the war. During Reconstruction, he resigned himself (at least implicitly) to most of the Republican Reconstruction measures, but he always maintained that southern honor and bravery should be acknowledged and respected. "Our people are dumb, struck speechless by their great misery," wrote one southern magazine in 1866. "[Bill Arp] is their spokesman."[4]

When Arp began writing for the *Atlanta Constitution* in 1878 he was still a spokesman for the South, but his role and his message were not as clear as they had been before. Historian Thomas D. Clark once wrote that "to understand the philosophy and methodology of Bill Arp is to grasp a fundamental knowledge of the intellectual development of much of the New South."[5] As a step in the direction Clark proposed, this chapter will look at Arp's audience and his message—the meaning of Bill Arp.

What a change has come over the world, some things for the better, some for the worse, and we must take life and progress as we find it," wrote Bill Arp in 1900. The question of change and continuity in the South is one that has perplexed scholars throughout this century. Philip Alexander Bruce and Holland Thompson, two early New South historians, stressed the ties (both familial and ideological) between leaders of the New South and the Old. The most famous expression of continuity came in 1941 when Wilbur J. Cash published *The Mind of the South*. "The extent of the change and of the break between the Old South that was and the South of our time has been vastly exaggerated," Cash wrote. The Civil War "left the essential Southern mind and will . . . entirely unshaken."[6]

A decade after *The Mind of the South* appeared, C. Vann Woodward turned Cash's world upside down. The New South leaders were no longer "of the old ruling class, the progeny of the plantation," as Cash had it; "they were of middle-class, industrial, capitalistic outlook, with little but a nominal connection with the old planter regime," Woodward wrote in *Origins of the New South*. Although he mentioned in the next sentence that some of the Redeemers (his word for the conservative whites who overthrew the Republican Reconstruction governments) "were more strongly associated . . . with the ante-bellum order," Woodward came down strongly on the side of discontinuity in southern history. "Redemption was not a return of an old system," he said, "nor the restoration of an old ruling class." [7]

Woodward's view of southern history remained virtually unchallenged on its fundamental points for almost a quarter of a century. In a 1977 survey of recent social scholarship, Harold D. Woodman described "the truly revolutionary change that emancipation brought to the South," especially in the area of economics, and concluded, as had Woodward and Arp, that "the New South . . . was new." A year after Woodman's article appeared, James Tice Moore, in an essay that examined more the political side of Woodward's interpretation, came to the opposite conclusion. Examples of discontinuity were superficial, Moore said, and he announced that "Professor Woodward's revisionist interpretation of Redeemer origins is itself in need of revision." This debate has been a valuable catalyst for research in southern history, but it has not settled the question of continuity or change. Actually, both sides are right: some things changed and others remained the same in the transition from the Old South to the New. As Woodward himself noted in a review of the debate, the question is one of degrees, not of absolutes. [8]

That some things changed in the South cannot be denied. In seven of the eleven former Confederate states the number of manufacturing plants at least doubled between 1880 and 1900, and in nine states the number of workers employed in manufacturing trebled.

These figures are impressive, though it must be remembered that figures for the whole South would be lower and that, because of the South's slow start in industrialization, the resulting growth in absolute terms was not as high and was certainly less than the New South prophets had anticipated. But there were other changes that accompanied industrialization and intensified its consequences. This was an age of urban growth, with the rise both of the New South cities (such as Birmingham and Durham) and of smaller urban areas (mill villages, mining towns, and so forth). In seven of the former Confederate states the urban population, as defined by the Census Bureau, more than doubled during the decade of the 1880s. In this new urban setting arose a new middle class of merchants, small businessmen, doctors, lawyers, and other professionals—a group of people who came to resemble, in attitude and influence, their counterparts in the big cities. Farmers were also affected, as changes in the production and distribution of cotton forced them into a more direct involvement with the market. A doubling of railroad mileage in the 1880s increased the integration of the farmer into the market economy as well as of the South into the rest of the nation.[9]

These changes did not occur overnight. As Gaines M. Foster observed, "The rise of an important industrial sector, the expansion of the market economy and a town culture, the growth of the middle class, and the integration into national systems all intensified later; the eighties marked the inauguration, not the culmination, of most of these trends."[10] But perception was much more important than reality. Just as the New South prophets announced the accomplishment of their program before it really got underway, so did the critics of the new order see around them the baneful effects of changes that were just beginning.

Bill Arp was one person who perceived great change in the South. Industrialization might bring wealth to the region, but the profits of the New South had to be weighed against the migration from countryside to city, a baser materialistic philosophy, and the disruption of the traditional family. The settlement of the race question, considered complete at the end of the 1870s, proved to be less perfect and less permanent than he had hoped. North and South had been reunited, but there remained a lingering sectional animosity. Low commodity prices depressed the South's economy, and Populism and organized labor threatened the South's political and social stability. According to Foster, "Southerners feared for the stability of their society and the maintenance of community in the midst of such challenges and worried about their own values in the face of increased commercialism."[11] Foster showed how these anxieties motivated and shaped Confederate celebrations late in the nineteenth century. These anxieties also caused many southerners, including Bill Arp, to look further back, to the days of the Old South.

For Bill Arp, the legacy of the Old South was a willingness to work, a strong sense of morality, and an ability and desire to be self-reliant. The New South, on the other hand, was indolence, an attitude fostered by the educational system, the ready availability of get-rich-quick schemes, and the general acceptance of a philosophy that emphasized the end (wealth) over the means. The New South also meant immorality, as seen in the rising divorce and crime rates. The growth of cities, the failure of schools to teach moral principles, and the breakup of the family all contributed to the New South's immorality, with the last mentioned being an unfortunate consequence as well. Dependence on others was a third attribute of the New South. The self-reliant southerners of antebellum days had given way to a society that, voluntarily or otherwise, surrendered its mind, will, and fortune to the control of others. The changes that the new age ushered into the South worked in various ways against the values and virtues of the antebellum days, and whenever Bill Arp explicitly condemned the New South, he did it in these terms.

Arp emphasized these same traditional values when he wrote on blacks and the North. His criticisms of the younger generation of blacks—their increasing participation in crime, decline in morality, and aversion to work—were the same ones he raised against the younger generation of white southerners, and he ascribed them to the same factors, such as the influence of cities, a faulty education, and the lack of proper guidance. This was true for Arp's writing on the North as well. Northerners, like young southerners, both black and white, and for many of the same reasons, were lazy, dishonest, and above all immoral. Furthermore, there were certain groups in the North—preachers, politicians, and journalists, among others—that continually found fault with the South, often belittling or denying the very virtues that Arp defended.

These traditional values were also the basis for Arp's homely philosophy. His writings on his family and farm, the past, and the common folk of Georgia were not simply the idyllic sketches that most scholars have assumed them to be. They were rather a further condemnation of the New South, because in them Arp stressed the values and virtues he saw missing from the new age.

"I believe it is true that nobody but the old men and women give praise to the old times and the customs of their fathers,"[12] Arp claimed in 1901, and almost everything he wrote in the *Atlanta Constitution* and elsewhere in the last quarter-century of his life had at its foundation a comparison of the New South to the Old. His writings were a mournful threnody for the traditional values of the Old South and a consistent (if occasionally subdued) criticism of both the changes that had made these values obsolete and the society that those changes had produced.

Arp was not the only person in the postwar South to look to the past. When Robert E. Lee surrendered in April 1865, the Old South became the Lost Cause and soon slipped into the realm of mythology. Rollin G. Osterweis, in a study of "the anatomy and development of the Lost Cause as social myth," showed how southerners (as well as northerners) manifested the myth in speeches, sermons, books and articles, drama, music, education, and organizations. Osterweis never really defined the Lost Cause, perhaps because it meant different things to different people. As mentioned in chapter 6, the New South prophets themselves were important propagators of the myth, or at least their version of it. "One of the major and inescapable concerns of the New South advocates was to emphasize the 'Southernness' of their movement and to romanticize the past out of which it came, to which it was related, and whose essential aspirations it was to fulfill," according to Paul Gaston, and so the New South prophets developed "historical formulas to underscore the degree to which the South had been both broadly nationalistic and economically progressive." In the words of Henry Grady, the New South was "simply the Old South under new conditions."[13]

The writers of the plantation romances were another group that looked to the South's past. The genre was a half-century old by the 1880s—most scholars look at John Pendleton Kennedy's *Swallow Barn*, published in 1832, as its primary progenitor—but "The Great Outburst" of plantation romances came only a decade or so after the Civil War with such writers as Thomas Nelson Page and F. Hopkinson Smith. According to Francis Pendleton Gaines, who was to historians of the plantation romance what Kennedy was to the plantation romance itself, one reason for the genre's popularity throughout the 1880s and 1890s was that the image it portrayed "stands as a kind of American embodiment of the golden age." This literature distorted most features of the Old South, but by showing something other than what might be called the darker side of southern history it provided an image that people of both sections, North and South, could agree was good and which could therefore serve as a basis for sectional reconciliation. Although these romances were apparently popular with many southerners, a more recent scholar has reminded us that the writers of the plantation romances "dealt almost exclusively with the aristocracy, a group that represented the highest aspirations of the Southern populace, but whose lives were not typical of the vast majority of Southerners."[14]

The Old South had different meanings for other southerners. Daniel J. Singal, in *The War Within*, interpreted postbellum southern intellectual history in terms of the transition from Victorian to "modernist" thought. "The very bedrock of [Victorian] thought," Singal said, was a "separation between the barbaric and the civilized, the animal and the human." Victorianism "settled in with a vengeance" in the late nineteenth-century South as southerners adopted an understanding of the Old South that included "the sustaining conviction that, in its day, theirs had been an aristocratic culture infinitely superior to the crass materialistic culture of their enemy." In other words, southerners embraced the Victorian myth of the Old South because it gave them a way to win the war that the sword had lost. Singal's study, however, suffered from a defect common to many intellectual histories: it omitted a lot of people. Singal divided the southern population into two groups. The first was made up of "the remnant of the old planter class as well as the growing middle-class elite—those actively involved in building the new order, such as lawyers, teachers, and the enlightened captains of industry." The second consisted of "the southern masses: the mill hands, dirt farmers, mechanics, and sharecroppers who formed the overwhelming majority of the southern population." By Singal's definition, Victorianism included only the first group; excluded were the masses, the agrarian yeomen and others whom John Spencer Bassett described in true Victorian fashion as "not yet out of the stage of uncultured animalism." [15]

Other historians have applied a different interpretive framework. Charles Reagan Wilson, for example, argued that the southerners' use of the past became a "civil religion." In *Baptized in Blood*, Wilson described various aspects of the Lost Cause, showing how each was expressed in religious terms and how each was "directed toward meeting the profound concerns of postwar Southerners." Although the religious imagery he showed is almost overwhelming, most of the celebrants of Wilson's "religion of the Lost Cause" were Protestant ministers and veterans. Lloyd Arthur Hunter, who used the phrase "*Kulturreligion*" rather than "civil religion," included more of the southern population in his study. [16]

Studies of the New South mentality and the mythology of the Old South have been, like those on the question of continuity and change in southern history, vigorous but nonconclusive. Some historians could benefit from remembering Timothy Curtis Jacobson's comment that "the task of identifying any single idea or set of ideas as the heart of the New South's perception of herself would be a futile exercise in oversimplification." [17] Along the same lines, many of these studies have confined themselves to certain groups of southerners: the journalists who were the New South prophets; the upper classes; the intellectual elite; Protestant ministers and veterans; and so on. But what of the masses—the non-Victorians of Singal's second group of southerners?

R. L. Foreman II, in an informal history of the *Atlanta Constitution*, suggested one way to get at this part of the southern mind:

> It is difficult today to measure the influence of the newspapers of the 70's and 80's with no telephone connection, no automobile for quick travel, no radio or television. There was nothing but the newspaper and an occasional visiting orator to bring news. The daily paper was the whole of outside life to the average man, a great majority of whom then lived on farms and in small cities. . . . It is easy to understand how a people starved by such a limited press would particularly welcome the special dishes offered by men like Grady, Harris, Bill Arp and Sam Small. Their remarks made the daily conversation in most households in the Atlanta territory.[18]

The people Foreman described in the above paragraph presumably cut across class lines—they included the masses as well as the middle-class elite and what was left of the planters, to return to Singal's division of the southern white population—but his conclusion on the importance of newspapers in the intellectual life of the South is a useful one. Thomas D. Clark made a similar point in his studies of the small southern country papers. Calling the country press "one of the most vigorous institutions in the New South," he showed how rural and small-town papers reflected both "the political flavor" and "the cultural level" of the areas they served.[19]

Bill Arp was the brightest star in the universe of the rural press. Arp's column, syndicated from the *Atlanta Constitution* by the Western Newspaper Union to newspapers all over the South, was, in Clark's words, "enormously popular" and "extremely influential." While many people enjoyed his writings, Arp "spoke for large numbers of inarticulate people," the masses whose perceptions of the New South seldom matched exactly those described by Singal, Wilson, Gaston, and other historians.[20] When Arp praised the simple and pristine life of the countryside and the Georgia folk, he implicitly condemned the New South, but he also suggested a utopian alternative. The world of Arp's homely philosophy was one filled with honest and industrious people who lived in the country and in small towns and who cared more for their families and fellow men than for wealth, power, or the fashions of society. Arp was so successful in creating this world that a generation of scholars has been fooled into thinking of him, this discontented old man, as a cheerful homely philosopher. Arp thought, wrote, and talked about the virtues of the past as a way of dealing with the wrongs of the present, and his popularity suggests that his weekly letter was a balm for other southerners as well, soothing the pain of irretrievable loss that they shared with him.

For Bill Arp and his readers, the Lost Cause was not moonlight and magnolias, a separate cultural identity, or a justification for industrialization and sectional reconciliation. For them, the Old South was the traditional values that they associated with good men and good living, values that were missing in the New South. The Old South that Arp implicitly pictured—hard work in the fields, the necessity of relying on oneself, the close ties of a rural family gathered at night around the humble hearth—was perhaps not as pretty as that of the plantation romances, but it was one that Arp and many other southerners could understand. For them, this was the Lost Cause, "a cause," Arp said, "for which we are still proud, for it gets brighter and purer as the years roll on." [21]

Notes

Introduction

1. *Atlanta Constitution* [hereafter cited as *Constitution*], 3 June 1969.
2. Ibid., 6 June 1969.
3. Annie May Christie, "Charles Henry Smith, 'Bill Arp': A Biographical and Critical Study of a Nineteenth-Century Georgia Humorist, Politician, Homely Philosopher"; William L. Brown, Atlanta, Ga., personal correspondence, 8 Jan. 1986.
4. James C. Austin, *Bill Arp*, [10], 107.
5. Charles Henry Smith, *Bill Arp's Peace Papers*, 19. Hereafter Charles Henry Smith is cited as CHS.
6. Walter Blair and Raven I. McDavid, Jr., eds., *The Mirth of a Nation: America's Great Dialect Humor*, xix; Walter Blair, *Native American Humor, 1800–1900*, 119.
7. John M. Harrison, *The Man Who Made Nasby, David Ross Locke*, 5.
8. David Ross Locke, *Divers Views, Opinions, and Prophesies*, 25–27.
9. *Constitution*, 27 April 1884.
10. Quoted in David B. Kesterson, *Josh Billings (Henry Wheeler Shaw)*, 13.
11. Henry Wheeler Shaw, *Josh Billings, Hiz Sayings*, 83, 85.
12. CHS, *The Farm and the Fireside: Sketches of Domestic Life in War and in Peace*, 252.
13. Charles Farrar Browne, *Artemus Ward, His Book*, 176.
14. Quoted in James C. Austin, *Artemus Ward*, 39–40.
15. John J. Pullen, *Comic Relief: The Life and Laughter of Artemus Ward, 1834–1867*, 114; *Constitution*, 16 Feb. 1896. The two did meet at some point, however, according to a later newspaper article: *Rome Weekly Courier*, 6 May 1870.
16. Brom Weber, "The Misspellers," 137; David B. Kesterson, "Those

Literary Comedians"; *Abe Lincoln Laughing: Humorous Anecdotes from Original Sources by and about Abraham Lincoln,* ed. P. M. Zall; Pullen, *Comic Relief,* 3 (Lincoln on Ward); Harrison, *Man Who Made Nasby,* 113 (on Nasby); Walter Blair and Hamlin Hill, *America's Humor: From Poor Richard to Doonesbury,* 293 (on Billings); Marian Smith, *I Remember,* 24 (on Arp).

17. Alan Gribben, *Mark Twain's Library: A Reconstruction* 1:xxxiii; Kenneth S. Lynn, *Mark Twain and Southwestern Humor;* David E. E. Sloane, *Mark Twain as a Literary Comedian.*

18. Sandy Cohen, "American Humor: A Historical Survey: South and Southwest," 597; Austin, *Bill Arp,* 97.

19. Wade Hall, *The Smiling Phoenix: Southern Humor from 1865 to 1914,* 261; Louis D. Rubin, Jr., *A Gallery of Southerners,* 121.

20. *Constitution,* 10 May 1879; *Mark Twain's Notebooks and Journals* 2: 361. The proposed anthology was never published, but it provided the inspiration for a later book, *Mark Twain's Library of Humor* (1888), which did not include any Arp selections.

21. W. J. Cash, *Mind of the South;* William R. Taylor, *Cavalier and Yankee: The Old South and American National Character;* Bertram Wyatt-Brown, *Southern Honor: Ethics and Behavior in the Old South;* Frank L. Owsley, *Plain Folk of the Old South.*

One. Lawrenceville: 1826–1851

1. CHS, *Bill Arp: From the Uncivil War to Date, 1861–1903,* Memorial Edition, 21–22; *Constitution,* 27 June 1880, 15 July 1888.

2. CHS, *Uncivil War to Date,* 23–24, 29; James C. Flanigan, *History of Gwinnett County, Georgia, 1818–1843* 1:387, 389; 2:149, 151; *Constitution,* 30 Sept. 1888, 6 Nov. 1881, 14 Sept. 1890.

3. Flanigan, *History of Gwinnett County* 1:83, 94–95, 387–88; 2:12–13, 116, 154; Alice Smythe McCabe, ed., *Gwinnett County, Georgia, Families, 1818–1968,* 517; interviews with members of the Gwinnett Historical Society, Lawrenceville, Ga., May 1986; *Constitution,* 6 Feb. 1887, 9 March 1884.

4. Flanigan, *History of Gwinnett County* 1:87 (quot.), 172, 176, 179, 389–90; "'Bill Arp'—Humorist," 28; *Constitution,* 20 March 1887, 29 May 1887, 17 Nov. 1889, 7 May 1899; CHS, *Peace Papers,* 184; Slave Schedule, Federal Censuses of 1830, 1840, and 1860, Gwinnett County, Ga.; A. R. Smith to Reuben S. Norton, 10 Dec. [1864], Norton Family Papers;

signed legal agreement, 18 July 1834, in Charles Henry Smith Collection, McCain Library, Agnes Scott College, Decatur, Ga. (hereafter cited as CHS Papers).

5. CHS, *Uncivil War to Date*, 18–26; Flanigan, *History of Gwinnett County* 1:387–88; CHS, "Caroline Ann Smith."

6. *Constitution*, 22 Feb. 1880; Flanigan, *History of Gwinnett County* 2:177; Christie, "Charles Henry Smith," 6–8; D. W. Newsom, "Bill Arp," 61 (quot.); CHS, *Bill Arp's Scrap Book: Humor and Philosophy*, 366; George Magruder Battey, Jr., *A History of Rome and Floyd County, State of Georgia, United States of America: Including Numerous Incidents of More Than Local Interest, 1540–1922*, 587. According to Joseph A. Cote, bibliographer for the Hargrett Library of the University of Georgia, no copies of the college paper are extant, correspondence with author, 12 Oct. 1987.

7. CHS, *Uncivil War to Date*, 28 (quot. 1); Flanigan, *History of Gwinnett County* 1:178, 182, 186, 344–48; 2:10, 18–19, 152, 498–500; Population and Slave Schedules, Federal Censuses of 1850 and 1860, Gwinnett County, Ga.; McCabe, *Gwinnett Families*, 259–62; *Constitution*, 29 Jan. 1893 (quot. 2).

8. *Constitution*, 31 Aug. 1884; C. H. Smith & Co., Account ledger, account of N. L. Hutchins, May–Nov. 1848, CHS Papers; CHS, *Uncivil War to Date*, 28 (quot.).

9. Salem Dutcher, "Bill Arp and Artemus Ward," 475 (quot.); *Constitution*, 30 April 1893; "Recollections of Long Ago," Aubrey Scrapbook; Joel Branham, *The Old Court House in Rome*, 54.

10. *Rome Tribune*, 2 Sept. 1894, quoted in Battey, *History of Rome*, 263; Marian Smith, *I Remember*, 26; W. Lafayette Smith to Laura Jane Smith, 24 Feb. 1893, Laura Jane Smith Papers, Perkins Library, Duke University; *Constitution*, 25 May 1891.

11. *Constitution*, 30 June 1878, 19 June 1887, 10 June 1883, 8 Feb. 1891, 5 June 1892 (quot.); Marian Smith, *I Remember*, 5; CHS, *Uncivil War to Date*, 29.

12. CHS, *Uncivil War to Date*, 31.

13. Flanigan, *History of Gwinnett County* 1:160–61.

14. Memorandum of an agreement between Nathan L. Hutchins and Charles H. Smith, January 16, 1850, CHS Papers; CHS, *Uncivil War to Date*, 30 (quot.). The two Lawrenceville children were Hines Maguire, born 19 Jan. 1850, and Wirt Walter, 19 Oct. 1851.

Two. Rome: 1851–1877

1. Branham, *Old Court House*, 52; Verdie Frances Miller, "Bill Arp (Charles Henry Smith): Georgia Author," 10; Marian Smith, *I Remember*, 15, 18; *Rome Tribune*, 2 Sept. 1894, quoted in Battey, *History of Rome*, 262; "Recollections of Long Ago," Aubrey Scrapbook; CHS to Nathan L. Hutchins, Jr., 3 Sept. 1856, CHS Papers. The house, no longer standing, was located at what is now 312 East Fourth Avenue.

2. Christie, "Charles Henry Smith," 14; Marian Smith, *I Remember*, 20; *Constitution*, 19 June 1887 (quot.); Roger Aycock, *All Roads to Rome*, 465; Reuben S. Norton to A. R. Smith, 13 Nov. 1864, and A. R. Smith to Reuben S. Norton, 10 Dec. 1864, Norton Family Papers; *Rome Tri-Weekly Courier*, 2 Oct. 1866.

3. This story was passed along by Marilu Young Munford, Jessie's daughter, of Cartersville, Ga., in May 1986. The remaining children were Ralph Royal, born 23 April 1854; Harriet Hutchins, 19 Jan. 1856; Frank Clifton, 15 April 1858; Victor James, 22 Jan. 1860; Marian Caroline, 17 July 1861; Stella Octavia, 23 June 1863; Charles Napoleon, 7 March 1865; Ralph Edward, 29 Nov. 1867; Laura Maria, 16 Dec. 1869; Carl Holt, 18 Aug. 1873; and Jessie Winfred, 13 Nov. 1874. The following died as infants: Wirt Walter, 25 May 1853; Charles Napoleon, 9 May 1866; and Laura Maria, 25 June 1870.

4. Christie, "Charles Henry Smith," 15; Marian Smith, *I Remember*, 12; CHS, *Farm and Fireside*, 78 (quot.).

5. Marian Smith, *I Remember*, 5; *Constitution*, 8 Feb. 1891, 25 Nov. 1883.

6. Slave Schedule, Federal Census of 1860, Floyd County, Ga.; CHS to Nathan L. Hutchins, Jr., 3 Sept. 1856, CHS Papers; CHS, *Farm and Fireside*, 315–16; *Constitution*, 10 June 1883.

7. CHS, *Scrap Book*, 283 (quot. 1); *Constitution*, 22 Dec. 1878 (quot. 2), 7 Oct 1888 (quots. 3, 6), 8 Feb. 1891 (quot. 4); CHS, *Farm and Fireside*, 316 (quot. 5).

8. Newsom, "Bill Arp," 62; James E. Ginther, "Charles Henry Smith, Alias 'Bill Arp,'" 315. The "Sam McCrackin" letters were apparently never published.

9. *Rome Tri-Weekly Courier*, 17 Jan. 1860, quoted in Battey, *History of Rome*, 236–37.

10. Branham, *Old Court House*, 51; CHS to Nathan L. Hutchins, Jr., 3 Sept. 1856, CHS Papers.

11. Christie, "Charles Henry Smith," 17; Battey, *History of Rome*, 394; Aycock, *All Roads to Rome*, 180; Walter S. Cothran to Harriet Aubrey, 21 Feb. 1939, and "A Visit to 'Little Rock,' Arkansas," in Aubrey Scrapbook; *Rome Weekly Courier*, 1 July 1870; Branham, *Old Court House*, 34.

12. *Rome Weekly Courier*, 10 Feb. 1860, 24 Feb. 1860; *Constitution*, 3 June 1888.

13. Reuben S. Norton, Diary, 2 July and [?] July 1861, Norton Family Papers.

14. *Constitution*, 16 Sept. 1888.

15. CHS, *Uncivil War to Date*, 42–43.

16. *Constitution*, 13 July 1884, 1 Jan. 1888, 7 Oct. 1888, 2 Jan. 1887; CHS, *Farm and Fireside*, 316; Marian Smith, *I Remember*, 9; Christie, "Charles Henry Smith," 21.

17. Battey, *History of Rome*, 162. Forrest's victory is described in greater detail in chapter 4.

18. Wade Banister Gassman, "A History of Rome and Floyd County, Georgia, in the Civil War," 85 (quot.); Christie, "Charles Henry Smith," 21.

19. Reuben S. Norton, Diary, 12 June 1864, quoted in Gassman, "History of Rome," 115; Marian Smith, *I Remember*, 6, 11–12 (quot. 2, 11); *Constitution*, 16 Feb. 1879, 2 Dec. 1888, 20 Jan. 1889; "The Negro," Aubrey Scrapbook.

20. *Constitution*, 18 May 1890; Marian Smith, *I Remember*, 3–9; Christie, "Charles Henry Smith," 21–23; U.S. Congress, Senate Committee on Education and Labor, *Report of the Committee of the Senate upon the Relations between Labor and Capital, and Testimony Taken by the Committee* 4:329 (testimony of Mrs. Margaret Ketchum Ward, hereafter cited as Ward, "Testimony").

21. CHS, *Bill Arp, So Called: A Side Show of the Southern Side of the War*, 84–109; *Constitution*, 20 Jan. 1889, 13 July 1884.

22. *Constitution*, 7 October 1888; Marian Smith, *I Remember*, 9; Christie, "Charles Henry Smith," 23; David S. Freeman, "Characteristics of Maj. Chas. H. Smith, 'Bill Arp' "; Branham, *Old Court House*, 51.

23. Gassman, "History of Rome," 117–23; *Constitution*, 12 Feb. 1888; Reuben S. Norton to A. R. Smith, 13 Nov. 1864, Norton Family Papers.

24. CHS, *Bill Arp, So Called*, 124; Battey, *History of Rome*, 177, 192; Marian Smith, *I Remember*, 7, 17; Maud H. Yancey, "When *Sherman* Visited Rome"; "The Negro," Aubrey Scrapbook.

25. Marian Smith, *I Remember*, 7 (quot.), 15; *Constitution*, 20 Jan. 1889.

26. *Constitution,* 2 Jan. 1887; Marian Smith, *I Remember,* 17; *Rome Tribune,* 2 Sept. 1894, reprinted in Battey, *History of Rome,* 263.

27. *Constitution,* 14 Dec. 1884, 8 Jan. 1888, 24 Feb. 1901; CHS, *Uncivil War to Date,* 37; Marian Smith, *I Remember,* 23 (quot.).

28. *Constitution,* 20 Jan. 1889.

29. Marian Smith, *I Remember,* 23; Ward, "Testimony," 341.

30. CHS to Samuel Gibbons, 12 Jan. 1865, quoted in Aycock, *All Roads to Rome,* 121; Gassman, "History of Rome," 124–25; U.S. Congress, Joint Select Committee on Condition of Affairs in the Late Insurrectionary States, *Report of the Joint Select Committee to Inquire into the Condition of Affairs in the Late Insurrectionary States So Far as Regards the Execution of the Laws and the Safety of the Lives and Property of the Citizens of the United States and Testimony Taken* 6:74 (hereafter cited as *KKK Report*).

31. *Constitution,* 20 Jan. 1889 (quot.), 30 Nov. 1890, 2 Jan. 1887.

32. Ibid., 30 Nov. 1890 (quot. 1); A. R. Smith to Reuben S. Norton, 10 Dec. 1864, Norton Family Papers (quot. 2); Marian Smith, *I Remember,* 11; *Constitution,* 20 Jan. 1889, 5 Jan. 1902; Freeman, "Characteristics of Maj. Chas. H. Smith"; Gassman, "History of Rome," 125; CHS to Nathan Louis Hutchins, 22 Aug. 1865, CHS Papers (quot. 3).

33. Austin, *Bill Arp,* 19.

34. CHS to W. E. Mitchell, 24 Oct. 1893, Joseph Regenstein Library, University of Chicago.

35. CHS, *Scrap Book,* 7–8. CHS told this story many times with only slight variation. See the letter to W. E. Mitchell, cited in n. 34; Newsom, "Bill Arp," 62–63; CHS to Joseph D. Shields, 1 June 1877, Joseph D. Shields Papers, Louisiana and Lower Mississippi Valley Collections, LSU Libraries; Josephus Daniels, *Editor in Politics,* 205.

36. Rabun Lee Brantley, *Georgia Journalism of the Civil War Period,* 121; Gerald J. Smith, "Bill Arp: A Lincoln Correspondent," 139. Christie suggested that the first publication of this letter might have been in the Richmond *Whig:* Christie, "Charles Henry Smith," 25. This letter is described in greater detail in chapter 4.

37. Louis Turner Griffith and John Erwin Talmadge, *Georgia Journalism, 1763–1950,* 86; Christie, "Charles Henry Smith," 27; Elmo Scott Watson, *A History of Newspaper Syndicates in the United States, 1865–1935,* 13; Louella Landrum, "Charles Henry Smith (Bill Arp): Georgia Humorist," 14.

38. CHS, *Bill Arp, So Called,* 10.

39. Ibid., 6; *Constitution,* 12 April 1883.

40. Brantley, *Georgia Journalism of the Civil War Period,* 46; *Constitution,* 31 July 1892, 1 Oct. 1899.

41. *Rome Courier,* 16 Nov. 1865, quoted in Christie, "Charles Henry Smith," 45.

42. CHS, *Peace Papers,* 127–28 (quot. 1); *Constitution,* 3 Aug. 1884 (quots. 2–4), 28 March 1891; *Rome Weekly Courier,* 15 March 1867; Marian Smith, *I Remember,* 10; Battey, *History of Rome,* 242–45; Frank A. Palumbo, *George Henry Thomas, Major General, U.S.A.: The Dependable General,* 377.

43. CHS to James Cothran, 9 April 1867, Thomas C. Perrin Papers, Perkins Library, Duke University.

44. *Rome Tri-Weekly Courier,* 22 Feb. 1866.

45. Branham, *Old Court House,* 53–54.

46. Battey, *History of Rome,* 250; Aycock, *All Roads to Rome,* 474; Raymond B. Nixon, *Henry W. Grady: Spokesman of the New South,* 77–78; CHS to Joseph D. Shields, 1 June 1877, Joseph D. Shields Papers, Louisiana and Lower Mississippi Valley Collections, LSU Libraries (quot.).

47. *Rome Weekly Courier,* 28 Oct. 1870.

48. CHS, *Scrap Book,* 366; *Constitution,* 4 Nov. 1900.

49. John F. Stover, *The Railroads of the South, 1865–1900: A Study in Finance and Control,* 32, 83–85; Mark W. Summers, *Railroads, Reconstruction, and the Gospel of Prosperity: Aid under the Radical Republicans, 1865–1877,* 264.

50. The relevant issues of the *Rome Daily Courier* apparently no longer exist, but the background is given with the exchange of letters in *Rome Weekly Courier,* 14 Oct. and 28 Oct. 1870.

51. *Constitution,* 11 Jan. 1880; *Rome Weekly Courier,* 15 Oct. 1869.

52. *Rome Weekly Courier,* 18 Nov. 1870, 25 Nov. 1870 (poem), 6 June 1871. Several years before, CHS, in a Bill Arp letter, criticized Joseph E. Brown for urging Georgians to accept the Reconstruction Acts. Arp suggested that Brown, formerly the wartime governor of Georgia, changed his mind on the issue because "somebody carried him up onto a high mountain, and showed him a Kingdom or two." Ibid., 15 March 1867. Certain lines in the above poem probably refer to that letter.

53. CHS to Nathan L. Hutchins, Jr., 27 Dec. 1871, CHS Papers.

54. *KKK Report* 6:44.

55. Ibid. 6:73–74, 87.

56. Allen W. Trelease, *White Terror: The Ku Klux Klan Conspiracy and Southern Reconstruction,* 239 (quot.); Stanley F. Horn, *Invisible Empire: The*

Story of the Ku Klux Klan, 1866–1871, 179; Marian Smith, *I Remember,* 11; *Constitution,* 10 Sept. 1882.
  57. *Rome Weekly Courier,* 4 Aug. 1871.
  58. Trelease, *White Terror,* 75, 325 (quot. 1); Theodore Barker Fitz-Simons, Jr., "The Ku Klux Klan in Georgia, 1868–1871," 39.
  59. *KKK Report* 6:65.
  60. *Louisville Courier-Journal,* n.d., quoted in Mildred Lewis Rutherford, *The South in History and Literature: A Hand-Book of Southern Authors from the Settlement of Jamestown, 1607, to Living Writers,* 390–91.
  61. "Recollections of Long Ago," Aubrey Scrapbook; *Constitution,* 31 May 1896; CHS to Nathan L. Hutchins, Jr., 8 Aug. 1867, 27 Dec. 1871, 26 July 1873, CHS Papers.
  62. Branham, *Old Court House,* 52; Christie, "Charles Henry Smith," 32; *Constitution,* 15 Jan. 1888.

Three. Cartersville: 1877–1903

  1. CHS, *Uncivil War to Date,* 31 (quot. 1); CHS to Nathan L. Hutchins, Jr., 19 June 1878, CHS Papers; *Constitution,* 23 May 1878 (quot. 2), 24 Aug. 1885, 14 Feb. 1886, 1 May 1887, 9 Dec. 1888; Newsom, "Bill Arp," 60 (quot. 3).
  2. CHS, *Scrap Book,* 72–75 (quot., 73); Agricultural Schedule, Federal Census of 1880, Bartow County, Ga.; *Constitution,* 23 May 1878, 14 March 1880, 19 Sept. 1880, 24 Aug. 1885, 1 May 1887, 12 Dec. 1887, 9 Dec. 1888.
  3. *Constitution,* 20 May 1883 (quot. 1); CHS, *Farm and Fireside,* 105 (quot. 2); CHS to Nathan L. Hutchins, Jr., 19 June 1878, CHS Papers.
  4. *Constitution,* 17 May 1878.
  5. Ginther, "Alias 'Bill Arp,'" 314; Nixon, *Henry W. Grady,* 68–93, 127–29, 202 (quot. 1, 76); *Constitution,* 28 May 1878 (quots. 2, 3).
  6. *Constitution,* 28 May 1878.
  7. Ibid., 11 Dec. 1881, 22 Jan. 1882.
  8. Ibid., 27 Dec. 1891.
  9. Ibid., 22 Nov. 1885–14 Feb. 1886. The missed column was for 17 Jan. 1886. Smith wrote two extra columns during this time, however; they appeared on 14 Dec. 1885 (a Monday) and 19 Dec. 1885 (a Saturday).
  10. Christie, "Charles Henry Smith," 134.

11. Watson, *History of Newspaper Syndicates*, 13, 33–41; Frank Luther Mott, *American Journalism: A History, 1690–1960*, 479.

12. Watson, *History of Newspaper Syndicates*, 53; Thomas D. Clark, *The Southern Country Editor*, 57, 59 (quot.); Ginther, "Alias 'Bill Arp,'" 317; Christie, "Charles Henry Smith," 134. I scanned small runs of 46 N.C. newspapers held on microfilm in the North Carolina Collection of the University of North Carolina at Chapel Hill Library. For daily papers, I looked at a couple of weeks, and for weeklies, a month or so. My admittedly unscientific survey turned up Arp columns in 16 of the 46 papers.

13. *Constitution*, 26 June 1878.

14. Christie, "Charles Henry Smith," 34, 41, 202–13; *Constitution*, 16 Jan. 1887 (quot.); David B. Parker, "Bill Arp: A Homely Philosopher in the New South," 82–83.

15. *Constitution*, 28 Nov. 1880, 12 Oct. 1891, 14 Nov. 1897, 17 Dec. 1899.

16. Ibid., 4 March 1894.

17. CHS, *Uncivil War to Date*, 33–46, 47–57; CHS to Nathan L. Hutchins, Jr., 19 June 1878, CHS Papers.

18. Christie, "Charles Henry Smith," 44.

19. W. Lafayette Smith to Laura Jane Smith, 24 Feb. 1893, Laura Jane Smith Papers, Perkins Library, Duke University.

20. *Overton* (Tex.) *Press*, 27 Feb. 1986. This clipping was supplied by William Y. Harvey, great-grandson of CHS.

21. *Constitution*, 3 Oct. 1880, 22 March 1885, 19 Dec. 1886.

22. Arp's letters from Texas appeared in the *Constitution* from 15 March to 3 May 1885. Comments on the letters appeared on 18 March (quot.), 19 April, 5 May, 10 May, and 14 May.

23. *Constitution*, 14 Aug. 1892, 21 Aug. 1892.

24. Ibid., 2 Oct. 1892.

25. Ibid., 13 May 1894 (quot.), 1 April 1894.

26. Ibid., 6 Dec. 1891, 8 March 1903.

27. Ibid., 15 July 1888, 19 March 1893.

28. CHS, *A School History of Georgia: Georgia as a Colony and a State, 1733–1893*, iii.

29. *Constitution*, 23 March 1902.

30. Ibid., 10 Dec. 1882 (Mormonism), 14 Dec. 1884, 12 Feb. 1888, 9 Dec. 1889, 16 March 1890 (sectional reconciliation), 4 Jan. 1885 (race relations), 11 April 1886 (labor unions).

31. Ibid., 2 Feb. 1888, 14 Oct. 1888, 17 May 1891, 12 Sept. 1897.
32. Ibid., 30 Sept. 1900, 20 Dec. 1891.
33. Ibid., 29 March 1903, and CHS to Mrs. B. H. Hannah, 1 Oct. 1899, CHS Papers (manuscripts); *Constitution,* 20 Dec. 1891 (jobs); CHS to T. K. Oglesby, 28 July 1888, and CHS to W. B. Collins, 20 Aug. 1894, both in Charles H. Smith Papers, Perkins Library, Duke University (biographies); *Constitution,* 18 April 1897 (contests).
34. *Constitution,* 19 Nov. 1896, 26 Aug. 1894.
35. Ibid., 18 Nov. 1894.
36. Ibid., 22 March 1903; Thaddeus Kosciusko Oglesby Papers, Duke University Library (quoted letters are from Ben P. Hunt, 17 April 1903, and R. H. De Witt, 30 March 1903.)
37. Marion R. Hemperley, comp., *Cities, Towns and Communities of Georgia between 1847–1962: 8500 Places and the County in Which Located,* 7, 15. I am grateful to John H. Seanor, Fannie Mae Davis, Marvin Purcell, Dixie L. Emch, and other kind Georgians who sent information on these communities.
38. *Constitution,* 20 Feb. 1887, 21 June 1894; "From Memory's Precious Treasures," Aubrey Scrapbook; Christie, "Charles Henry Smith," 47; Freeman, "Characteristics of Maj. Chas. H. Smith"; Rutherford, *South in History and Literature,* 391.
39. *Constitution,* 19 Aug. 1900, 16 Sept. 1900, 21 Oct. 1900.
40. Ibid., 3 Feb. 1901.
41. Ibid., 28 Sept. 1884, 7 Dec. 1884, 7 Dec. 1890; Lucy Josephine Cunyus, *History of Bartow County, Formerly Cass,* 152.
42. Freeman, "Characteristics of Maj. Chas. H. Smith"; Marian Brumby Hammond, quoted in "How Bill Arp Got His Name," 16; Joseph H. Baird, "Bill Arp's Humor in the Bleak South," 19; Elaine Rolan, "Charles Henry Smith, Alias Bill Arp," 19–20; *Constitution,* 26 May 1901, 4 May 1902.
43. *Constitution,* 26 Feb. 1899, 5–11 March 1899, 19 March 1899; *Cartersville Daily Tribune,* 17 September 1975; *Louisville Home and Farm,* [n.d.], clipping in my possession, supplied by Jeff Gordon, Roopville, Ga. Information about the cake cutter came from Marilu Munford, CHS's granddaughter.
44. *Constitution,* 2 April 1893, 11 June 1893, 18 June 1893.
45. Ibid., 16 July 1899, 19 Jan. 1896, 9 Feb. 1902, 11 Jan. 1903.
46. Ibid., 15 June 1902, 22 June 1902, 27 July 1902, 28 Sept. 1902.

47. Ibid., 10 Sept. 1899, 29 Sept. 1901; Freeman, "Characteristics of Maj. Chas. H. Smith"; Marian Smith, "The Home Life of Bill Arp," 13; *Constitution*, 1 March 1903, 17 May 1903.

48. *Constitution*, 16 Aug. 1903.

49. Ibid., 22 Aug. 1903.

50. Ibid., 27 Aug. 1903; Marian Smith, "Home Life of Bill Arp," 14.

Four. War and Reconstruction

1. *Constitution*, 7 June 1891, 21 June 1891.

2. Richard Dilworth Rust, *Glory and Pathos: Responses of Nineteenth-Century American Authors to the Civil War*, 185; James Wood Davidson, *The Living Writers of the South*, 530; quoted in Mary Elizabeth Massey, *Refugee Life in the Confederacy*, 138; D. G. Tyler to [Mrs. Julia Gardiner Tyler], 14 July 1866, quoted in "Bill Arp—Humorist," 26.

3. *Mary Chesnut's Civil War*, ed. by C. Vann Woodward, 79; CHS, *Peace Papers*, 20.

4. *Mary Chesnut's Civil War*, 806; CHS, *Bill Arp, So Called*, 137 (Arp's original statement: "I ain't agoing to support nary one of 'em, and when you hear anybody say so, you tell 'em 'it's a lie,' *so-called*. I golly, I ain't got nuthin to support myself on."); *The Private Mary Chesnut: The Unpublished Civil War Diaries*, ed. by C. Vann Woodward and Elisabeth Muhlenfeld, 236–37, 85; Elisabeth Muhlenfeld, *Mary Boykin Chesnut: A Biography*, 197.

5. CHS, *Peace Papers*, 19.

6. I. W. Avery, *The History of the State of Georgia from 1850 to 1881*, 149–55 (quot. on 149); Michael P. Johnson, "A New Look at the Popular Vote for Delegates to the Georgia Secession Convention."

7. CHS, *Peace Papers*, 19.

8. Ibid., 20.

9. Ibid., 20, 21, 22.

10. Ibid., 23.

11. Ibid., 24.

12. Ibid., 31.

13. Ibid., 32, 34.

14. Ibid., 28–29.

15. Ibid., 27–28.

16. Ibid., 104–5.

17. Battey, *History of Rome*, 161; Robert Selph Henry, *"First with the Most" Forrest*, 155–57 (quot. on 157); John Allan Wyeth, *That Devil Forrest: Life of General Nathan Bedford Forrest*, 194–95.

18. CHS, *Peace Papers*, 36.

19. Ibid., 40.

20. Ibid., 65–66. Identification of the first publication of this letter (and others later in this chapter) is from Christie, "Charles Henry Smith," 215–19.

21. CHS, *Peace Papers*, 71.

22. Ibid., 72.

23. Ibid., 90.

24. CHS, *Bill Arp, So Called*, 110–11.

25. Ibid., 32.

26. CHS, *Peace Papers*, 106, 63.

27. Ibid., 78.

28. Louise Biles Hill, *Joseph E. Brown and the Confederacy*, 89; CHS, *Bill Arp, So Called*, 78; CHS, *Peace Papers*, 45.

29. CHS, *Bill Arp, So Called*, 78; CHS, *Peace Papers*, 50.

30. T. Conn Bryan, *Confederate Georgia*, 46.

31. Joseph H. Parks, *Joseph E. Brown of Georgia*, 267–72; Avery, *History of the State of Georgia*, 271; Hill, *Brown and the Confederacy*, 206; Herbert Fielder, *A Sketch of the Life and Times and Speeches of Joseph E. Brown*, 290.

32. Parks, *Joseph E. Brown*, 282–83; Avery, *History of the State of Georgia*, 270–71; Hill, *Brown and the Confederacy*, 210, 218–19.

33. The *Rome Tri-Weekly Courier* printed the piece on 26 March 1864, noting that it was copied from the *Atlanta Register*.

34. CHS, *Peace Papers*, 53.

35. Ibid., 54–55.

36. Ibid., 56, 60.

37. Ibid., 57; Richard Malcolm Johnston and William H. Browne, *The Life of Alexander H. Stephens*, 409; CHS, *Peace Papers*, 58–59.

38. CHS, *Bill Arp, So Called*, 63.

39. Ibid., 119; David B. Parker, "Bill Arp, Joe Brown, and the Confederate War Effort."

40. John Morris, "Smith, Charles Henry," 4886; CHS, *Peace Papers*, 109–10.

41. CHS, *Peace Papers*, 112–13.

42. Ibid., 115.

43. Ibid., 116–17.

44. Ibid., 119, 121.

45. Ibid., 124–25. The issue of the *Chattanooga Gazette* that carried this editorial has not been found.

46. CHS, *Bill Arp, So Called*, 11; CHS, *Peace Papers*, 110.

47. CHS, *Bill Arp, So Called*, 9–11.

48. Elisabeth Muhlenfeld, "The Civil War and Authorship," 184.

49. CHS, *Bill Arp, So Called*, 6–7.

50. Ibid., 10–11.

51. CHS, *Peace Papers*, 11–12, 14.

52. Hall, *Smiling Phoenix*, 83.

53. Alan Conway, *The Reconstruction of Georgia*, 142.

54. CHS, *Peace Papers*, 159–60. This incident is described in greater detail in chapter 2.

55. Ibid., 163, 165.

56. Ibid., 180, 181, 183.

57. Ibid., 149, 155.

58. Ibid., 127; Havilah Babcock, "Some Aspects of the Literary Influence of the Civil War," 242.

59. CHS, *Bill Arp, So Called*, 6; CHS, *Scrap Book*, 8 (quots. 2, 3); CHS, *Farm and Fireside*, 10.

60. Richard Bridgman, *The Colloquial Style in America*, 58; James C. Austin and Wayne Pike, "The Language of Bill Arp," 85; Margaret Gillis Figh, "A Word-List from 'Bill Arp' and 'Rufus Sanders,'" 3.

61. Thomas J. Cusker, "Revolt of the Titans: The Civil War Era as Seen through the Works of James R. Lowell, David R. Locke and Charles H. Smith," 51; Walter Blair, *Horse Sense in American Humor: From Benjamin Franklin to Ogden Nash*, 161.

62. Ginther, "Alias 'Bill Arp,'" 316.

Five. The New South

1. Quoted in Cunyus, *History of Bartow County*, 295.

2. *Constitution*, 17 May 1878.

3. Ibid., 27 Feb. 1898.

4. Ibid., 30 June 1901.

5. Ibid., 23 April 1882.

6. These examples are all from CHS, *Farm and Fireside.*

7. Ibid., 68–69.

8. *Constitution,* 4 April 1880, 15 June 1884, 26 Aug. 1888.

9. CHS, *Farm and Fireside,* 159–60.

10. Quoted in Rutherford, *South in History and Literature,* 392.

11. CHS, *Farm and Fireside,* 52, 140.

12. Christie, "Charles Henry Smith," 4–5. See also Margaret Gillis Figh, "Life in Nineteenth Century Georgia as Reflected in Bill Arp's Works."

13. CHS, *Farm and Fireside,* 11, 15; Shields McIlwaine, *The Southern Poor-White: From Lubberland to Tobacco Road,* 63.

14. CHS, *Farm and Fireside,* 128; Margaret Gillis Figh, "Tall Talk and Folk Sayings in Bill Arp's Works" (examples of folk sayings); CHS, *Farm and Fireside,* 238–39, 157; Margaret Gillis Figh, "Folklore in Bill Arp's Works."

15. Morris, "Smith, Charles Henry," 4886; Napier Wilt, *Some American Humorists,* 238; Hall, *Smiling Phoenix,* 20.

16. Blair and Hill, *America's Humor,* 295; Blair, *Horse Sense in American Humor,* 175, 186; Joseph Litsch, "Arp, Born at 35, Kept 'Em Laughing, Even in Dark Days," 108; William Lenz, "Charles Henry Smith," 451.

17. Christie, "Charles Henry Smith," 140, 214–37. To the best of my knowledge, Christie is the only other scholar in the last seventy-five years to attempt to read all of Arp's writings.

18. *Constitution,* 20 Jan. 1884, 27 Jan. 1884; CHS, *Scrap Book,* 295–303.

19. Paul M. Gaston, *The New South Creed: A Study in Southern Mythmaking,* 7, 54.

20. Ibid., 63–68.

21. Ibid., 71–75, 123, 127–28, 181–82.

22. Ibid., 49.

23. Nixon, *Henry W. Grady,* 241–53; Barton C. Shaw, "Henry W. Grady Heralds 'The New South.'"

24. Quoted in Joel Chandler Harris, ed., *Life of Henry W. Grady, Including His Writings and Speeches,* 204–5.

25. Jack Claiborne, *The Charlotte Observer: Its Time and Place, 1869–1986,* 82 (quot. 1); Gaston, *New South Creed,* 48–53; C. Vann Woodward, *Origins of the New South,* 144–48; Clark, *Southern Country Editor,* 29 (quot. 2).

26. Nixon, *Henry W. Grady*, 215; *Constitution*, 18 Jan. 1885, 11 March 1888, 4 Sept. 1892, 10 June 1883 (quot. 1), 25 Nov. 1894 (quot. 2).

27. *Constitution*, 27 July 1890, 11 Dec. 1881, 14 March 1880, 3 Nov. 1895.

28. Ibid., 12 Aug. 1888, 3 Dec. 1899, 7 June 1897, 2 May 1897.

29. Ibid., 31 Oct. 1886, 18 Feb. 1900. For a discussion of the New South prophets' views on the success of their programs, see Gaston, *New South Creed*, 189–98, and Arp's column in the *Constitution*, 5 May 1889.

30. *Constitution*, 30 Dec. 1883, 20 May 1888, 12 Aug. 1888.

31. Ibid., 9 Aug. 1885, 11 April 1886, 28 Aug. 1892.

32. CHS, *Leisure Hours in Florida on the West Coast Plant System: The Weal and Wonder of the Peninsula*, [i]; *Constitution*, 14 Jan. 1894, 26 May 1895; Woodward, *Origins of the New South*, 293; *National Cyclopaedia of American Biography* 18:287.

33. *Constitution*, 16 Jan. 1887, 27 March 1881, 10 July 1881, 19 June 1881, 17 July 1881.

34. Ibid., 19 Sept. 1880, 15 May 1881, 15 Aug. 1880 (quot. 1), 16 Jan. 1881 (quot. 2).

35. *Southern Cultivator* 41 (Oct. 1883): 18; ibid., 42 (Oct. 1884): 324 (quot. 1); ibid., 42 (Dec. 1884): 399, 418 (quot. 2); ibid., 42 (Jan. 1884): 11 (quot. 3).

36. Ibid., 41 (Nov. 1883): 21 (quot. 1); ibid., 42 (Nov. 1884): 358; ibid., 42 (March 1884): 94 (quot. 2).

37. Ibid., 42 (April 1884): 140; 42 (Dec. 1884): 392, 394, and cover.

38. Landrum, "Charles Henry Smith," 95.

Six. The Old South

1. Gaston, *New South Creed*, 48, 252–53 (n. 11); Wayne Mixon, *Southern Writers and the New South Movement, 1865–1913*, 6; Paul H. Buck, *The Road to Reunion, 1865–1900*, 170–74.

2. Mixon, *Southern Writers*, 8; Gaston, *New South Creed*, 160.

3. For example, *Constitution*, 16 Dec. 1883, 5 July 1885, 25 June 1899.

4. Ibid., 24 April 1887; Wilbur Fisk Tillett, "The White Man of the New South," 776.

5. *Constitution*, 3 April 1881.

6. Ibid., 5 Dec. 1897.

7. Ibid., 24 May 1885, 9 Feb. 1902, 20 June 1897. The list at the end of the paragraph was compiled from the *Constitution*, 28 Feb. 1886, 29 Aug. 1886, 12 Aug. 1900, 15 June 1902.

8. Ibid., 13 Jan. 1901, 29 May 1887.

9. Ibid., 21 Feb. 1886, 1 July 1883, 29 May 1881; CHS, *Farm and Fireside*, 121.

10. *Constitution*, 8 May 1881, 27 Jan. 1889, 20 July 1890, 5 July 1891, 12 June 1881.

11. Ibid., 12 June 1881, 3 May 1886.

12. Ibid., 9 Aug. 1896, 28 Nov. 1886, 25 March 1883, 4 Jan. 1885, 10 April 1887, 21 May 1899, 2 July 1882.

13. Ibid., 28 Sept. 1890, 10 April 1887, 26 Aug. 1888.

14. Ibid., 22 March 1889 (Webb's letter), 31 March 1889 (Arp's response).

15. Ibid., 13 Jan. 1901.

16. Ibid., 16 June 1895, 1 Oct. 1893 (quots. 2, 3).

17. Ibid., 17 Sept. 1899, 10 April 1887.

18. Ibid., 3 Nov. 1901, 21 Aug. 1881, 10 April 1887, 24 March 1901.

19. Ibid., 5 Dec. 1897, 16 June 1895, 28 July 1895, 13 Feb. 1887, 31 May 1896.

20. Donald J. Fay, "Bill Arp—Unreconstructed but Domesticated," 33; *Constitution*, 13 Jan. 1901, 10 Aug. 1884.

21. *Constitution*, 10 June 1886, 26 Sept. 1886, 7 Sept. 1890.

22. Ibid., 10 April 1887, 1 April 1888, 26 Aug. 1888, 5 Oct. 1902.

23. Ibid., 29 Oct. 1893, 13 Jan. 1901, 6 Dec. 1896.

24. Fay, "Bill Arp," 33; *Constitution*, 25 Sept. 1881, 22 Aug. 1886, 1 Oct. 1893.

25. *Constitution*, 12 March 1893, 1 July 1894 (quot. 2 and last two).

26. Ibid., 15 Feb. 1885, 29 June 1890, 19 Aug. 1883; *Southern Cultivator* 42 (Feb. 1884): 54.

27. *Constitution*, 28 March 1880, 1 June 1890, 31 March 1901, 25 June 1885, 12 May 1889, 19 Feb. 1893.

28. Ibid., 3 Dec. 1882; CHS, *Farm and Fireside*, 137.

29. *Constitution*, 9 June 1878, 20 May 1883, 11 Sept. 1892, 15 July 1883.

30. Ibid., 20 July 1884, 15 April 1888, 5 Feb. 1882, 4 Feb. 1900.

31. Ibid., 5 March 1886, 7 Sept. 1884, 27 Dec. 1891.

32. Ibid., 23 Sept. 1894; Bruce Palmer, *"Man over Money": The Southern*

Populist Critique of American Capitalism. See Ellis Merton Coulter, *Georgia: A Short History*, 385–88, for a discussion of Georgia's independent political movements of the late 1870s. For examples of Arp's criticisms of these movements, see his columns on the race for Georgia's 7th congressional district, *Constitution*, 7 July–10 Nov. 1878.

33. Fred Hobson, *Tell About the South: The Southern Rage to Explain*, 11.

34. *Constitution*, 5 Aug. 1888.

35. Ibid., 10 Jan. 1897, 17 May 1903.

36. Ibid., 19 Oct. 1879. A few scholars have offered limited statements on this theme; see, for example, Hall, *Smiling Phoenix*, 316, and Fay, "Bill Arp," 33–34.

Seven. The Negro and Race Relations

1. Christie, "Charles Henry Smith," 67, 72; Marian Smith, *I Remember*, 5.

2. CHS, *Scrap Book*, 313. This extract is from an essay, here titled "The Negro," that first appeared in the *Constitution*, 27 July 1883.

3. *Constitution*, 22 Oct. 1882, 10 Feb. 1889; CHS, *Scrap Book*, 322.

4. CHS, *Peace Papers*, 113.

5. *Constitution*, 29 Sept. 1878; CHS, *Scrap Book*, 154; *Constitution*, 9 April 1882, 8 Oct. 1885.

6. *Constitution*, 12 May 1901; CHS, *Scrap Book*, 312–13.

7. *Constitution*, 7 March 1880, 22 Oct. 1882; *Southern Cultivator* 41 (Dec. 1883): 15; *Constitution*, 13 Aug. 1889.

8. *Constitution*, 19 March 1882, 17 June 1888, 21 Oct. 1883, 28 Oct. 1888.

9. Definitions are from *Webster's New Collegiate Dictionary* (1975).

10. *Constitution*, 23 July 1882.

11. Ibid., 7 Nov. 1880, 21 Oct. 1883, 27 Oct. 1901.

12. Ibid., 7 Aug. 1887, 2 March 1890, 23 July 1893.

13. Ibid., 13 Aug. 1889, 19 March 1882, 14 Dec. 1885.

14. Ibid., 30 August 1885, 12 Jan. 1890, 27 Oct. 1901, 26 Sept. 1886, 4 Jan. 1885, 9 May 1886.

15. Ibid., 19 March 1882, 30 April 1882, 25 Nov. 1883, 12 Jan. 1890, 2 July 1899, 12 May 1901.

16. Ibid., 1 Dec. 1901, 7 Oct. 1888.

17. Ibid., 7 Oct. 1888, 7 Oct. 1883, 8 Feb. 1891 (Tip), 17 Oct. 1886 (Mims), 4 June 1899 (Heyward), 6 Aug. 1882 (Richardson), 25 Aug. 1889 (Hutchins), 3 Sept. 1899 (Sam); *Southern Cultivator* 41 (Dec. 1883): 15 (Carter); *Constitution*, 27 Nov. 1881 (Bell), 20 Aug. 1899 (Jordan); *Southern Cultivator* 41 (Dec. 1883): 15.

18. *Constitution*, 9 Dec. 1900.

19. Ibid., 4 Oct. 1891.

20. CHS, *Scrap Book*, 313; *Constitution*, 4 Jan. 1885, 16 May 1886; CHS, *Scrap Book*, 154; *Constitution*, 25 June 1899, 7 Nov. 1886, 1 July 1894.

21. *Constitution*, 3 March 1889, 21 May 1899.

22. Ibid., 4 Dec. 1898, 5 Dec. 1886, 27 Aug. 1899, 30 April 1882.

23. Ibid., 12 Aug. 1900, 28 April 1890, 20 May 1900.

24. Ibid., 6 Oct. 1889, 22 Oct. 1882; CHS, *Peace Papers*, 183; *Constitution*, 6 May 1883.

25. *Constitution*, 1 Aug. 1897, 6 May 1883, 1 Oct. 1882, 6 Aug. 1882, 20 Aug. 1899, 14 Jan. 1900.

26. Ibid., 1 Dec. 1901, 6 Aug. 1899, 3 March 1901, 22 Feb. 1903, 27 Oct. 1901.

27. Ibid., 1 Dec. 1901, 21 July 1885, 28 Aug. 1887, 22 Feb. 1903, 22 Jan. 1882. This was also the topic of CHS, "Have American Negroes Too Much Liberty?"

28. *Constitution*, 30 Sept. 1900.

29. Ibid., 5 Dec. 1886, 28 April 1890, 25 Jan. 1891, 14 Aug. 1892, 16 July 1893, 6 Aug. 1893.

30. Ibid., 6 May 1883, 20 Sept. 1885.

31. Ibid., 20 Sept. 1885, 16 March 1890.

32. Ibid., 8 June 1893, 16 July 1893, 30 April 1899, 1 Aug. 1897, 16 July 1893, 23 July 1893, 1 Aug. 1897.

33. Ibid., 18 May 1902, 4 Oct. 1891, 12 Aug. 1900. Carroll's *The Negro a Beast, or In the Image of God* (1900) argued that blacks, a separate creation of God, were the highest order of apes rather than a race of Homo sapiens.

34. *Constitution*, 15 Jan. 1899, 27 Aug. 1899, 20 May 1900, 7 July 1901.

35. Ibid., 12 Nov. 1893, 4 July 1897, 20 May 1900, 5 May 1901, 1 Dec. 1901, 9 Nov. 1902.

36. National Association for the Advancement of Colored People, *Thirty Years of Lynching in the United States, 1889–1918*, 29, 31–32. These figures are considered fairly reliable, but other sources differ slightly. See, for ex-

ample, James Elbert Cutler, *Lynch-Law: An Investigation into the History of Lynching in the United States*, 155–92.

37. Some of the major works in this field include C. Vann Woodward, *Origins of the New South* and *The Strange Career of Jim Crow;* J. Morgan Kousser, *The Shaping of Southern Politics: Suffrage Restrictions and the Establishment of the One-Party South, 1880–1910;* Howard N. Rabinowitz, *Race Relations in the Urban South, 1865–1890;* John W. Cell, *The Highest Stage of White Supremacy: The Origins of Segregation in South Africa and the American South;* David Herbert Donald, "A Generation of Defeat"; Joel Williamson, *The Crucible of Race: Black-White Relations in the American South since Emancipation;* George M. Fredrickson, *The Black Image in the White Mind: The Debate on Afro-American Character and Destiny, 1817–1914;* and Edward L. Ayers, *Vengeance and Justice: Crime and Punishment in the 19th-Century American South.*

38. Fredrickson, *Black Image in the White Mind,* 273; Austin, *Bill Arp,* 43; Christie, "Charles Henry Smith," 70; Landrum, "Charles Henry Smith," 97.

Eight. The North and Sectional Reconciliation

1. Quoted in Nixon, *Henry W. Grady,* 344. The Arp quotation appeared, in a slightly different form, in CHS, *Scrap Book,* 378.

2. *Constitution,* 15 Sept. 1878, 9 June 1889.

3. Ibid., 23 Feb. 1879, 17 Aug. 1890, 13 Nov. 1892, 17 Nov. 1895, 24 Nov. 1895, 3 May 1896.

4. CHS to Ben W. Austin, 22 March 1886, Historical Society of Pennsylvania.

5. *Constitution,* 30 Nov. 1879.

6. Ibid., 11 Feb. 1879, 16 Feb. 1879.

7. Ibid., 16 Feb. 1879, 12 June 1881, 16 Sept. 1888.

8. Ibid., 18 May 1890, 5 June 1892.

9. Ibid., 9 Aug. 1903.

10. Austin, *Bill Arp,* 24; *Constitution,* 22 Jan. 1882.

11. *Constitution,* 30 Nov. 1879, 7 Aug. 1898, 29 Feb. 1880, 12 Feb. 1888.

12. Ibid., 27 Oct. 1878, 17 Aug. 1884.

13. Ibid., 12 June 1887, 1 Feb. 1903.

14. Ibid., 9 Feb. 1890, 23 May 1897, 1 Feb. 1903, 23 May 1897, 26 Sept. 1897, 5 April 1903.

15. Ibid., 13 July 1890, 17 Aug. 1890.

16. Ibid., 16 Dec. 1883, 28 April 1890.

17. Ibid., 14 Oct. 1894, 26 June 1887, 15 Jan. 1888.

18. Ibid., 30 Nov. 1879, 1 Jan. 1899, 5 May 1901, 23 May 1897.

19. Ibid., 26 Oct. 1884, 18 April 1886, 27 July 1890, 26 Feb. 1899, 28 May 1899.

20. Ibid., 22 Aug. 1897, 10 Nov. 1889, 15 March 1903, 10 June 1894, 3 Nov. 1901, 15 March 1903.

21. Ibid., 17 May 1891 (Oglesby), 18 June 1899 (Greg and Grady), 6 Aug. 1893 (McKinley), 12 Aug. 1894 (Rutherford), 28 April 1901 (Cussons), 9 Sept. 1888 and 17 May 1891 (Appleton).

22. Ibid., 26 April 1891, 18 Nov. 1900, 29 Nov. 1891, 13 Feb. 1898, 12 July 1891.

23. Ibid., 19 March 1893; CHS, *History of Georgia*, 90, 92–93.

24. CHS, *History of Georgia*, 117–35 (quots. on 125, 130, 121); CHS to Mrs. B. H. Hanna, 1 Oct. 1899, CHS Papers.

25. *Constitution*, 24 April 1887, 10 June 1894, 19 March 1882, 29 Nov. 1891, 12 Oct. 1902.

26. *Constitution*, 28 Sept. 1902, 12 Oct. 1902, 25 Jan. 1903, 23 Aug. 1885 (Davis), 16 July 1899 (Andersonville), 10 Feb. 1895 (Grant), 20 July 1902 (Hart).

27. Ibid., 29 May 1892, 21 Oct. 1883, 18 May 1880.

28. Ibid., 1 Jan. 1899, 27 May 1900.

29. Ibid., 17 May 1891, 10 June 1894, 30 Sept. 1900, 21 Oct. 1900.

30. Ibid., 29 April 1900, 20 May 1900.

31. Ibid., 14 Oct. 1883, 28 Nov. 1886, 22 Aug. 1897.

32. Ibid., 3 March 1889, 28 May 1899, 18 June 1899, 12 June 1892.

33. Ibid., 12 Nov. 1893, 28 May 1899.

34. Buck, *Road to Reunion*, 298; *Constitution*, 29 Sept. 1901.

35. Christie, "Charles Henry Smith," 200; Hall, *Smiling Phoenix*, 126.

36. Landrum, "Charles Henry Smith," 106; Jay B. Hubbell, *The South in American Literature, 1607–1900*, 686; Paul Richard Hilty, Jr., "Nasby vs. Arp: Yankee vs. Rebel Satire in the Civil War," 89, 105; Jennette Tandy, *Crackerbox Philosophers in American Humor and Satire*, 116; Lenz, "Charles Henry Smith," 451; Blair, *Horse Sense in American Humor*, 186. Jack K. Wil-

liams, in "Three Georgians on Sectional Reconciliation," discussed Arp's writings only through Reconstruction.

37. George H. Aubrey, "Charles Henry Smith (Bill Arp)," 393. Aubrey married Harriet Smith, CHS's daughter.

38. *Constitution*, 3 March 1889.

39. Ibid., 26 June 1887, 7 Dec. 1890, 12 June 1892, 2 June 1901.

Nine. The Meaning of Bill Arp

1. *Constitution*, 23 Dec. 1985, 8 Jan. 1986, 31 Jan. 1986.

2. A copy of the program for Brown's presentation, "Bill Arp, the Georgia Philosopher, Lectures on Bill Arp, the UnCivil War, Politics, Bill Tell, and the Farm and the Fireside," is at the Carnegie Library in Rome, Ga.

3. Figh, "Life in Nineteenth Century Georgia," 22; "F. C. S.," Preface, in CHS, *Bill Arp's Peace Papers*, American Humorist Series, vol. 24 (Upper Saddle River, N.J.: Literature House/Gregg Press, 1969), [vi]; Aubrey, "Charles Henry Smith," 396 (others repeat this quotation with minor variations).

4. *Home Monthly* 1 (Aug. 1866): 96, quoted in Ray Morris Atchison, "Southern Literary Magazines, 1865–1887," 336.

5. Thomas D. Clark, *The Rural Press and the New South*, 33.

6. *Constitution*, 12 Aug. 1900; Philip Alexander Bruce, *The Rise of the New South;* Holland Thompson, *The New South: A Chronicle of Social and Industrial Evolution;* Cash, *Mind of the South*, x, 105.

7. Cash, *Mind of the South*, 209; Woodward, *Origins of the New South*, 20–22.

8. Harold D. Woodman, "Sequel to Slavery: The New History Views the Postbellum South," 554; James Tice Moore, "Redeemers Reconsidered: Change and Continuity in the Democratic South, 1870–1900," 367; C. Vann Woodward, *Thinking Back: The Perils of Writing History*, 59–79.

9. This paragraph relies heavily on Gaines M. Foster, *Ghosts of the Confederacy: Defeat, the Lost Cause, and the Emergence of the New South, 1865–1913*, 79–80.

10. Ibid., 80.

11. Ibid., 87.

12. *Constitution*, 11 Aug. 1901.

13. Rollin G. Osterweis, *The Myth of the Lost Cause, 1865–1900*, 8; Gaston, *New South Creed*, 160, 167, 165 (Grady quot.).

14. Francis Pendleton Gaines, *The Southern Plantation: A Study in the Development and the Accuracy of a Tradition*, 4 (quot. 1), 63, 74 (quot. 2); Alfred Y. Wolff, Jr., "The South and the American Imagination: Mythical Views of the Old South, 1865–1900," 218.

15. Daniel Joseph Singal, *The War Within: From Victorian to Modernist Thought in the South, 1919–1945*, 5, 8–9, 29 (quots. 3, 4), 30.

16. Charles Reagan Wilson, *Baptized in Blood: The Religion of the Lost Cause, 1865–1920*, 11; Lloyd Arthur Hunter, "The Sacred South: Postwar Confederates and the Sacralization of Southern Culture."

17. Timothy Curtis Jacobson, "Tradition and Change in the New South, 1865–1910," xiii.

18. R. L. "Trot" Foreman II, "Early Days of the Atlanta Constitution," typescript (n.d.) in Rosalie Howell Collection, Mss 119, Box 5, Folder 3, Atlanta Historical Society. Sam Small, an Atlanta journalist, was associated with the *Constitution* from time to time between 1869 and 1932.

19. Clark, *Southern Country Editor*, 1 (quot. 1); Clark, *Rural Press and the New South*, 32.

20. Clark, *Rural Press and the New South*, 32 (quots. 1, 2); Clark, *Southern Country Editor*, 58.

21. *Constitution*, 29 April 1900.

Bibliography

Manuscripts

The largest collection of Charles Henry Smith's papers is at McCain Library, Agnes Scott College, but a few useful materials turned up at Perkins Library, Duke University; Woodruff Library, Emory University; the Georgia Historical Society; Hill Memorial Library, Louisiana State University; Joseph Regenstein Library, University of Chicago; the Pennsylvania Historical Society; the Atlanta Historical Society; and the Georgia Department of Archives and History. In addition, several of Smith's descendants allowed me to see items in their possession; especially helpful were a typescript of the Norton Family Papers, provided by W. T. Maddox, and Harriet Smith Aubrey's scrapbook, provided by Marian Granger Stout.

Published Works by Charles Henry Smith

Bill Arp, So Called: A Side Show of the Southern Side of the War. New York: Metropolitan Record Office, 1866.

Bill Arp's Peace Papers. New York: Carleton, 1873.

Bill Arp's Scrap Book: Humor and Philosophy. Atlanta: J. P. Harrison, 1884.

The Farm and the Fireside: Sketches of Domestic Life in War and in Peace. Atlanta: Constitution Publishing Co., 1891.

Introduction to *The Wanderer Case: The Speech of the Hon. Henry R. Jackson . . . Speech of Daniel Webster at Capon Springs, Virginia, June, 1851.* Atlanta: E. Holland, [1891?].

A School History of Georgia: Georgia as a Colony and a State, 1733–1893. Boston: Ginn, 1893.

Bibliography

"Have American Negroes Too Much Liberty?" *Forum* 16 (Oct. 1893): 176–83.

Leisure Hours in Florida on the West Coast Plant System: The Weal and Wonder of the Peninsula. N.p., [1895?].

"Caroline Ann Smith." In *The Mothers of Some Distinguished Georgians of the Last Half Century,* compiled by Sarah Harriet Butts, 31–33. New York: J. J. Little, 1902.

Bill Arp: From the Uncivil War to Date, 1861–1903. Atlanta: Byrd, 1903.

Bill Arp: From the Uncivil War to Date, 1861–1903. Memorial Edition. Atlanta: Byrd, 1903.

Newspapers and Periodicals

Atlanta Constitution, 1878–1903
Rome (Ga.) *Courier,* 1860–1872
Southern Cultivator, 1882–1886

Government Documents

Federal Census. Population Schedule, 1850, Gwinnett County, Ga.; 1860–1870, Floyd County, Ga.; 1880, Bartow County, Ga. Agriculture Schedule, 1880, Bartow County, Ga. Slave Schedule, 1830–1860, Gwinnett County, Ga.; 1860, Floyd County, Ga.

United States. Congress. Joint Select Committee on the Condition of Affairs in the Late Insurrectionary States. *Report of the Joint Select Committee to Inquire into the Condition of Affairs in the Late Insurrectionary States So Far as Regards the Execution of the Laws and the Safety of the Lives and Property of the Citizens of the United States and Testimony Taken.* 13 vols. H. Rept. 22, 42nd Congress, 2nd sess., 1871.

United States. Congress. Senate. Committee on Education and Labor. *Report of the Committee of the Senate upon the Relations between Labor and Capital, and Testimony Taken by the Committee.* Senate Rept. 1262, 48th Cong., 2nd sess., 1884.

Bibliography

Books

Austin, James C. *Artemus Ward*. Twayne's United States Authors Series, no. 51. New York: Twayne, 1964.

————. *Bill Arp*. Twayne's United States Authors Series, no. 162. New York: Twayne, 1969.

Avery, I. W. *The History of the State of Georgia from 1850 to 1881*. New York: Brown & Derby, 1881.

Aycock, Roger. *All Roads to Rome*. 2nd ed. Roswell, Ga.: Rome Area Heritage Foundation, 1982.

Ayers, Edward L. *Vengeance and Justice: Crime and Punishment in the 19th-Century American South*. New York: Oxford University Press, 1984.

Battey, George Magruder, Jr. *A History of Rome and Floyd County, State of Georgia, United States of America: Including Numerous Incidents of More Than Local Interest, 1540–1922*. Atlanta: Webb and Vary, 1922.

Bier, Jesse. *The Rise and Fall of American Humor*. New York: Holt, Rinehart and Winston, 1968.

Blair, Walter. *Horse Sense in American Humor: From Benjamin Franklin to Ogden Nash*. Chicago: University of Chicago Press, 1942.

————. *Native American Humor, 1800–1900*. New York: American Book Company, 1937.

Blair, Walter, and Hamlin Hill. *America's Humor: From Poor Richard to Doonesbury*. New York: Oxford University Press, 1978.

Blair, Walter, and Raven I. McDavid, Jr., eds. *The Mirth of a Nation: America's Great Dialect Humor*. Minneapolis: University of Minnesota Press, 1983.

Branham, Joel. *The Old Court House in Rome*. Atlanta: Index Printing Co., 1921.

Brantley, Rabun Lee. *Georgia Journalism of the Civil War Period*. Contributions to Education, no. 58. Nashville: George Peabody College for Teachers, 1929.

Bridgman, Richard. *The Colloquial Style in America*. New York: Oxford University Press, 1966.

Browne, Charles Farrar. *Artemus Ward, His Book*. New York: Carleton, 1862.

Bruce, Philip Alexander. *The Rise of the New South*. The History of North America, vol. 17. Philadelphia: G. Barrie, 1905.

Bryan, T. Conn. *Confederate Georgia*. Athens: University of Georgia Press, 1953.

Bibliography

Buck, Paul H. *The Road to Reunion, 1865–1900*. Boston: Little, Brown, 1937.

Cash, W. J. *The Mind of the South*. New York: Knopf, 1941; reprint ed., New York: Random House, Vintage Books, 1969.

Cell, John W. *The Highest Stage of White Supremacy: The Origins of Segregation in South Africa and the American South*. Cambridge: Cambridge University Press, 1982.

Chesnut, Mary Boykin. *Mary Chesnut's Civil War*. Edited by C. Vann Woodward. New Haven: Yale University Press, 1981.

———. *The Private Mary Chesnut: The Unpublished Civil War Diaries*. Edited by C. Vann Woodward and Elisabeth Muhlenfeld. New York: Oxford University Press, 1984.

Claiborne, Jack. *The Charlotte Observer: Its Time and Place, 1869–1986*. Chapel Hill: University of North Carolina Press, 1986.

Clark, Thomas D. *The Rural Press and the New South*. Baton Rouge: Louisiana State University Press, 1948; reprint ed., New York: Greenwood, 1970.

———. *The Southern Country Editor*. Indianapolis: Bobbs-Merrill, 1948.

Clemens, Samuel L. *Mark Twain's Notebooks and Journals*. 3 vols. Edited by Frederick Anderson, Lin Salamo, and Bernard L. Stein. Berkeley: University of California Press, 1975.

Conway, Alan. *The Reconstruction of Georgia*. Minneapolis: University of Minnesota Press, 1966.

Coulter, Ellis Merton. *Georgia: A Short History*. Revised Edition. Chapel Hill: University of North Carolina Press, 1947.

Cunyus, Lucy Josephine. *The History of Bartow County, Formerly Cass*. Cartersville, Ga.: Tribune, 1933.

Cutler, James Elbert. *Lynch-Law: An Investigation into the History of Lynching in the United States*. London: Longmans, Green, and Co., 1905.

Daniels, Josephus. *Editor in Politics*. Chapel Hill: University of North Carolina Press, 1941.

———. *Tar Heel Editor*. Chapel Hill: University of North Carolina Press, 1939.

Davidson, James Wood. *The Living Writers of the South*. New York: Carleton, 1869.

Fielder, Herbert. *A Sketch of the Life and Times and Speeches of Joseph E. Brown*. Springfield, Mass.: Springfield Publishing Co., 1883.

Bibliography

Flanders, Bertram Holland. *Early Georgia Magazines: Literary Periodicals to 1865.* Athens: University of Georgia Press, 1944.

Flanigan, James C. *History of Gwinnett County, Georgia, 1818–1843.* 2 vols. Hapeville, Ga.: Tyler, 1943, 1959 [vol. 2, reprint ed., Lawrenceville, Ga.: Gwinnett Historical Society, 1984].

Foster, Gaines M. *Ghosts of the Confederacy: Defeat, the Lost Cause, and the Emergence of the New South, 1865–1913.* New York: Oxford University Press, 1987.

Fredrickson, George M. *The Black Image in the White Mind: The Debate on Afro-American Character and Destiny, 1817–1914.* New York: Harper & Row, 1971.

Gaines, Francis Pendleton. *The Southern Plantation: A Study in the Development and the Accuracy of a Tradition.* New York: Columbia University Press, 1925.

Gaston, Paul M. *The New South Creed: A Study in Southern Mythmaking.* New York: Knopf, 1970.

Gribben, Alan. *Mark Twain's Library: A Reconstruction.* 2 vols. Boston: G. K. Hall, 1980.

Griffith, Louis Turner, and John Erwin Talmadge. *Georgia Journalism, 1763–1950.* Athens: University of Georgia Press, 1951.

Hall, Wade. *The Smiling Phoenix: Southern Humor from 1865 to 1914.* Gainesville: University of Florida Press, 1965.

Harris, Joel Chandler, ed. *Life of Henry W. Grady, Including His Writings and Speeches.* New York: Cassell, 1890.

Harrison, John M. *The Man Who Made Nasby, David Ross Locke.* Chapel Hill: University of North Carolina Press, 1969.

Hemperley, Marion R., comp. *Cities, Towns and Communities of Georgia between 1847–1962: 8500 Places and the County in Which Located.* Easley, S.C.: Southern Historical Press, 1980.

Henry, Robert Selph. *"First with the Most" Forrest.* Indianapolis: Bobbs-Merrill, 1944.

Hill, Louise Biles. *Joseph E. Brown and the Confederacy.* Chapel Hill: University of North Carolina Press, 1939.

Hobson, Fred. *Tell About the South: The Southern Rage to Explain.* Baton Rouge: Louisiana State University Press, 1983.

Horn, Stanley F. *Invisible Empire: The Story of the Ku Klux Klan, 1866–1871.* Boston: Houghton Mifflin, 1939.

Hubbell, Jay B. *The South in American Literature, 1607–1900.* Durham: Duke University Press, 1954.

Johnston, Richard Malcolm, and William H. Browne. *The Life of Alexander H. Stephens.* Philadelphia: J. B. Lippincott, 1878.

Kesterson, David B. *Josh Billings (Henry Wheeler Shaw).* Twayne's United States Authors Series, no. 229. New York: Twayne, 1973.

Kousser, J. Morgan. *The Shaping of Southern Politics: Suffrage Restrictions and the Establishment of the One-Party South, 1880–1910.* New Haven: Yale University Press, 1974.

Locke, David Ross. *Divers Views, Opinions, and Prophesies.* 6th ed. Cincinnati: Carroll, 1867.

Lynn, Kenneth S. *Mark Twain and Southwestern Humor.* Boston: Little, Brown, 1960.

McCabe, Alice Smythe, ed. *Gwinnett County, Georgia, Families, 1818–1968.* Atlanta: Cherokee Publishing Co., 1980.

McIlwaine, Shields. *The Southern Poor-White: From Lubberland to Tobacco Road.* Norman: University of Oklahoma Press, 1939.

Mark Twain's Library of Humor. New York: Charles L. Webster, 1888.

Massey, Mary Elizabeth. *Refugee Life in the Confederacy.* Baton Rouge: Louisiana State University Press, 1964.

Mixon, Wayne. *Southern Writers and the New South Movement, 1865–1913.* James Sprunt Studies in History and Political Science, vol. 57. Chapel Hill: University of North Carolina Press, 1980.

Mott, Frank Luther. *American Journalism: A History, 1690–1960.* 3rd ed. New York: Macmillan Co., 1962.

Muhlenfeld, Elisabeth. *Mary Boykin Chesnut: A Biography.* Baton Rouge: Louisiana State University Press, 1981.

National Association for the Advancement of Colored People. *Thirty Years of Lynching in the United States, 1889–1918.* New York: NAACP, 1919.

Nixon, Raymond B. *Henry W. Grady: Spokesman of the New South.* New York: Knopf, 1943.

Osterweis, Rollin G. *The Myth of the Lost Cause, 1865–1900.* Hamden, Conn.: Archon Books, 1973.

Owsley, Frank L. *Plain Folk of the Old South.* Baton Rouge: Louisiana State University Press, 1949.

Palmer, Bruce. *"Man over Money": The Southern Populist Critique of American Capitalism.* Chapel Hill: University of North Carolina Press, 1980.

Palumbo, Frank A. *George Henry Thomas, Major General, U.S.A.: The Dependable General.* Dayton, Ohio: Morningside House, 1983.

Parks, Joseph H. *Joseph E. Brown of Georgia.* Baton Rouge: Louisiana State University Press, 1977.

Pullen, John J. *Comic Relief: The Life and Laughter of Artemus Ward, 1834–1867.* Hamden, Conn.: Archon Books, 1983.

Rabinowitz, Howard N. *Race Relations in the Urban South, 1865–1890.* New York: Oxford University Press, 1978.

Rubin, Louis D., Jr. *A Gallery of Southerners.* Baton Rouge: Louisiana State University Press, 1982.

Rust, Richard Dilworth. *Glory and Pathos: Responses of Nineteenth-Century American Authors to the Civil War.* Boston: Holbrook Press, 1970.

Rutherford, Mildred Lewis. *The South in History and Literature: A Hand-Book of Southern Authors from the Settlement of Jamestown, 1607, to Living Writers.* Atlanta: Franklin-Turner, 1906.

Shaw, Henry Wheeler. *Josh Billings, Hiz Sayings.* New York: Carleton, 1868.

Sibley, Celestine. *Day by Day with Celestine Sibley.* New York: Doubleday, 1975.

Singal, Daniel Joseph. *The War Within: From Victorian to Modernist Thought in the South, 1919–1945.* Fred W. Morrison Series in Southern Studies. Chapel Hill: University of North Carolina Press, 1982.

Sloane, David E. E. *Mark Twain as a Literary Comedian.* Baton Rouge: Louisiana State University Press, 1979.

Smith, Marian. *I Remember.* Jacksonville, Fla.: Ambrose Printing Co., 1931.

Stover, John F. *The Railroads of the South, 1865–1900: A Study in Finance and Control.* Chapel Hill: University of North Carolina Press, 1955.

Summers, Mark W. *Railroads, Reconstruction, and the Gospel of Prosperity: Aid under the Radical Republicans, 1865–1877.* Princeton: Princeton University Press, 1984.

Tandy, Jennette. *Crackerbox Philosophers in American Humor and Satire.* New York: Columbia University Press, 1925.

Taylor, William R. *Cavalier and Yankee: The Old South and American National Character.* New York: Harper & Row, 1961.

Thompson, Holland. *The New South: A Chronicle of Social and Industrial Evolution.* The Chronicles of America, vol. 42. New Haven: Yale University Press, 1919.

Trelease, Allen W. *White Terror: The Ku Klux Klan Conspiracy and Southern Reconstruction.* New York: Harper & Row, 1971.

Bibliography

Watson, Elmo Scott. *A History of Newspaper Syndicates in the United States, 1865–1935*. Chicago: n.p., 1936.

Williamson, Joel. *The Crucible of Race: Black-White Relations in the American South since Emancipation*. New York: Oxford University Press, 1984.

Wilson, Charles Reagan. *Baptized in Blood: The Religion of the Lost Cause, 1865–1920*. Athens: University of Georgia Press, 1980.

Wilt, Napier. *Some American Humorists*. New York: Nelson, 1929.

Woodward, C. Vann. *Origins of the New South*. A History of the South, vol. 9. Baton Rouge: Louisiana State University Press, 1951.

———. *The Strange Career of Jim Crow*. 3rd ed. New York: Oxford University Press, 1974.

———. *Thinking Back: The Perils of Writing History*. Baton Rouge: Louisiana State University Press, 1986.

Wyatt-Brown, Bertram. *Southern Honor: Ethics and Behavior in the Old South*. New York: Oxford University Press, 1982.

Wyeth, John Allan. *That Devil Forrest: Life of General Nathan Bedford Forrest*. New York: Harper & Row, 1959.

Zall, P. M., ed. *Abe Lincoln Laughing: Humorous Anecdotes from Original Sources by and about Abraham Lincoln*. Berkeley: University of California Press, 1982.

Articles

Aubrey, George H. "Charles Henry Smith (Bill Arp)." In *Men of Mark in Georgia*, edited by William J. Northen, 3:393–96. Atlanta: Caldwell, 1911.

Austin, James C., and Pike, Wayne. "The Language of Bill Arp." *American Speech* 48 (1973): 84–97.

Baird, Joseph H. "Bill Arp's Humor in the Bleak South." *Atlanta Journal and Constitution Magazine* (18 Oct. 1970): 18–21, 37–39.

" 'Bill Arp'—Humorist." *Tyler's Quarterly Historical and Genealogical Magazine* 31 (1949): 25–33.

Cohen, Sandy. "American Humor: A Historical Survey: South and Southwest." In *American Humorists*, edited by Stanley Trachtenberg, 2:597–603. Detroit: Gale, 1982.

Christie, Anne M. "Civil War Humor: Bill Arp." *Civil War History* 11 (Sept. 1956): 103–19.

Cooper, Cornelia E. "Bill Arp, the Cherokee Philosopher." *Georgia Magazine* 8 (April–May 1965): 12–15.

Donald, David Herbert. "A Generation of Defeat." In *From the Old South to the New: Essays on the Transitional South,* edited by Walter J. Fraser, Jr., and Winfred B. Moore, Jr., 3–20. Westport, Conn.: Greenwood Press, 1981.

Dutcher, Salem. "Bill Arp and Artemus Ward." *Scott's Monthly Magazine* 2 (June 1866): 472–78.

Eidson, John O. "Smith, Charles Henry." In *Dictionary of Georgia Biography,* edited by Kenneth Coleman and Charles Stephen Gurr, 894–96. Athens: University of Georgia Press, 1983.

Fay, Donald J. "Bill Arp—Unreconstructed but Domesticated." *Proceedings and Papers of the Georgia Association of Historians* 5 (1984): 24–36.

Figh, Margaret Gillis. "Folklore in Bill Arp's Works." *Southern Folklore Quarterly* 12 (1948): 169–75.

———. "Life in Nineteenth Century Georgia as Reflected in Bill Arp's Works." *Georgia Historical Quarterly* 35 (1951): 16–22.

———. "Tall Talk and Folk Sayings in Bill Arp's Works." *Southern Folklore Quarterly* 13 (1949): 206–12.

———. "A Word-List from 'Bill Arp' and 'Rufus Sanders.' " *Publication of the American Dialect Society* 13 (1950): 3–15.

Freeman, David S. "Characteristics of Maj. Chas. H. Smith, 'Bill Arp.' " *Atlanta Constitution,* 29 March 1903.

Ginther, James E. "Charles Henry Smith, Alias 'Bill Arp.' " *Georgia Review* 4 (1950): 312–22.

———. "Charles Henry Smith, the Creator of Bill Arp." *Mark Twain Journal* 10 (Summer 1955): 11–12, 23–24.

"How Bill Arp Got His Name." *Atlanta Journal Magazine* (10 Jan. 1932): 12, 16.

Kesterson, David B. "The Literary Comedians and the Language of Humor." *Studies in American Humor,* n.s. 1 (1982): 44–51.

———. "Those *Literary* Comedians." In *Critical Essays on American Humor,* Critical Essays on American Literature, edited by William Bedford Clark and W. Craig Turner, 167–83. Boston: G. K. Hall, 1984.

Johnson, Michael P. "A New Look at the Popular Vote for Delegates to the Georgia Secession Convention." *Georgia Historical Quarterly* 56 (1972): 259–75.

Lenz, William. "Charles Henry Smith." In *American Humorists,* edited by Stanley Trachtenberg, 2:447–52. Detroit: Gale, 1982.

Litsch, Joseph. "Arp, Born at 35, Kept 'Em Laughing, Even in Dark Days." *Atlanta* 14 (March 1975): 108, 110.

Miller, Hattie Parks. "How Bill Arp Got His Name." *Bob Taylor's Magazine* 4 (Oct. 1906): 100–106.

Moore, James Tice. "Redeemers Reconsidered: Change and Continuity in the Democratic South, 1870–1900." *Journal of Southern History* 44 (1978): 357–78.

Morris, John. "Smith, Charles Henry." In *Library of Southern Literature,* edited by Edwin Anderson Alderman, Joel Chandler Harris, and Charles William Kent, 11:4885–87. New Orleans: Martin & Hoyt, 1907.

Muhlenfeld, Elisabeth. "The Civil War and Authorship." In *The History of Southern Literature,* edited by Louis D. Rubin, Jr., 178–87. Baton Rouge: Louisiana State University Press, 1985.

Newsom, D. W. "Bill Arp." *Trinity College Historical Society Publications,* 5th ser., 20 (1900): 57–66.

Parker, David B. "'Answers to Our Correspondents': Examples of Henry W. Grady's Humor." *Atlanta Historical Journal* 30 (Summer 1986): 67–74.

———. "Bill Arp and Blacks: The Forgotten Letters." *Georgia Historical Quarterly* 67 (1983): 336–49.

———. "Bill Arp and the New South." *Southern Historian* 8 (1987): 74–81.

———. "Bill Arp and the North: The Misreading of a Southern Humorist." *Southern Studies* 25 (1986): 257–73.

———. "Bill Arp, Joe Brown, and the Confederate War Effort." *Georgia Historical Quarterly* 73 (1989): 80–87.

———. "'I Thought He Looked Like a Baptist': Another 'New' Zeb Vance Story for the Collection." *The State* (Raleigh, N.C.) 55 (July 1987): 7.

Shaw, Barton C. "Henry W. Grady Heralds 'The New South'." *Atlanta Historical Journal* 30 (Summer 1986): 55–66.

Simms, L. Moody, Jr. "Smith, Charles Henry." In *Encyclopedia of American Humorists,* edited by Steven H. Gale, 398–400. New York: Garland Publishing, 1988.

"Smith, Charles Henry." In *National Cyclopaedia of American Biography,* 3: 308. New York: James T. White, 1893.

Smith, Gerald J. "Bill Arp: A Lincoln Correspondent." *Lincoln Herald* 79 (1979): 139–41.

Smith, Marian. "The Home Life of Bill Arp." Introduction to Charles

Henry Smith's *Bill Arp: From the Uncivil War to Date, 1861–1903*. Memorial Edition. Atlanta: Byrd, 1903.

Steadman, J. M., Jr. "Smith, Charles Henry." In *Dictionary of American Biography*, edited by Dumas Malone, 17:248–49. New York: Scribner's, 1935.

Tillett, Wilbur Fisk. "The White Man of the New South." *Century* 33 (March 1887): 769–76.

Weber, Brom. "The Misspellers." In *The Comic Imagination in American Literature*, edited by Louis D. Rubin, Jr., 127–37. New Brunswick: Rutgers University Press, 1973.

Williams, Jack K. "Three Georgians on Sectional Reconciliation." *Emory University Quarterly* 7 (1951): 217–24.

Woodman, Harold D. "Sequel to Slavery: The New History Views the Postbellum South." *Journal of Southern History* 43 (1977): 523–54.

Yancey, Maud H. "When *Sherman* Visited Rome." *Atlanta Journal*, 24 July 1932.

Dissertations and Theses

Atchison, Ray Morris. "Southern Literary Magazines, 1865–1887." Ph.D. dissertation, Duke University, 1956.

Babcock, Havilah. "Some Aspects of the Literary Influence of the Civil War." Ph.D. dissertation, University of South Carolina, 1927.

Christie, Annie May. "Charles Henry Smith, 'Bill Arp': A Biographical and Critical Study of a Nineteenth-Century Georgia Humorist, Politician, Homely Philosopher." Ph.D. dissertation, University of Chicago, 1952.

Cusker, Thomas J. "Revolt of the Titans: The Civil War Era as Seen through the Works of James R. Lowell, David R. Locke and Charles H. Smith." M.A. thesis, Seton Hall University, 1961.

Fitz-Simons, Theodore Barker, Jr. "The Ku Klux Klan in Georgia, 1868–1871." M.A. thesis, University of Georgia, 1957.

Gassman, Wade Banister. "A History of Rome and Floyd County, Georgia, in the Civil War." M.A. thesis, Emory University, 1966.

Hilty, Paul Richard, Jr. "Nasby vs. Arp: Yankee vs. Rebel Satire in the Civil War." M.A. thesis, Columbia University, 1961.

Hunter, Lloyd Arthur. "The Sacred South: Postwar Confederates and the Sacralization of Southern Culture." Ph.D. dissertation, Saint Louis University, 1978.

Jacobson, Timothy Curtis. "Tradition and Change in the New South, 1865–1910." Ph.D. dissertation, Vanderbilt University, 1974.

Landrum, Louella. "Charles Henry Smith (Bill Arp): Georgia Humorist." M.A. thesis, Duke University, 1938.

Miller, Verdie Frances. "Bill Arp (Charles Henry Smith): Georgia Author." M.A. thesis, University of Georgia, 1927.

Parker, David B., Jr. "Bill Arp: A Homely Philosopher in the New South." Ph.D. dissertation, University of North Carolina at Chapel Hill, 1988.

Rolan, Elaine. "Charles Henry Smith, Alias Bill Arp." M.A. thesis, Samford University, 1970.

Smith, Rebecca Washington. "The Civil War and Its Aftermath in American Fiction, 1861–1899, with a Dictionary Catalogue and Indexes." Ph.D. dissertation, University of Chicago, 1932.

Wolff, Alfred Y., Jr. "The South and the American Imagination: Mythical Views of the Old South, 1865–1900." Ph.D. dissertation, University of Virginia, 1971.

Index

Index

Underwood, John (lawyer), 12–13

Vandever, General William, 17, 60

Ward, Artemus, xv–xvii, 159 (n. 15);
letter from Bill Arp, 29, 40, 52,
67–71, 113
Washington, Booker T., 116
Watterson, Henry, 89, 96
Webb, G. P., 102–3
Weber, Brom, xvi
Webster, Daniel, 44
Western and Atlantic Railroad, 24

Western Newspaper Union, 35, 157
Whittier, John Greenleaf, 143
Wilson, Charles Reagan, 156–57
Wilt, Napier, 84
Woodman, Harold D., 151
Woodward, C. Vann, 52, 151

Young, Caroline, 46
Young, Jessie Smith, 10, 46, 80
Young, Marilu, 46
Young, P. M. B., 24, 26
Young, Will, 46